ISSUE IN DOUBT

ISSUE IN DOUBT

Naval Powers in the Pacific, 1941–1942

ROGER BARES
with Pat Collins Bares

M·P·P
www.MissionPointPress.com

Readers are encouraged to go to MissionPointPress.com to contact the author or to
find information on how to buy this book in bulk at a discounted rate.

Published by Mission Point Press

 Mission Point Press

2554 Chandler Rd.
Traverse City, MI 49696
(231) 421-9513
MissionPointPress.com

ISBN: 978-1-965278-63-5

Library of Congress Control Number: 2025905084

Printed in the United States of America

Cover photo: USS Enterprise (CV-6), a Yorktown class aircraft carrier, was the first
US Navy warship to sink a Japanese warship, Submarine I-70. She covered the
Doolittle Raid in April 1942 and, among other battles, participated in the Battle of
Midway where her planes helped sink three Japanese aircraft carriers.

For all people who seek truth and work for peace

CONTENTS

PART TWO (NOVEMBER 1941–APRIL 1942)

PART THREE (MAY 1942–DECEMBER 1942)

PREFACE

Sixty-five years after the Japanese attack on Pearl Harbor and the United States' entry into World War II, interest in the history of the war is taking hold in a new generation of Americans, a generation of young people who will most likely never serve in the military. At the same time, the people who served in World War II are being lost to us each day. Perhaps that is the reason I feel so strongly the responsibility of my generation, those of us born during the war and the baby boomers whose births followed the return of the veterans, to record as best we can the events of those times.

Over the years, I've read volumes about the war in the Pacific, and I've spoken to countless men who served in it aboard ships of the United States Navy, sailors and marines. A common impression I received from everyone to whom I've spoken was the importance, after all this time, that each man still placed on his ship and the attachment he held for her.

For these reasons I decided to write about a most critical time in American naval history, the first year of the Pacific War. After some background chapters, this book focuses on the period from Pearl Harbor through the last sea battle for Guadalcanal. In those days, often with the Japanese Navy and always with the US Navy, the issue of victory was in doubt. I wanted to produce an accurate and readable account of the battleships, carriers, cruisers and destroyers that were available to the Pacific combatants—Japanese, American, British, Australian and Dutch—where they were and in what actions they took part.

The United States entered the Second World War when the first wave of 183 Japanese fighter and bomber aircraft attacked US air and naval installations on the island of Oahu. The war ended 45 months later, after a single US bomber detonated a solitary bomb over the city of Nagasaki.

Roger Bares, Saluda, North Carolina
April 20, 2006

INTRODUCTION

This is not my book. It is my husband's. I merely did rewriting and editing. Born on Hitler's 50th birthday in 1939, Roger Alan Bares was steeped in the history of World War II by osmosis. When his uncles held him as a toddler, they were in uniforms of the United States Army and Navy. One uncle served aboard destroyer USS *Allen*, one of the few US Navy ships completed during World War I that also served in World War II. From early in our marriage in the 1960s, Roger read almost exclusively books on US military history and later, more exclusively, histories of the war in the Pacific. Veterans of both the European and Pacific theaters enjoyed talking with him because he understood their service and even if reluctant to share their military experience with family and friends, they opened up to Roger. He knew the geography, the statistics, the officers, the battles on land and at sea. After extended visits with Riverside, Illinois, neighbor and Marine veteran George Myrtle who served on Guadalcanal, Roger honored him by joining the Guadalcanal-Solomon Islands War Memorial Foundation as a Charter Member in 1987. In 1996, we visited the Solomon Islands where our friend, former "Shanghai Marine" Jack Nelson, had served aboard cruiser USS *Vincennes* when it was sunk on August 9, 1942. Nelson said that after being hit by at least eighty-five 130- and 200-millimeter shells and two Japanese long lance torpedoes, the ship listed to port so significantly that Navy and Marine personnel merely walked off the deck into Iron Bottom Sound off Savo Island where they waited to be rescued.

While writing *Issue in Doubt*, Roger took time out to write a novel set between Manila and Sydney in the early months of war, *Beyond the Sea: A Tale of Love & War in the South Pacific*. It recounts the fictional exploits of a motor torpedo or PT Boat in the early months of war, the men who manned her and loved her as the Eight Boat and the women who loved the men. This endeavor led him to book signings where he met more veterans with more stories to share.

By the time Roger Bares died in early 2020, he had most chapters of *Issue in Doubt* completed or close to completion. I promised I would do my best to get it into print—someday. Any errors are strictly mine.

Pat Collins Bares, Carmel, Indiana
December 7, 2024

Honiara Hotel, Guadalcanal, Solomon Islands, 1996

Part One

1834–1941

Old men forget: yet all shall be forgot,
But he'll remember with advantages
What feats he did that day: then shall our names . . .
Be in their flowing cups freshly remembered.
This story shall the good man teach his son.

—King Henry in William Shakespeare's *Henry V*, Act IV, Scene III

Chapter I

EVOLUTION OF THE FLEETS

One Navy Matures, Another Is Born, and Three Are Destroyed
Twenty years after the United States launched its first steam-powered commercial vessel, the US Navy began construction of its first steam warship, USS *Fulton*. The year was 1834. The *Fulton* was still in dry dock at Norfolk, Virginia, three years later when the American journal, *Naval Magazine*, published an article which disturbed and inspired officials of the young American naval service. The journal evaluated the world's naval powers. Not surprisingly, it ranked the United States Navy well behind those of Great Britain, France and Russia. What was truly disturbing, however, was America's ranking below the navies of Turkey, the Netherlands, Sweden and Egypt.

When the *Fulton* was launched in 1837, the Navy ordered Captain Matthew Perry to sail its newest warship from Norfolk to Washington, DC, to show President Van Buren and members of Congress a modern naval vessel firsthand. Subsequently, Congress passed the Naval Appropriations Act of 1839 and ordered construction of three more steam-powered warships.

Also at this time, the United States began an effort to reopen the Empire of Japan to western trade. In late 1852, now Commodore Matthew Perry sailed an eastern route to Japan carrying a personal letter to its Emperor from President Millard Fillmore. Perry's order: to open trade negotiations with the feudal empire after its 200 years of strict, self-imposed isolation. His fleet: the East India Squadron of three steam-powered frigates; four three-masted, square-rigged sloops; and three store ships. Perry dropped anchor off the east coast of Honshu Island in Edo (now Tokyo) Bay in July 1853 with two frigates and two sloops. The remainder of the fleet dropped anchor in the Okinawa Islands well to the south. The following year, after a show of force by Perry's entire squadron, the Japanese signed the Treaty of Kanagawa that called for "lasting and unlimited peace between the United States of America and the Empire of Japan." The treaty opened ports on the islands of Honshu and Hokkaido to American vessels for fuel, water and the humane treatment of shipwrecked seamen. Within three years, Japan signed similar treaties with Great Britain, Russia and the Netherlands and used assistance from these and other European countries to begin to amass a modern fleet.

For centuries, Japanese and Chinese forces had been fighting over various disputed lands and territorial waters. A lopsided Japanese victory in the Sino-Japanese War of 1894–95 resolved some of these long-standing differences while at the same time, it decimated the old, inefficient Chinese Fleet. More importantly, perhaps, it showed the Japanese to have the most powerful navy in Asia although European and American naval officials still thought it no match for western powers.

In the Caribbean, a mysterious explosion aboard the USS *Maine* in February 1898 claimed the lives of 260 American officers and men in Cuba's Havana Harbor. In the short course of the Spanish-American War that ensued, US naval forces destroyed two Spanish fleets, one in the Caribbean and another in the Philippines at Manila Bay. In the Peace Treaty of Paris signed by the combatants that December, Spain ceded its colonies of Puerto Rico and of Guam in the Marianas to the United States and allowed the US to purchase the Philippine Islands for $20 million, effectively ending Spain's worldwide empire. Together with a US claim on Wake Island for use in a cable line to the Philippines and the annexation of the Hawaiian Islands that same year, it became clear that the United States on the brink of the 20th century found itself in definite need of a two-ocean navy.

In 1900, European imperialism was assaulted in the Chinese capital of

Peking (now Beijing) during the Boxer Rebellion. Triggered by a command from the Chinese Dowager Princess Tz'u-Hsi to "Kill all foreigners," the rebellion was actually a limited and insignificant land conflict by 20th century standards. It did, however, provide a rare opportunity for the foreigners involved. In the Chinese Gulf of Taku, the world saw for the first and only time the navies of Great Britain, France, Russia, Germany, Italy and Austria along with those of the United States and the Empire of Japan moored side by side in a common cause. At the turn of the 20th century, world naval rankings placed the United States Navy fourth after Great Britain, France and Russia. The Japanese Navy, which did not exist 45 years earlier, ranked sixth after fifth-place Germany.

Two wars involving Japan and her neighbors confirmed the rise in power and ranking of the Japanese Navy. In the Sino-Japanese War of 1894–95, China and Japan fought over control of the Korean peninsula that both countries ruled as a co-protectorate. The Chinese, despite being considered the stronger of the two forces, were defeated both on land and at sea and in the treaty that ended the war, they agreed to the independence of Korea and ceded several strategic areas to Japan, including Taiwan, the Pescadores Islands, and Port Arthur on the Liaotung Peninsula on the Chinese mainland west of Korea. Demands from France, Germany and Russia, however, convinced Japan to return several confiscated areas to the Chinese, one being Port Arthur that China immediately leased to Russia. In the wake of the Sino-Japanese War in a move to gain additional trade concessions from Japan, Great Britain agreed in 1896 to oversee the training of Japanese naval crews and to provide designs and build armored cruisers and battleships for the Imperial Japanese Navy. British trade with Japan also included the sale of guns, ammunition and coal.

As the 19th century drew to a close, Japanese officials became increasingly concerned over Russian intrusions into northern Manchuria and into Korea. They worried about the possibility of an attack from the Korean Peninsula, an area that some in Japan perceived as "an arrow pointed at the heart of Japan." With Russia's Pacific Fleet now at Port Arthur, the Japanese viewed their situation as untenable. In February 1904, without formal declaration, the Japanese Navy launched an attack there, beginning the Russo-Japanese War. Torpedo attacks by Japanese destroyers were only moderately successful but an effective blockade kept the Russian fleet in port while a unit of the Japanese Army laid siege to Port Arthur by land.

Russia dispatched its old Baltic Fleet on a circuitous 18,000-mile course to the Pacific. With poorly trained crews and outdated vessels, the fleet reached Tsushima Strait between Korea and Japan six months later in May 1905 after numerous breakdowns, major malfunctions and a near war with Great Britain over the Dogger Bank Incident. There at Tsushima, 600 miles southeast of Port Arthur, 36 antiquated and battered Russian ships engaged 12 modern warships of the Japanese Navy on May 27, 1905. After five hours, a decimated Russian Baltic Fleet retired, having lost one-third of its force. The short Russo-Japanese War served to shuffle again the status and rankings of the world's navies. With Russia eliminated, the United States Navy ranked third after France. Germany was fourth and the Imperial Japanese Navy was raised to fifth place.

Dreadnought, the Ultimate Naval Weapon

Great Britain remained the undisputed leader among the world's naval forces and about the time of the Russo-Japanese War, Admiral Sir John Fisher, Britain's First Sea Lord, designed a vessel that would further extend that lead. Displacing 18,000 tons, with armor of up to 12 inches in thickness, powered by new steam turbine engines and armed with ten 12-inch guns, HMS *Dreadnought* became the most revolutionary warship afloat. Completed in just 14 months, it embodied its designer's big gun theory, armed only with large guns of a single caliber. When launched in 1906, *Dreadnought* made all existing warships obsolete. Proclaiming that speed is armor, Fisher later conceived and developed the battle cruiser. Envisioned as the cavalry of the sea, battle cruisers possessed the endurance, maneuverability and speed of cruisers with armor protection and firepower of the battleship. After Great Britain introduced the *Dreadnought* battleship and the armored battle cruiser, European shipbuilders lost interest in old-line naval vessels and concentrated on building battleships, battle cruisers, light cruisers and destroyers.

In 1905 the US Congress authorized the construction of two Dreadnought-type battleships, *Michigan* and *South Carolina*. In short order, Congress approved the building of two more warships of a similar design, *Arkansas* and *Wyoming*. USS *Michigan* and USS *South Carolina* were completed in 1910. USS *Arkansas* and USS *Wyoming,* launched in 1912, were at 26,000 tons the largest warships of the day, and armed with twelve 12-inch guns housed in six turrets, the most powerful. By 1911, battleships *Texas* and *New York* were under construction and the following year, work began on *Oklahoma* and *Nevada*. The four were armed with ten 14-inch guns and displaced either 26,000 or 27,000 tons. In 1913 USS *Pennsylvania*, with main armament of twelve 14-inch guns, was laid down at the Newport News Shipyard. Months later, a battleship similar in all respects to *Pennsylvania* was under construction. It was USS *Arizona*.

By 1914 the US Navy had six modern battleships in service and four in various stages of construction. Each reached a top speed of 21 knots and their lattice-work masts made them the most recognizable capital ships afloat. In addition, the Navy had a dozen armored cruisers that were built at the turn of the century, nearly 50 destroyers of various ages and an assortment of auxiliary vessels.

The Japanese Navy's first Dreadnought-type warship, *Kongo,* was completed in 1913. At 29,000 tons and with a maximum speed of 30 knots, it was larger and faster than any American battleship then in service. Battleship *Hiei*, one of *Kongo's* three sister ships, was launched in 1914, while *Haruna* and *Kirishima* were still under construction. In addition the Imperial Japanese Navy had two modern heavy armored cruisers, one old heavy cruiser, three light cruisers and 54 modern British-designed destroyers.

Great Britain formed alliances with Japan in 1902, with France in 1904 and with Russia in 1907, while Germany was empowered by its Triple Alliance with Austria-Hungary and Italy. Germany had been an innovator in lighter-than-air aviation with its turn-of-the-century zeppelin and also with heavier-than-air aviation, but it was the British Royal Navy that introduced heavier-than-air *naval* aviation in 1912, when an aeroplane was catapulted from the deck of an anchored British naval vessel. Later that year the Royal Navy launched an aeroplane from a moving warship and in 1913 the HMS *Hermes*, an old British cruiser, was recommissioned as the world's first aircraft carrier.

Responding to Britain's naval buildup and to challenge the Royal Navy's Grand Fleet for control of European waters, Germany developed its High Seas Fleet. By 1914 Great Britain and Germany were both involved in extensive shipbuilding programs. Britain knew it had to outproduce Germany by 60 percent to maintain the naval superiority necessary to protect its worldwide shipping interests. Further the British could not rely on naval support from France's four modern battleships, three of which operated from the Atlantic port of Brest and a fourth which was committed in the Mediterranean. The warships of Germany's High Seas Fleet were stationed at ports on the Baltic and on the North Sea. Like Great Britain, Germany could not rely on allied naval assistance since the navies of Austria-Hungary and Italy, with three modern battleships each, were restricted to operations in Mediterranean home waters. Great Britain had 21 modern battleships to Germany's 13. She had nine battle cruisers in service and a tenth nearing completion. The German Navy had five battle cruisers with a sixth about to be launched. Britain had 18 modern light cruisers to Germany's eight and 225 destroyers to Germany's 152. However, 125 of the Royal Navy's ships were new destroyers, compared to 108 modern German destroyers.

By 1914 the major navies of the world were organized into units called battle squadrons that included battleships, cruisers or battle cruisers, and destroyers. Battleship squadrons had two divisions of three or four ships each. Cruiser squadrons of four to six ships accompanied battleship squadrons or operated independently. Destroyer squadrons contained from six to 12 destroyers while flotillas contained as many as 36 destroyers.

The War to End All Wars

When the Great War began in August 1914, a stronger British Grand Fleet attempted to blockade the German High Seas Fleet, confining Germany's naval activities to the North Sea. However, breakouts by German surface raiders and deployment of the submarine greatly reduced blockade effectiveness and within five months, the global scale of naval engagements clearly demonstrated the enormous scope of the conflict.

In November 1914, the Battle of Coronel in the Pacific Ocean west of Chile saw the British and the German navies in their first significant engagement of the war. The following month, in the Atlantic Ocean, the Battle of the Falkland Islands took place off the coast of Argentina, and in January 1915, the Battle of Dogger Bank was fought in the North Sea. In May 1916, the last major naval engagement of what had truly become the first world war was fought in the North Sea off the coast of Denmark at the Battle of Jutland.

Great Britain had launched three new battleships in 1915 and another eight the following year. During the remainder of the war, however, the Royal Navy produced only a few additional light cruisers and destroyers. The German Navy received no surface ships during the war. What vessels it did receive were submarines. In 1915 over 850,000 tons of Allied shipping were lost to German submarines. To combat this threat, the Allies implemented naval escort procedures for merchantmen and defensive fire techniques for armed merchant ships and destroyers. They developed hydrophone systems for submarine detection, dropped depth charges and towed paravanes with explosive charges that initially destroyed submarines only by accident. Japan in 1914, eyeing Germany's holdings in China and the Pacific colonial islands, honored an old alliance with Great Britain and joined the Allied cause. The United States on the other hand took a passive role at the outbreak of war and remained neutral.

The last two battleships of the Japanese Navy's *Kongo* class, *Haruna* and *Kirishima*, were completed in 1915. In the same year, the battleship *Fuso* was launched, the first of two ships of the *Fuso* class, and her sister ship *Yamashiro* was laid down. Work on the battleship *Ise*, slightly larger than the ships of the *Fuso* class, was also begun. In 1916 construction began on *Hyuga*, sister ship of *Ise*. Japan authorized and initiated two light cruiser shipbuilding programs during the war. The namesake of the two-ship *Tenryu* class was laid down in May 1917 and construction on the *Tatsuta* was started in July. The *Tenryu* class cruisers displaced 3,200 tons and were armed with four 5.5-inch guns and six torpedo tubes. A second Japanese light cruiser program authorized five ships under the *Kuma* class. Armed like the *Tenryu* class but displacing 5,100 tons, two of the five were under construction by war's end.

In the United States, two new battleship programs had been authorized and in January 1915, USS *Idaho*, first of three *New Mexico* class ships, was laid down. The *Idaho* was followed by USS *Mississippi* in April and USS *New Mexico* in October. In 1916, battleships *Nevada, Oklahoma, Pennsylvania* and *Arizona* were completed and construction of the *Tennessee* class *California* was begun. USS *Tennessee* was laid down in 1917.

On May 7, 1915, the Cunard liner *Lusitania* on its way from New York to

England was torpedoed and sunk by a German submarine in the North Atlantic with the loss of nearly 1,200 passengers and crew. World opinion at the time forced Germany to ban further attacks on passenger liners, however, a second civilian liner was sunk by the Germans the following August. Protests by the United States after that incident prompted Germany to cease all submarine warfare on the west coast of Great Britain and in the English Channel. By February 1917, however, Germany again initiated unlimited submarine warfare.

That spring, the United States entered the war on the side of the Allies. Congress voted for war on April 6, 1917, and on April 24, the US Navy transferred six old destroyers from the East Coast to Great Britain. As America went to war, a massive shipbuilding effort was underway on her east coast. The battleship *Maryland* was laid down at Newport News Shipyard, first of the three-ship *Maryland* class. It was followed by USS *Colorado* and USS *West Virginia*. Armed with eight 16-inch guns and protected by 16 inches of belt armor, the ships of the *Maryland* class were the most heavily armored warships in the world and represented the last US battleships to be produced until the late 1930s.

The first modern US destroyer built was USS *Bainbridge*. It was ready for service in 1901. By 1917, the 66th modern US destroyer, and the last completed before the US joined the war, was close to completion at the Bath Iron Works in Maine—the USS *Allen*. That same year, a US naval program was authorized that would eventually produce 275 more of these flush-deck, four-stack destroyers. They were built in six phases representing six production groups (6th Group through 1st Group) and by the end of the war, 62 were completed and 138 more were in production. USS *Pruitt* with hull number 347 was launched in 1920 and was the last of the four-stackers. After *Pruitt* went into service, 14 years would pass before the Navy received another new destroyer.

The War to End All Wars had become, instead, the conflict that revolutionized the manner in which nations would thereafter go to war. Innovative technologies upped the fearsome stakes of battle on land, on the seas and now, in the air. The armed forces of the 20th century had new weapons systems, the wireless, turbine-driven warships, the submarine, the airplane and the aircraft carrier. In just four years of war, Great Britain sustained over three million human casualties. The Royal Navy at the battles of Coronel and Jutland alone lost 19 warships with an additional 22 ships significantly damaged. Her war debt was massive. France had casualty and war debt figures doubling Great Britain's but less severe naval losses. Germany sustained over seven million casualties. All her surviving surface vessels and submarines of the High Seas Fleet were scuttled after the war. United States' casualties totaled 331,000 and losses for Japan were set at 1,200. Naval experts still considered Great Britain "Ruler of the Waves" but the US Navy was now a close second and the Japanese Navy a very close third. A naval design so indispensable an element to a modern fleet, the super-warship HMS *Dreadnought,* never appeared in battle. Hailed by naval experts in 1906 as able to hold her own against any three pre-Dreadnought warships and years after giving her name to a whole new generation of warships, HMS *Dreadnought* never sortied with the Grand Fleet at the Battle of Jutland. During the most monumental naval battle since Trafalgar, *Dreadnought* was assigned defense duty off the coast of England.

Shipbuilding Programs

In the 80 years between the launching of USS *Fulton* in 1837 and the signing of the Armistice in November 1918, the United States developed into a major naval power. At the same time, Japan with her Imperial Navy took a place among the world's powers. She joined the League of Nations and as a signatory to the Treaty of Versailles, received Germany's holdings in the central Pacific—the Caroline, Mariana, Marshall and Papau island groups. Great Britain won the eastern half of the large island of New Guinea, the Bismarck Archipelago and the Solomon Islands and gave over other German South Pacific holdings to her self-governing colonies of Australia, New Zealand and South Africa. Responding to its citizens' strong leanings toward separatism and isolationism, the United States neither joined the League of Nations nor signed the Treaty of Versailles.

American shipbuilding programs underway at war's end were continued but previously authorized programs not yet begun were abandoned. The last battleship of the *New Mexico* class, USS *Idaho*, was ready for service in March 1919. USS *Tennessee* of the *California* class went into service in June 1920 and USS *California* in 1921. The namesake of the four-ship *Maryland* class was completed in July 1921; *Colorado* would be ready for service in August 1923 and *West Virginia* that December. *Washington*, the fourth ship of the class, remained under construction. Although Americans looked for disarmament and reduced taxes, destroyers of the Flush Deck Program of 1917 continued to be produced at a cost of just under $2,000,000 per vessel, and work on a previously authorized 10-ship, light cruiser program began a few months after the war ended. In December 1918, two of these *Omaha* class ships, *Omaha* and *Milwaukee,* were laid down at the Todd Company Shipyard in Tacoma, Washington. They would be completed in 1923, the remaining eight by 1925.

Japan continued her buildup as well. She entered the Great War with a navy of modern warships, including 54 destroyers. At war's end, she authorized 35 new destroyers to be produced in four groups, two groups totaling thirteen 2nd class destroyers with displacement not to exceed 1,000 tons and two groups totaling 22 larger 1st class destroyers. The 2nd class destroyers were designated as the five-ship *Kuri* class and the eight-ship *Wakatake* class programs, the 1st class destroyers as the 12-ship *Akikaze* class and the nine-ship *Kamikaze* class programs. Four 1st class destroyers of the *Akikaze* class were in production before the war ended and two of the *Kuri* 2nd class destroyers were laid down a few months after the armistice. Work on the 2nd class *Wakatake* and 1st class *Kamikaze*, namesakes of their classes, was begun in December 1921. Most of the 35 destroyers were in service by 1922, although it was not until December 1925 that the last ship of the *Kamikaze* class, *Hayate*, was completed. By 1919, Japan had the remaining three light cruisers of the *Kuma* class under construction, and she authorized a third light cruiser program, the six-ship, 5,200-ton *Natori* class. The five ships of the *Kuma* class were ready for service by October 1921. Of the *Natori* class, *Natori*, *Isuzu* and *Nagara* were laid down in 1920. Construction on the remaining three began the following year. Three were ready for service in 1922, two more in 1923, and the last of the class, *Abukuma,* in 1925. Japan authorized no heavy cruiser programs during the war; however, she did have six battleships under construction. The 30,000-ton *Hyuga* was completed in 1918, *Nagato* in 1920, and *Mutsu*, sister ship of *Nagato*, in 1921. Completion of *Mutsu* gave the Japanese Navy a total of 10 modern battleships.

While battleships, battle cruisers, cruisers and destroyers were receiving the highest military and budgetary consideration during and after the war, an innovation begun humbly in those years would lead to massive changes in naval warfare in the decades to follow—the aircraft carrier. The Royal Navy's HMS *Hermes* was home base for a mere nine biplanes when it was recommissioned in 1913 as the world's first carrier. The United States Navy ordered its 11,000-ton fleet collier *Jupiter* to the Norfolk Naval Yard in 1920 for conversion; it emerged as the aircraft carrier USS *Langley* the following year. As *Jupiter* was being converted, construction began on two 35,000-ton battle cruisers, one at the New York Shipbuilding Company and another at the Fore River Shipbuilding Company. Authorized as battle cruisers, the ships would come into service years later as the aircraft carriers *Saratoga* and *Lexington*.

In December 1919, more than a year before the US Navy's *Jupiter* underwent conversion, construction began on Japan's first aircraft carrier at the Asano Shipyard at Tsurumi. The 7,500-ton *Hosho* was completed in three years and was to be followed by her sister ship, *Shokaku*. As *Hosho* was being built, the keel for Japan's first battle cruiser, *Amagi*, was laid down at the Yokosuka Dockyard. Although launched in 1923, the 42,000-ton *Amagi* was so severely damaged by an earthquake and ensuing fire that final construction was abandoned. In July 1920 a battleship of 39,000-ton displacement was laid down at the Kawasaki Company Yard in Kobe and in December of that year, a battle cruiser, a near sister ship to the ill-fated *Amagi,* was laid down at the Kure Shipyard.

Treaties and Agreements

Woodrow Wilson was first elected to the White House in 1912 and reelected in 1916. In the 1920 presidential election, Wilson's Democrats lost to Republican Warren Harding. Bolstered by a Republican Congress, Harding forged a new foreign policy approach, parity through arms control. American voters wanted lower taxes, decreased spending and military disarmament and the new administration hoped to placate them through international agreements. After the war, the United States continued to close the naval gap with Great Britain. By 1921 the British, still recovering from the devastating economic effects of the war, had produced only a few 4,900-ton D-class light cruisers, one 9,800-ton heavy cruiser, and a lone battle cruiser of 41,000 tons, the HMS *Hood*. Japan, on the other hand, initiated a number of ship-building programs and was narrowing the interval with both the US Navy and the Royal Navy.

When approached by the Harding administration concerning a conference on naval limitations and controls, Great Britain welcomed the idea. Officially called the International Conference on Naval Limitation, the Washington Conference was held in Washington, DC, from November 1921 to February 1922. Nine countries took part in the conference, and during its course, the various attending powers signed six treaties, one declaration and 12 resolutions. The Five Power Treaty adopted at the final plenary session on February 6, 1922, was signed by the United States, Great Britain, France, Japan and Italy. It limited naval armament so that the United States retained 18 capital ships, Great Britain 22 and France, Italy and Japan, 10 each. Further it placed future capital ship replacement tonnage for the United States and Great Britain at 525,000 tons each and for Japan at 315,000 tons, the 5-5-3 ratio. France and Italy could build and maintain navies at 50 percent of Japan's strength.

The agreement judged aircraft carriers with battleships as capital vessels. It placed a 10-year moratorium on new battleship construction and limited their displacement to 35,000 tons and gun caliber to 16 inches. Cruiser displacement could not exceed 10,000 tons. Heavy cruisers could carry armament no larger than 8-inch guns and light cruisers no larger than 6-inch guns. Some concessions were granted between nations on completed warships and those under construction. The United States was allowed to convert two partially completed battle cruisers into aircraft carriers if Japan were allowed the same conversions for a battleship and a battle cruiser. The two US battle cruisers had been laid down in the year prior to the Washington Conference. When finally converted to 33,000-ton fleet carriers, they were named USS *Saratoga* and USS *Lexington* and became the mainstays of the United States Navy's carrier force. Under the treaty, the fourth battleship of the *Maryland* class, USS *Washington*, though nearing completion, was scrapped. The Japanese battleship initially laid down at Kobe in 1920 was towed to Yokosuka for conversion. Under Japan's 1923 Shipbuilding Program, it became the Imperial Navy's first fleet carrier, *Kaga*. Japan's battle cruiser was redeveloped into the fleet carrier *Akagi* and together these warships became the backbone of Japan's carrier force. *Shokaku*, sister ship of the carrier *Hosho*, was scrapped under terms of the treaty. A carrier built in the 1930s would carry her name. Under a three-nation compromise, Japan was allowed to retain the 32,700-ton warship *Mutsu* that had been built with funds contributed by Japanese school children. The US could retain two of its Navy's newest but still incomplete battleships, *Colorado* and *West Virginia*. Great Britain could keep its newest battle cruiser HMS *Hood*.

In addition to revising shipbuilding programs and redefining future naval strength, the Five Power Treaty required that signatories eliminate some warships already in service. The United States scrapped two of its first Dreadnought-type battleships, *Michigan* and *South Carolina*. Other outmoded ships were scrapped or decommissioned. In the early 1920s, Brigadier General William "Billy" Mitchell used the old USS *Alabama* as a target ship in a military experiment to prove the vulnerability of naval vessels to air attack.

The Five Power Treaty was seen by many as a significant step toward lasting world peace, but for some Americans, it did not go far enough. Although proponents saw it leading to a more reasonable world order, militarists and isolationists alike opposed the treaty, arguing it allowed too little or too much, respectively. All dissenters agreed, however, that the treaty's success would rely on allies trusting allies and, for that matter, a former enemy, to faithfully follow treaty terms. Japan was dissatisfied with the limitations imposed on her Imperial Navy but initially she adhered to the terms and conditions of the treaties of the Washington Conference.

In the years between 1912 and 1923, the US built 14 battleships, one aircraft carrier and roughly 300 destroyers. Under the Five Power Treaty, American shipbuilding programs authorized production of eight heavy cruisers, the first scheduled for construction in 1926. The Navy received the battleship *Colorado* in August 1923, *West Virginia* that December and six of the 10 *Omaha* class light cruisers during the year. Still, US naval officials saw a service they judged to be well behind envisioned standards and strength. Even programs unaffected by cancellations required more time for completion due to funding cuts. Over the same period, the Imperial Japanese Navy grew by 10 battleships, an aircraft carrier, 10 light cruisers and 19 destroyers. By the end of 1923, Japan received two additional light cruisers and six more destroyers with a light cruiser and six destroyers still under construction. Within the terms of the Five Power Treaty, Japan launched new shipbuilding programs authorizing eight heavy cruisers, four light cruisers and 12 destroyers.

The United States would realize the least from treaties of the Washington Conference. Despite Britain's heavy naval losses during the Great War, the Royal Navy retained her ranking. Allowing Great Britain to take a passive approach and enjoy the luxury of not having to build warships or expend funds to keep up with her treaty partners was to her definite advantage. Ranked behind Great Britain and the United States, Japan desired military expansion, could afford it and had the most to gain from the treaties. Her Navy sought rapid expansion in order to close the gap with England and the United States.

The Post-War Arms Race

Within two weeks of the close of the Washington Conference, the Japanese had under construction at the Mitsubishi Yard in Nagasaki the light cruiser *Sendai,* first of the three-ship *Jintsu* class. Work began that June on the second of the class, *Naka,* and in August on *Jintsu.* These 5,200-ton cruisers, an improved version of the *Natori* class, were completed in 1924 and 1925. In June 1922, a lone 2,900-ton light cruiser, *Yubari*, was laid down at the Sasebo Dockyard. By December of that year, the first two heavy cruisers of the four-ship, 7,100-ton *Kako* class were started, *Kako* and *Furutaka*. They were constructed at the Kawasaki Yard in Kobe and at the Mitsubishi Shipyard, respectively. The cruisers were followed nearly two years later by *Kinugasa* and *Aoba*. The four ships of the *Kako* class were ready for service in 1927. In October 1924 the first of four 10,000-ton heavy cruisers of the *Nachi* class, *Myoko*, was laid down at the Kure Shipyard. She was followed a month later by *Nachi*. Work on *Haguro* began in March 1925 and *Ashigara* was laid down that April. In April 1927 another Japanese heavy cruiser program began when the 9,900-ton *Atago* was laid down at the Kure Shipyard. That same month, *Takao,* a second cruiser in the four-ship *Atago* class, was laid down at the Yokosuka Shipyard. By 1928, the remaining heavy cruisers, *Chokai* and *Maya,* were in production.

Work began early in 1924 on the Japanese Navy's 12-ship 1st class destroyer program for the 1,315-ton *Mutsuki* class, and in 1926, Japan autho-rized construction of 24 destroyers of the *Fubuki* class. Larger than the ships of the *Mutsuki* class, the 1,700-ton *Fubuki* warships were classified into three groups: eight destroyers of the *Shinonome* type, 12 of the *Amagiri* type and four of the *Hibiki* type. Japan's first fleet carrier, *Akagi*, initially laid down as a battle cruiser in 1920, was converted to an aircraft carrier under the Five Power Treaty. At 33,000 tons, *Akagi* was completed and ready for service in March 1927. A year later, a former battleship and Japan's second fleet carrier, the 35,000-ton *Kaga*, was completed. In November 1929 the smaller 7,600-ton carrier *Ryujo* was under construction at the Yokosuka Shipyard.

America's first naval building program after the Washington Conference was approved in December 1924. It was for heavy cruisers of the two-ship, 9,100-ton *Pensacola* class. *Pensacola* was laid down in October 1926 at the New York Naval Yard, and in June 1927, work began on *Salt Lake City* at the New York Shipbuilding Company. In March 1928, the 9,200-ton heavy cruiser *Chester,* first of six *Northampton* class cruisers, was laid down at the New York Shipbuilding Company. She was followed by *Northampton, Houston, Augusta, Louisville* and *Chicago*, all of which were under construction by October 1928. The last of the six ships, USS *Chicago*, was completed in March 1931. America's first fleet carrier USS *Saratoga* was completed in November 1927. USS *Lexington* was ready for service soon after. It had taken seven years for *Lexington*'s conversion to a fleet carrier from the battle cruiser she was first destined to be.

As the decade of the '20s ended and when existing shipbuilding programs were completed, Great Britain's Royal Navy had 14 battleships, a battle cruiser, six aircraft carriers (four fleet carriers and two light carriers), 16 heavy cruisers, 24 light cruisers and 76 destroyers. The Japanese Navy included 10 battleships, four aircraft carriers (two fleet carriers and two light carriers), 12 heavy cruisers, 17 light cruisers and 71 destroyers. United States naval power included 16 battleships, three aircraft carriers (two fleet carriers and a light carrier), eight heavy cruisers, 10 light cruisers and more than 200 destroyers.

By 1931, and under terms of the Five Power Treaty, the United States and the Royal Navy were considered in parity in the categories of battleships and carriers. US destroyers outnumbered Britain's significantly, but the Royal

Navy was ahead in all other categories. The Japanese Navy was to maintain a naval force equal to 60 percent of her major treaty partners, but in reality, only her battleship and destroyer numbers met treaty requirements. Though she observed the Five Power Treaty moratorium on battleship construction, Japan exceeded the treaty's requirements on aircraft carrier and heavy and light cruiser production.

Chapter II

ROAD TO WAR

Collision Course

The signers of the 1854 Treaty of Kanagawa that opened the Empire of Japan to foreign trade and foreign influence could not have foreseen the speed with which Japan would integrate herself into the world community. Japan's leaders went to the source for the best ideas that foreigners had to offer—to Britain for shipbuilding and weaponry, to Germany for a template on which to fashion a strong national army, even modeling their general staff on the Prussian system, to Italy for looms for a lucrative textile industry. By the turn of the 20th century, Japan had thousands of factories using imported technologies to manufacture textiles, machine tools, metals, chemicals, weapons and warships. In 1889 Japan adopted a western-style parliament with a two-house legislature. Her businesses were organized on a German model, with large holding companies controlled by important families receiving huge government supports. She brought in British instructors to train officers for her growing Navy, an essential element if Japan were to be a great power in the industrialized world. Some said that by the 1920s, certain areas of Tokyo looked more like Chicago.

One area of life in Japan remained unalterably Japanese and that was devotion to the Emperor, a deity to his people. Crown Prince Hirohito was named regent in 1921 at age 20 and became Emperor five years later. Every Japanese pledged to serve the Emperor unto death. Hirohito ascended the Imperial throne in difficult days for his country, however, and various segments of the Japanese citizenry held different views on how service to him could best be achieved.

With a land area about the size of the state of California, Japan had a population of 80 million in 1931 and was growing by over one million a year. The economic successes of the late 19th and early 20th centuries disintegrated in the 1920s and especially in the worldwide depression of the 1930s. Jobs became scarce in urban areas and depressed silk and produce prices brought many farmers to near starvation. Young Japanese saw political changes in Europe and in Russia after the World War and looked for ways to correct the social injustices they saw in their own country. The average Japanese blamed politicians, statesmen, bankers, manufacturers and businesspeople for their country's economic and social ills. There was a rise of unions and new political parties and of nationalist organizations with revolutionary ideas. Elements of the military formed secret societies.

Japan had long viewed China as her chief military threat but by the turn of the 20th century, she passed that honor to Russia. That policy changed as well, though, after the Japanese Navy's decisive victory over the Russian Navy in 1905 and with Russia's lessened involvement in Asia during the Bolshevik Revolution. After the World War, the Japanese military formulated a new defense policy that saw the United States as its primary adversary and with good reason. The treaties of the Washington disarmament conference that pledged respect for the sovereignty and territorial integrity of China and that limited Japanese warship production to a ratio of US and British numbers were seen as unfair by the Japanese. Japanese nationalists saw the US as imperialistic, much too powerful militarily, economically and politically in the international arena. And many Japanese were incensed by the increasingly anti-Japanese tone the US press took in the 1920s and by the passage of the US Immigration Act of 1924 that severely limited the number of Japanese allowed to migrate to America.

About this time the Japanese Army and the Japanese Navy came to a crucial policy disagreement. The Japanese Army decided that once more, all future military planning and maneuvers should be directed against Russia whose army was again building in strength. The Japanese Navy, however, continued planning and preparedness maneuvers with a view toward the United States as the primary foe.

Some elements of the Japanese Army found a way to deal with the Russians and, at the same time, the Chinese. In summer 1931, General Kanji Ishiwara and Colonel Seishiro Itagaki moved Japan's Kwantung Army north to Mukden in Manchuria under the same pretense Adolf Hitler would use seven years later in Czechoslovakia and a year after that in Poland—more living room. Believing they were conquering territory for the good of the Emperor, these extreme militarists sought to provide Japan with the markets and materiel needed for her industries. Ishiwara and Itagaki envisioned the transformation of the sparsely populated, resource-rich Manchuria into an independent refuge for Japanese citizens, Chinese, Koreans and even White Russians. In Tokyo neither government and military officials nor the Emperor condoned or sanctioned the action of the Kwantung Army that was meekly ordered by the War Ministry to refrain from any new project such as becoming independent from the Imperial Army and seizing control of Manchuria and Mongolia. The Emperor, who never spoke in public, issued a written statement that was equally mild.

The Army itself was divided. Some thought only the conquest of all northern China would guarantee security against Russian attack. Others viewed an industrialized Manchuria as protection enough against the Communist threat. Whatever opinions were expressed by these factions or whether actions of the Kwantung Army were completely independent or sanctioned in Tokyo, by 1933 the Japanese Army occupied Manchuria. The United States' response was to condemn Japan's movement and subsequent occupation as armed aggression. The League of Nations labeled the Japanese as aggressors, and in retaliation, Japan withdrew from the League in spring 1933. The news from Japan became more disconcerting as the decade of the 1930s wore on. Secret societies within her military singled out business and political leaders for assassination with support from the public who had come to believe in a military-led reform. In the February 26 Incident in 1936, Army rebels acting in support of the Kwantung Army occupied a square mile of Tokyo, the Diet and the square around the Prime Minister's home and murdered seven senior Japanese statesmen.

In the United States after the World War, the numbers of returning servicemen coupled with reductions in military spending after the national elections of 1920, 1924 and 1928, created a short labor market. At times when employment figures did improve, serious inflation followed. The Republican Party retained the White House in 1924 with the election of Calvin Coolidge and again in 1928 with Herbert Hoover and continued the Harding administration's pacifist bent that reflected the wishes of most Americans. Hoover's election coincided with the tenth anniversary of the signing of the Versailles Treaty denouncing war. Although the United States had not signed the treaty, it did join 14 other nations in signing the Kellogg-Briand Pact, a multilateral treaty to settle international disputes by peaceful means. Since new weapons would never be used, it was reasoned, funding for previously approved weapons programs was frozen and new weapons programs were canceled. After a dozen years in the White House, the Republicans lost the 1932 election to Democrat Franklin Delano Roosevelt. As the new president took office, Japan was in control of all northern China. Roosevelt did not trust the Kellogg Pact. He envisioned the United States a leader in world affairs with a strong national defense and a forceful, global American military presence. As a former Assistant Secretary of the Navy, he worked to bring the Navy up to required strength and called for more shipbuilding programs.

Short of War

In 1936 Japan renounced the treaties of the Washington disarmament conference of 1922 and signed an Anti-Comintern Pact with Germany. In June 1937 Prince Fumimaro Konoye, a 46-year-old moderate from a well-respected family, became Japan's Prime Minister. Within two months he found himself dealing with an incident at the Marco Polo Bridge. After China's Boxer Rebellion in 1900, some foreign powers, including Japan, were allowed to occupy areas near Peking for the maintenance of open communications between the capital and the sea. Japanese troops were barracked near the city and were accustomed to training near Chinese troops. On the night of July 7, 1937, a company of Japanese troops held an exercise near the ancient stone

Marco Polo Bridge 15 miles southwest of Peking. They were camped within a mile of a Chinese Army unit and as maneuvers were ending, shots were fired from the Chinese lines. The Japanese troops returned fire. Although officers from both units successfully restored order, similar incidents occurred in the weeks that followed, and the Japanese Army continued sending reinforcements to the area. On the night of July 25, an incident at the railroad station in Langfang, 50 miles south of Peking, turned into a major confrontation. Japanese reinforcements were sent in, Japanese planes bombed the Chinese Army barracks, and by noon, Japanese troops occupied the city of Langfang. Continuing its hold on Manchuria, Japan launched other campaigns into China, all part of what had become to them the China Incident. There was a battle at Shanghai in August 1937 and what came to be called the Rape of Nanking that December.

In July 1939, the United States refused to renew an old trade pact with Japan, and in September 1940, all US iron exports to Japan were banned. The United Kingdom banned rubber exports to Japan in May 1941, and the following month, negotiations between Japan and the Netherlands for supplying oil and rubber to Japan failed. In July, the United States and the United Kingdom froze all Japanese assets in those countries. Three days later, the Japanese Army entered French Indochina, and on the same day, American, English and Dutch assets in Japan were frozen. On August 1, 1941, the United States placed an oil embargo against Japan as an aggressor nation.

Meanwhile, as economic and diplomatic sanctions were being imposed on Japan, the US Navy had made a significant change in the placement of its warships. America's Asiatic Fleet had for years been stationed at Manila Bay in the Philippines but, in spring 1940, what was previously the United States Fleet headquartered at Norfolk, Virginia, and at San Diego, California, became the Atlantic Fleet and the Pacific Fleet. The Pacific Fleet was now headquartered at the anchorage known as Pearl Harbor on Oahu in the Hawaiian Islands.

In April 1941 President Roosevelt signed an unpublicized executive order, authorizing reserve officers and enlisted men to resign from the Army Air Corps and the Naval and Marine Air Services to join an American volunteer group being formed to support the Chinese against the Japanese. Claire

Chennault, a former US Army Air Corps colonel serving as a brigadier general in the Chinese Air Force, headed a group of 100 of these American pilots and several hundred ground-crew personnel under the guise of the Central Aircraft Manufacturing Company of China. Officially set up to manufacture, service and operate aircraft in China, Chennault's Flying Tigers unofficially trained in Burma as a clandestine American military operation against Japan. It wasn't long before the Japanese recognized the Chennault operation as a hostile act.

On September 6, 1941, at a Japanese Imperial Conference, an agreement was reached that unless negotiations underway with the US government resulted in a relaxation of sanctions against the Empire of Japan, plans for war against the United States of America and the European colonies of Southeast Asia would go forward. On October 17, Prince Konoye stepped down after four years as Prime Minister. He was replaced by General Hideki Tojo of the Imperial Japanese Army, leaving the Empire of Japan under the firm control of its military. Early in November a deadline of November 25 was set to confirm that a settlement was reached with the Americans—or not.

Japanese Air Power

The adversarial climate that developed over two decades between Japan and the western powers was accompanied by an unprecedented buildup of military machinery in Japan that included not just naval power but air power as well. Japan began importing British aircraft in the early 1920s. The Imperial Japanese Army's primary warplane was a British biplane, the Gloster Sparrowhawk. In 1923 an agreement was reached between the Mitsubishi conglomerate and Great Britain's Sopwith Aircraft Company to produce the first Japanese-made military aircraft, the Mitsubishi 1MF1 biplane fighter. The 1MF1s were assigned to the Japanese Naval Air Force and were stationed on board Japan's first aircraft carrier, *Hosho*. By the late 1920s, in addition to Mitsubishi, the Nakajima and the Kawasaki manufacturing companies were primary sources for the design and production of Japanese aircraft. The first of many Kawasaki fighters, the Type 92 biplane, powered by the Japanese version of a German BMW air-cooled engine, became operational in the service of the Army Air Force in 1930. The following year Nakajima produced Japan's first monoplane fighter for the Army, the Type 91. In production until 1934, the Type 91 was the first airplane of complete Japanese design; it replaced all foreign-designed aircraft in the Japanese Army Air Force.

In 1934 Kawasaki produced the Ki-10 biplane for the Army as Nakajima released its A4N1 biplane to the Navy. Both aircraft types would remain operational until 1941, but they were the last biplane fighters to be accepted by the Japanese armed forces. Also in 1934, Mitsubishi developed and delivered a single-seat, open-cockpit, monoplane fighter with a fixed undercarriage, the A5M4. Nicknamed Claude by the Allies, it remained the Japanese Navy's primary fighter aircraft until Mitsubishi made its Zero operational in 1940. Along with the Zero, Mitsubishi produced the Navy's and Japan's first medium bomber, the G3M Nell based on a design by the German aircraft company Junkers. These twin-tailed, twin-engine monoplanes entered service in 1937 and initially operated as civil transports. By 1937, a Nakajima fighter, the Ki-27 Nate became operational in the service of Army squadrons stationed in Manchuria and replaced Kawasaki Ki-10 biplanes there. The Nate, with its stubby nose, low wing, and fixed undercarriage, resembled Mitsubishi's Claude fighter but had the added advantage of an enclosed cockpit.

The first of the Japanese Navy's new carrier-based attack bombers, the Nakajima B5N Kate, was produced in 1937 and became the Navy's main torpedo bomber. The single-engine monoplane carried up to three men in an enclosed cockpit and could carry an 1,800-pound torpedo or an equivalent bomb load with a range of over 1,000 miles. In 1938 Mitsubishi produced the first medium bomber for Japan's Army Air Force, the Ki-21 Sally. A second Mitsubishi twin-engine aircraft, the Ki-46 Dinah reconnaissance light bomber was operational by 1940. Nakajima produced the Ki-43 Oscar fighter for the Army Air Force in 1940 and Kawasaki delivered the first Ki-61 Tony fighters to the Army a year later. Both aircraft were used defensively to protect the Japanese homeland and its previously conquered territories.

A Japanese aircraft designer and manufacturer that had not previously been authorized to provide warplanes, Aichi, won a 1936 competition to produce the Navy's principal dive bomber, the D3A Val. The Val entered service in 1940 with the Japanese Combined Fleet. She carried 900 pounds of bombs, had a range of 1,200 miles and was used in level bombing and in dive bombing. By 1940, two designs from Mitsubishi provided the Japanese Navy with its premier fighter and medium bomber aircraft. The fighter was the A6M Zero or Zeke, a high-speed, highly maneuverable, single-seat aircraft armed with two 7.7-mm machine guns and a 20-mm cannon. The G4M Betty was a versatile, twin-engine bomber that carried 2,000 pounds of bombs or a torpedo internally. The Betty was armed with four 20-mm cannons and one 7.7-mm machine gun. Both the Zero and the Betty saw service throughout the Pacific War.

As an island nation with a penchant for seaplanes on all types of warships from battleships to light cruisers, Japan, with few exceptions, modified existing single-engine aircraft for seaplane duty. Aichi's Jake was a modified Val, and both Mitsubishi and Nakajima produced float versions of the Zero. By late 1941, principal aircraft aboard Japanese carriers included the Mitsubishi Zero as the only carrier fighter, the Nakajima Kate as the main torpedo and level bomber and the Aichi Val as the primary dive bomber. Battleship, heavy cruiser and light cruiser aircraft included Jakes and Zeros, both single-engine floatplanes. Land-based naval units used Zeros as fighters, Vals as level and dive bombers and Mitsubishi Bettys and Nells as level and torpedo bombers. One of Japan's largest aircraft, the four-engine Kawanishi H6K flying boat, the Mavis, was used in long-range reconnaissance, along with Jakes and float Zeros.

US Air Power

Glenn Hammond Curtiss, an airplane designer and builder in Hammondsport, New York, provided Great Britain with designs for Royal Navy flying-boats during the World War and in 1922, designed a two-seat fighter for the US Navy's first aircraft carrier. In 1925 the US Army accepted the P-1 (Pursuit-one) Hawk, a biplane fighter designed and built by Curtiss Aeroplane and Engine Company. The same design modified for carrier operations was approved by the Navy as the F6C (Fighter-six-Curtiss). Curtiss's plan for a two-seat, open cockpit biplane fighter able to double as a light bomber was approved by the Marine Corps in 1927. Designated the F8C Helldiver, it became America's first dive bomber and first of the long series of

Curtiss Helldivers. Only one other major aircraft design and production facility was in operation in the US in the 1920s, the Seattle-based Boeing Airplane Company. By the mid-1930s, however, Boeing and Curtiss found themselves in competition for government contracts with more than a dozen aircraft manufacturers. In 1929, Curtiss merged with the Wright Aeronautical Corporation to form the Curtiss-Wright Corporation. In the same year, the Boeing Airplane Company began filling the largest military contract order for a single aircraft series to date. Boeing produced over 580 single-seat biplane fighter aircraft designated P-12 for the Army and F4B for the Navy. Boeing F4Bs became the primary aircraft aboard the carriers USS *Lexington* and USS *Saratoga*. In 1931 the Army Air Corps accepted a Boeing design for America's first monoplane bomber, the twin-engine, all metal B-9. Two years later Boeing received a contract to manufacture the country's first pursuit monoplane fighter, the P-26 Peashooter. It was the first American fighter of all metal construction and the first powered by a fuel-injected engine.

By 1933 a new company located on Long Island, the Grumman Aircraft and Engineering Corporation, was awarded two contracts by the US Navy. The first design was for a two-seat biplane fighter with enclosed cockpit and retractable landing gear. The second design, a single-engine amphibious biplane, was a seaplane with landing gear that retracted into the sides of the main float. The Navy designated Grumman's fighter the FF-1 and the amphibious floatplane, the JF Duck.

In 1934, the Army contracted with the Glenn L. Martin Company of Cleveland, Ohio, to produce streamlined, twin-engine monoplane bombers with enclosed cockpits and retractable landing gear. However, in 1936, as these B-10s were entering production, the Army decided on a new and different low-wing, twin-engine design for its standard medium bomber and awarded a contract to the Douglas Aircraft Company of Santa Monica, California, for the B-18 Bolo. It went back to Martin in 1939 for a new twin-engine medium bomber, the B-26.

In 1934 the US Army asked Boeing to design a four-engine bomber to patrol America's coastlines for the purpose of protecting the nation from enemy invasion from the sea. Since the new design was judged strictly defensive, the plane was dubbed the Flying Fortress and the B-17 came to life as America's first heavy bomber.

In 1935 Grumman was awarded a naval contract for a biplane fighter to replace its FF-1. The new F2F was a single-seat biplane that was faster and operated at higher altitudes with a greater range. Within a year, production on the second model ceased and the F2F was replaced by an improved version, the F3F. A Douglas Aircraft design for a three-seat, monoplane torpedo bomber was submitted to the Navy in 1934 and within three years, the Douglas TBD Devastator became the Navy's principal torpedo aircraft. That same year, on a request from the Navy for a carrier-borne dive bomber, Vought-Sikorsky designed a two-seat, single-engine aircraft, the SB2U Vindicator. In 1940, Grumman Aircraft began delivering the Navy's newest torpedo bomber, the TBF Avenger that became the primary US torpedo bomber for most of World War II. The Navy contracted with Consolidated Aircraft Corporation of San Diego, California, to produce a long-range flying boat, and in 1937, the first twin-engine PBYs were delivered. Dubbed Catalinas by the British, the PBY's wing was mounted on a pylon above the fuselage and its floats retracted to form wing tips. An amphibious version, the PBY-A, was produced with retractable landing gear.

By 1937 the Army Air Corps ordered 76 single-seat monoplane fighters from the Republic Aviation Corporation of Long Island, New York. Developed initially from privately funded experimental aircraft, the P-35 with enclosed cockpit and retractable landing gear was one of the fastest aircraft to date, at 290 mph. Later an improved version with a speed of 350 mph, the P-43 Lancer, was accepted by the Army, and in 1941, a faster version yet, the P-47 Thunderbolt at 450 mph was accepted.

The Army received a modified design of Douglas's commercial airliner, the twin-engine DC-3, in 1938 and began placing orders for large numbers of the aircraft in 1940. With reinforced floors, strengthened fuselage and increased power, the cargo-transport aircraft was designated the C-47 Skytrain by the Army and the R4D Skytrain by the Navy. Affectionately dubbed Gooney-Bird, the DC-3 became the primary workhorse for the entire US military with over 10,000 built by the end of 1945.

The Curtiss-Wright Corporation provided the Army with a single-seat, monoplane fighter design with enclosed cockpit and retractable landing gear, and in 1938, the first P-36 Hawks were delivered. A similar export version, the P-75 Mohawk, was produced for America's European allies. By 1941 after more modifications to the aircraft, the Army received 130 of the new Curtiss P-40 Warhawk fighters, some of which first saw combat with Chennault's Flying Tigers in China. In 1939, the Army took delivery of a new single-seat, pursuit fighter from the Bell Aircraft Corporation of Buffalo, New York. The streamlined P-39 Airacobra was armed, unlike any previous American fighter, with a 37-millimeter cannon in its nose. Because of this armament arrangement, the P-39's engine was centered in the fuselage directly behind the cockpit.

By 1940 the Army began receiving the first of another new light bomber design, the B-25 Billy Mitchell from North American Aviation Incorporated of Inglewood, California. The B-25 carried a crew of six. At the same time, the Douglas Aircraft Company designed a twin-engine, low-level attack medium bomber that the Army designated A-20 Havoc. The first A-20s became operational in 1942.

The Navy in the late 1930s received two types of amphibious floatplanes from Grumman and from Vought-Sikorsky. The Grumman aircraft was a twin-engine, amphibious flying boat designated JRF Goose. The Vought-Sikorsky floatplane was a single-engine aircraft, the OS2U Kingfisher.

Seventeen years after the first Curtiss design was accepted by the United States Navy, the Curtiss-Wright Corporation produced the last of the US Navy's biplanes. The SBC Helldiver, a two-seat, biplane fighter with enclosed cockpit and retractable landing gear, was delivered to the Navy in March 1939. A month later the Navy placed an order with the Douglas Aircraft Company for 144 single-wing dive bombers, the SBD Dauntless. The Dauntless, with retractable landing gear and enclosed cockpit for a crew of three, became the US Navy's primary dive bomber. In June 1939 the US Navy received a monoplane fighter from the Brewster Aeronautical Corporation of Long Island City, New York. The stubby, single-seat F2A Buffalo became the Navy's main fighter, but in less than a year, the Buffalo was replaced by Grumman's first monoplane fighter, the F4F Wildcat. The Wildcat was a better-armed, faster and more maneuverable plane and served as the Navy's principal fighter until 1943. The design for a tactical fighter with long-range capabilities was completed by the Lockheed Aircraft Corporation of Burbank, California, in 1937. In 1941, the first of these unique single-seat, twin-engine, twin-fuselage, twin-tailed P-38 Lightning fighters were ready for service with the Army Air Corps. Another Lockheed design, the A-28 Hudson light bomber and reconnaissance transport aircraft, was developed for Great Britain's Royal Air Force in 1939. By 1941, A-28s were in service in Great Britain and modified versions were developed, A-29s for the US Army Air Corps and AT-18s for the US Navy. A Vought-Sikorsky design for a single-seat, single-engine, gull-winged fighter was first flown in 1940. Designated the F4U Corsair, it was manufactured as a high-speed Navy and Marine carrier- and land-based aircraft. The first F4Us were delivered in October 1942.

In 1941, the aircraft of air groups aboard US Navy carriers included fighters, scout/dive bombers and torpedo bombers. The Grumman F4F Wildcat was the principal naval fighter; the SBD Dauntless and TBD Devastator, both manufactured by Douglas, were the carriers' primary scout/dive bomber and torpedo bomber aircraft, respectively. Battleships and cruisers usually launched floatplanes for reconnaissance/scout missions from aft catapults and recovered aircraft by cranes. The Grumman JF Duck biplane and the Vought-Sikorsky OS2U Kingfisher became the US Navy's predominant ship-borne reconnaissance aircraft. Naval land-based air units used Wildcats, Dauntlesses, Ducks and Kingfishers as well. The Consolidated PBY Catalina flying boat was employed for long-range reconnaissance and transport duties. For cargo and transport missions, the principal aircraft was the Douglas R4D Skytrain. Marine Corps land-based air units included fighters and scout/dive bombers. Marine pilots were flying Grumman biplanes, Grumman F4F Wildcats and Brewster F2A Buffalo fighters. Scout/dive bombers assigned to Marine Air Units included Curtiss SBC Helldiver biplanes, Vought-Sikorsky SB2U Vindicators and the Douglas SBD Dauntless.

Back in 1915, the United States had barely enough trained pilots to staff its meager air service of some 20 planes. By 1941, the US had become the world's leading manufacturer and exporter of military aircraft. Yet impressive as this production appeared over the decades of the '20s and '30s, the bulk of America's Pacific force consisted mainly of old biplanes and obsolete monoplanes. The combined strength of all US Army, Navy and Marine planes totaled 5,000, divided about equally between the Army and the Navy. Of these, 2,000 aircraft could be considered modern and combat ready.

More than half of these modern aircraft were housed on the US mainland, engaged in training exercises for the expected war with Germany. Numbers of new planes in production were promised to England as part of the Lend-Lease Act. Only 688 US land-based aircraft of all types and quality were in service in the Pacific in December 1941, some on the Hawaiian island of Oahu and others on Luzon in the Philippines, on Midway Island and on Wake Island. The US had another 225 aircraft based on the Navy's Pacific Fleet carriers, *Enterprise, Lexington* and *Saratoga*. The United Kingdom had 300 aircraft in the Pacific stationed at Singapore on the Malay Peninsula and on Borneo. The Dutch protected their interests in the Netherlands East Indies with about 200 planes, many of them obsolete. By comparison, the 3,000 planes of the Japanese Army and Navy were modern, combat-ready aircraft, more maneuverable and with more range and firepower than the military planes of the Allies. Japanese pilots and aircrews were well-trained and had become experienced in air combat over China. While some British and Dutch pilots had seen combat in Europe, American pilots were less well-trained and lacked combat experience.

Warships at the Ready—US Navy

In the aftermath of the treaties of the 1922 Washington disarmament conference, most signatories held to building new ships within the numbers and sizes allotted. The United States built fewer than prescribed. Japan built more. By 1930, however, and especially with the advent of the Roosevelt administration, warship construction in the US increased significantly. On February 17, 1930, the first of two heavy cruisers and the namesake of its class, *Portland* was laid down at the Bethlehem Steel Company in Quincy, Massachusetts. Four weeks later construction began on her sister ship, *Indianapolis*, at the New York Shipbuilding Company. *Indianapolis* was completed in November 1932 and *Portland* was ready for service by February 1933. The US named both its heavy and light cruisers for American cities. The first of the seven-ship *Minneapolis* class of heavy cruisers, *Astoria*, was laid down at the Puget Sound Navy Yard in September 1930. She was followed by *New Orleans* in March 1931, *Minneapolis* in June, and *Tuscaloosa* and *San Francisco* in September. Work on *Quincy* began in November 1933 at the Bethlehem Steel Company and the final cruiser of the class, *Vincennes*, was laid down there in January 1934. The last American heavy cruiser to be built during the 1930s, *Wichita*, was laid down as a single ship in October 1935 at the Philadelphia Navy Yard. Like cruisers of the *Portland* and the *Minneapolis* classes, *Wichita* displaced nearly 10,000 tons and was the last American heavy cruiser of its size. Eight 13,600-ton heavy cruisers of the *Baltimore* class were ordered in 1940 from the Bethlehem Steel Company and were in various stages of construction in late 1941. Construction on *Baltimore* began in May 1941 and on *Boston* and on *St. Paul* by December.

More than 15 years after the US Navy initiated its 10-ship *Omaha* class light cruiser program, work began on the larger and more heavily armed nine-ship *Brooklyn* class. *Savannah* was laid down in May 1934 and *Brooklyn* in March 1935. It was late 1939 when all *Brooklyn* class light cruisers were ready for service. The largest shipbuilding program for US Navy cruisers began July 1, 1940, when *Cleveland*, first of the 32-ship light cruiser *Cleveland* class, was laid down at the New York Shipbuilding Corporation. The ships of both the *Brooklyn* class and the *Cleveland* class displaced 10,000 tons. The *Cleveland* class had fewer main 6-inch guns than the *Brooklyn* class but more 5-inch, dual-purpose secondary batteries that were used for anti-aircraft as well as surface fire. Nineteen *Omaha* and *Brooklyn* class light cruisers were in service in late 1941 and 12 of the *Cleveland* class were under construction.

A new and distinct type of warship was placed in production in 1940, built specifically to protect and screen other warships from enemy attack by air. Armed with 12 dual-purpose, 5-inch, .38-caliber guns, the eight anti-aircraft light cruisers of the *Atlanta* class were produced at the Federal Shipbuilding Company at Kearny, New Jersey, at the Bethlehem Steel facilities at Quincy, and at San Francisco. *San Diego* was laid down in March 1940, *Atlanta* in April, and *San Juan* and *Juneau* that May. Construction on *Oakland* and *Reno* began in 1941 and work on *Spokane* and on *Tucson* was scheduled for 1942. None of the *Atlanta* class anti-aircraft light cruisers were in service by December 1941.

Though the US Navy had never produced a battle cruiser to completion, the *Alaska* class of six battle cruisers was scheduled for production at the New York Shipbuilding Corporation in early 1942. At 28,000 tons standard displacement and named for US possessions, only two ships, USS *Alaska* and USS *Guam*, were eventually completed as battle cruisers.

US Navy destroyers were named for men who had served the country, officers and enlisted men of the Navy and the Marine Corps, Secretaries of the Navy, members of Congress and some for American inventors. With the commissioning of the USS *Allen* in 1917 and until December 1941, the US Navy took delivery of 374 destroyers. Over the years, most of the old flush-deck, four-stack destroyers produced before 1920 were removed from active duty, decommissioned and placed in moth balls. Others were converted to minesweepers while some were modified into tenders and transports. Some were transferred to the US Coast Guard and some were sold for scrap. A dozen years after the last of the flush-decks was laid down, construction on destroyers of the post-war programs began in earnest. The first destroyer and namesake of the eight-ship *Farragut* class was laid down at the Bethlehem Steel Company in Quincy in September 1932. The *Farragut* class was followed by the eight-ship *Porter* class in 1933, the 18-ship *Mahan* class in 1934, the five-ship *Somers* class and the 22-ship *Gridley* class in 1934, the 12-ship *Sims* class in 1937 and the 24-ship *Benson* class in 1938. The 1940 Programme, also called the 193 + 80 Programme, initially authorized 115 destroyers of the *Fletcher* class and 78 destroyers of the *Bristol* class, with an additional 80 destroyers to be built later. *Bristol* was laid down at the Federal Shipbuilding and Dry Dock Company in December 1940 and it was the only destroyer in the 78-ship class that was ready for service by December 1941. Fifty-one destroyers of the *Bristol* class were under construction and only 22 of the 115 planned warships of the *Fletcher* class were laid down by that time. With passage by the US Congress of the Lend-Lease Act in March 1941, the United States began the transfer of 50 of the decommissioned flush decks to the British Royal Navy. In April 1941 the United States Navy totaled its number of destroyers ready for service at 174. By December the last three ships of the *Benson* class were ready and the first destroyer of the 78-ship *Bristol* class, USS *Bristol*, was completed. USS *Dahlgren* was modified for training duty, destroyers *Hamilton, Southard, Zane, Wasmuth, Trever, Perry, Hovey* and *Long* converted to minesweepers, and USS *Noa* recommissioned as a seaplane tender.

Sixteen battleships were built for the United States Navy between 1912 and 1923. They were named for states of the Union as were all subsequent American battleships. USS *Arkansas* and her sister ship USS *Wyoming* were the oldest. Between 1926 and 1931, all US battleships underwent varying degrees of modification and modernization. The older ships—*Arkansas, Wyoming, New York, Texas, Nevada, Oklahoma, Pennsylvania* and *Arizona*—received extensive alterations and refits that increased standard displacement by 3,000 tons or more. The more modern battleships built in the 1920s received less extensive modifications along with superstructure alterations. One modification done on all refitted ships was replacement of old secondary batteries with new 5-inch, dual-purpose, rapid-fire guns. The first battleships to be built since USS *West Virginia* in 1923 were USS *North Carolina* and USS *Washington*; they were completed late in 1941. Laid down at the New York Navy Yard in 1937, *North Carolina* was the first of six, 35,000-ton *Washington* class fast battleships. *Alabama, Indiana, Massachusetts* and *South Dakota* were under construction at that time. In 1940, USS *Wyoming* was demilitarized for use as a training ship. Also that year, six more fast battleships, this time of 45,000-ton displacement, were planned and by that September, *Iowa* was laid down at the New York Navy Yard and *New Jersey* was under construction at the Philadelphia Navy Yard. *Missouri* and *Wisconsin* were laid down the following January. Hulls of the last two ships planned for the class, *Illinois* and *Kentucky*, were never produced as battleships. The Navy anticipated that by 1942, USS *Arkansas* and USS *Texas* would be replaced by USS *North Carolina* and USS *Washington*. The four remaining battleships of the *Washington* class would be ready in 1942, and the first completed ships of the *Iowa* class would be ready in 1943. The Navy expected that in 1943, USS *New York* would be replaced by USS *Indiana*, USS *Nevada* by USS *Massachusetts*, USS *Oklahoma* by the new *Alabama*, and USS *Pennsylvania* by USS *South Dakota*. It was also planned that by 1944, the four ships of the *Iowa* class would replace *Arizona* and the three old *New Mexico* class battleships.

America's first aircraft carrier, USS *Langley*, was converted from a fleet collier in 1921, and in 1937, she was converted again from an aircraft carrier (CV 1) to an aircraft tender (AV 3). The first US fleet carriers were converted battle cruisers, *Lexington* and *Saratoga*. At the Newport News Shipbuilding

Company in September 1931, the US Navy's newest warship, *Ranger*, was the first American vessel to be laid down as an aircraft carrier. At 14,500 tons, she went into service in June 1934 and was the first of many thoroughbreds that followed. The three carriers of the 20,000-ton *Yorktown* class were also constructed at Newport News. Work began on *Yorktown* in May 1934 and on *Enterprise* two months later. Because of serious construction problems in reduction gearing and boiler tubing, *Enterprise* was not completed until July 1938 and *Yorktown* that November. Consequently, the third carrier of the *Yorktown* class, *Hornet*, was not laid down until September 1939 and was completed in October 1941. A lone carrier of 14,700 tons, *Wasp*, was laid down in April 1936 at the Bethlehem Steel Company. Completed in April 1940, USS *Wasp* along with USS *Hornet* became the last American fleet carriers constructed before war began, although *Hornet* was not yet ready for service. *Lexington, Saratoga* and *Yorktown* were named for historic battles, *Ranger, Enterprise* and *Hornet* for old naval vessels.

Work on an 11-ship fast fleet carrier class began in April 1941 when namesake *Essex* was laid down at the Newport News Shipbuilding Company. Four months later construction began on *Cabot* at the Bethlehem Steel Company and on December 1, *Intrepid* was laid down at Newport News, Virginia. Two of the 27,000-ton carriers, USS *Essex* and USS *Intrepid*, were completed and ready for service by the end of 1942. By summer 1941, three of eight light aircraft carriers of the new *Independence* class were under construction at New York: *Independence, Princeton* and *Belleau Wood*. That November, *Cowpens* was laid down at the New York Yard and late in December, work began on *Monterey*. The remaining three carriers of the class were started in 1942.

By 1939 four 7,800-ton merchantmen, diesel-powered C-3 merchant ships were undergoing modification into a new and different type of warship, the Escort Aircraft Carrier. A fifth and similar vessel, the merchantman *Mormacmail*, was refitted and renamed USS *Long Island* for launch in January 1940. Commissioned in 1941 as the US Navy's first escort carrier, *Long Island* was the forerunner of more than 100 escort carriers, 10 of which were under construction by December 1941, six of the 7,800-ton *Bogue* class and four of the 12,000-ton *Sangamon* class.

Warships at the Ready—Imperial Japanese Navy

The thrust of Japan's shipbuilding programs in the 1930s was directed at new destroyer and aircraft carrier construction. Earlier, the 2nd class destroyers built in the 1920s had been given botanical names. Like the 1st class ships of the previous decade, the new Japanese destroyers carried meteorological and seasonal names in a poetic style. *Shigure* translated to English as autumn showers, *Shiratsuyu* as white dew, and, of course, *Kamikaze* as divine wind. Most aircraft carriers were named for dragons and birds. *Ryujo* meant sacred dragon and *Zuikaku*, happy crane. The carriers *Akagi* and *Kaga* were laid down earlier in the century as a battle cruiser and a battleship, respectively, and were named differently. *Akagi* translated as red castle and *Kaga* as increased joy.

In May 1931 at Sasebo Shipyard, work began on *Hatsuharu*, the first of six destroyers of the 1,400-ton *Hatsuharu* class. Two others were laid down the same year and the remaining ships of the class were under construction early in 1933. The last destroyer of the class, *Yugure*, was laid down in April 1933 and was ready for service by April 1935. At Sasebo Yard in November 1933, the destroyer *Shiratsuyu* was the first of 10 ships of the *Shigure* class to undergo construction. These were similar in size, speed and armament to the *Hatsuharu* class, and by mid-1935, all the class had been laid down. The last to be completed, *Suzukaze*, was ready for service by September 1937. The first ship and namesake of the slightly larger 10-ship *Asashio* class was started in September 1935, also at the Sasebo facility. All the class were under construction by November 1937. The last destroyer in the class, *Kasumi*, was completed and ready for service by July 1938. The 18 ships of the *Kagero* class were the last group of Japanese destroyers completed before the war. *Shiranuhi* and *Kuroshio* were laid down in late August 1937 and *Kagero* started that September. All *Kagero* class destroyers were laid down by 1940 and all were ready for service by December 1941. Each displaced 2,000 tons and was armed with six 5-inch guns and eight torpedo tubes. Similar but slightly larger than the *Kagero* class vessels, the *Yugumo* program planned to produce 28 destroyers. Construction began in 1939 but only *Akigumo* was completed by December 1941. *Akigumo* was followed by *Yugumo* in late December and destroyers *Kazagumo* and *Makigumo* in March 1942. Work began in July 1940 on the namesake of the *Akizuki* class, the first of a 16-ship program for the largest of all Japanese destroyers. Four of the 2,700-ton vessels were under construction by December 1941. A lone destroyer, *Shimakaze,* was laid down in August 1941 at Maizuru Naval Yard.

Of the two fleet carriers of the *Soryu* class, *Soryu* was started in November 1934 at Kure Shipbuilding Yard and was completed in December 1937. The second ship of the class, *Hiryu,* was laid down at Yokosuka Naval Yard in July 1936 and completed two years later. The last two Japanese fleet carriers built before the war were *Shokaku* and *Zuikaku. Shokaku* was laid down in December 1937 at Yokosuka Naval Yard and *Zuikaku* was started the following year at Kawasaki Shipbuilding Company. By late 1941 both Imperial Japanese Navy's 20,000-ton aircraft carriers were ready to join the Combined Fleet. Work on two additional fleet carriers, *Junyo* and *Hiyo,* had begun. *Shoho* and *Zuiho*, originally laid down as submarine tenders, went into service in 1941 as light carriers. Japan's first escort carrier, *Taiyo,* converted from a former transport, went into service that year also. Two other escort carriers, *Chuyo* and *Unyo,* would eventually follow. Fleet carrier *Taiho*, Japan's answer to America's new *Essex* class carrier, was about to be laid down in December 1941, and the super-carrier *Shinano*, a 64,000-ton warship, was in the planning stage. By December 1941, Japan had produced 10 aircraft carriers, built an eleventh from a converted transport ship, and had three carriers at various stages of construction. Another vessel, completed as the submarine depot *Taigei* in 1933, would emerge in November 1942 as the 7,100-ton light carrier, *Ryuho.*

Most Japanese battleships that came into service earlier in the 20th century were given geographical names of old provinces. *Mutsu* was named for a province at the northern tip of the island of Hokkaido, *Yamashiro* for the province of the city of Kyoto. The 62,000-ton super battleships under construction in 1940, the last two battleships Japan would produce, were *Yamato* and *Musashi. Yamato*, translated as an ancient word for Japan, was completed and ready for service early in 1942. *Musashi* was completed later that year.

In 1932, as the four heavy cruisers of the *Atago* class were nearing completion, work was underway on the first two of the four-ship *Mogami* class. *Mogami* was laid down at Kure Shipyard and *Mikuma* at the Mitsubishi shipbuilding facility. Both were completed in 1935 and were followed by sister ships *Suzuya* and *Kumano* in 1937. The heavy cruiser *Chikuma* was ready for service in 1939. She followed *Tone*, her sister ship, which had been completed in November 1938. The 8,500-ton *Chikuma* of the *Tone* class was the last Japanese heavy cruiser built. The Japanese named most of their heavy cruisers for mountains and their light cruisers for rivers. After the *Jintsu* class of 1925, the Japanese produced no light cruisers until 1940. The *Katori,* first of three 5,500-ton light cruisers, came into service in April 1940. It was followed by *Kashima* in May of that year and *Kashii* in July 1941. Designed as training vessels, the ships were slow and void of armor. Three of four light cruisers of the 6,650-ton *Agano* class were laid down by late 1941, along with a lone light cruiser, 8,160-ton *Oyodo*.

World Events Escalate

On September 3, 1939, two days after Germany invaded Poland, the United Kingdom and France declared war against Germany. The Royal Navy remained the world's most powerful, with a force slightly larger than the US Navy. As war in Europe escalated, however, and as the United Kingdom attempted to protect her colonial holdings and other interests abroad, the ships of the Commonwealth became sparsely dispersed around the globe. Early in the war, Britain controlled the eastern Atlantic and provided maritime security between the Americas and England, but by 1941, Germany occupied the west coast of France and U-boat attacks became more frequent. Britain lacked the naval resources to continue her protection of the region and looked to the United States for assistance and materiel. To supply England, now threatened with starvation, with goods and armaments, the Roosevelt administration enacted the Lend-Lease Act with an initial appropriation of $7 billion. Said to be of mutual benefit to the United States and her allies, Lend-Lease rewards accrued mainly to Great Britain. In addition to the old flush-deck, four-stack destroyers England received, the US launched a shipbuilding program that eventually produced more than 200 anti-submarine convoy destroyer escorts for the Royal Navy. The United States also agreed to protect the convoys that crossed the Atlantic with supplies for Great Britain. In September 1941, the destroyer USS *Greer* was attacked without success by a German U-boat, while a second American destroyer, USS *Kearny*, was torpedoed and badly damaged. Two weeks after the attack on the *Kearny*, one of the first Lend-Lease long-hulled destroyer escorts, USS *Reuben James*, was torpedoed and sunk with the loss of 150 American officers and men. Although no declaration of war had been made by either country, by October 1941 a state of undeclared war existed between the United States and Germany.

With war against Germany imminent, the United States continued diplomatic attempts to avert hostilities with Japan. However, if conflict were to erupt on both fronts, Allied strategy called for America to join in unlimited warfare against Germany first while holding Japan in check in the Pacific until Germany was defeated. Most US military experts reasoned that if Japan expanded her war, she would strike first in the Dutch East Indies for oil. Other strategists believed that Japan would strike in the Philippines or against the US Pacific Island possessions of Guam, Wake and Midway.

Washington and London agreed that Britain's Singapore, the Gibraltar of the Pacific, could control Japanese naval advances to the south and east. Singapore would become the western anchor of the Malay Barrier, creating an 1,800-mile-long natural barricade from Singapore to New Guinea. Formed by islands of the Netherlands East Indies, the Malay Barrier protected Australia and New Zealand from attack from the north. It was reasoned that Japanese movement south through the China Sea or the Philippine Sea would be detected long before a Japanese naval force could cross the equator. If such movement were to occur, the US Navy, British Royal Navy and the Royal Netherlands Navy would all respond. Should Japan strike the Philippines first, the Manila-based Asiatic Fleet, aided by the remaining warships of the Pacific Fleet, could contain Japan's initial advance to the south.

By November 1941, Japan's plans for war against the United States and the Pacific colonial powers were set. Naval and land combat contingencies were in place. Her strategy of attack in the Pacific mostly paralleled the Allies' expectations, with some striking exceptions including the approach the Japanese would take to Singapore and the attack on Hawaii. Before striking Guam, Wake or Midway and prior to amphibious landings in the Philippines and the oil fields of the Dutch East Indies, Japan planned to invade the Malay Peninsula, not by sea from the south as the Allies imagined but over land from the North. She would neutralize the only British base in the region, at Singapore, to secure her oil supply. To protect her flank while moving down the Malay Peninsula, Japan planned to invade the Philippines and take out her only other deterrent in the region, the US fleet at Manila. After defeating the British at Singapore and the Americans at Manila, Japan planned to move south to the oil fields and the rubber and tungsten deposits of the Dutch East Indies. A southward advance, however, required containment of the one force able to cut the Japanese Navy's line of communication, the US Pacific Fleet based at Pearl Harbor on the Hawaiian island of Oahu.

To secure her major objectives in the Pacific, Japan had to establish a defensive perimeter. Beginning north of Japan at the Kurile Islands, this perimeter would continue southeast to the equator and the Gilbert Islands (now Kiribati). Below the equator, her line of defense would extend through the island of Bougainville in the Solomons, take in northern New Guinea, all the Dutch East Indies and then run west, encompassing the large island of Sumatra and into the Indian Ocean to include Burma. To secure the area within these defensive perimeters, the Japanese planned major attack objectives during the opening phase of war. They would invade the American possessions of Wake and Guam and bombard Midway Island. Their amphibious forces would land on the Malay Peninsula and on Luzon in the Philippines. The cities of Rangoon and Hong Kong would be secured by Japanese land troops while the islands of New Britain and New Ireland in the Bismarck Archipelago would be attacked from the sea.

With the defense perimeter in place, the sea lanes between the United States and the Philippines would be cut and the island of Fiji and the islands of the New Hebrides (now Vanuatu) threatened. China would be isolated and Japan could continue to ravage this old enemy while watching any movement from Russia in the north. The perimeter would further threaten America's lines of communication with Australia and New Zealand.

To accomplish these planned objectives, the Imperial Japanese Army and the Imperial Japanese Navy must overcome their dissension. It would be up to the Navy's Combined Fleet to take the impending war—and the Army— to the enemy.

Chapter III

ON THE EVE OF ATTACK

Introduction

Japan renounced the treaties of the Washington disarmament conference in 1936, yet by November 1941 her battleship and destroyer numbers remained in parity with those of the United States. The Imperial Japanese Navy had 10 battleships to the United States' 17, 110 destroyers to the US's 168. In carrier numbers, the Japanese moved beyond the old guidelines of the disarmament treaties. She had 11 aircraft carriers; the United States had one escort carrier and six fleet carriers with a seventh, USS *Hornet*, due for service early in 1942. The Japanese Navy had no battle cruisers and none planned while the US Navy was authorized to build six. Both navies had 18 heavy cruisers in service by late 1941. Japan had 20 light cruisers, the US 19 with approval to build six anti-aircraft light cruisers. Japan had none of these. After two years of war with Germany, Great Britain still ruled the waves, the United States Navy was ranked second and the Imperial Japanese Navy, a close third.

Imperial Japanese Navy—Leaders and Fleets

Hirohito was 40 years old in 1941 and in his fifteenth year as Japan's Emperor. In essence he was supreme Commander-in-Chief of the Army and of the

Navy. Admiral Osami Nagano served as Chief of the Naval General Staff, Admiral Isoroku Yamamoto was Commander in Chief of the Navy's Combined Fleet and Rear Admiral Matome Ugaki served as Yamamoto's Chief of Staff. The admirals reverenced the Emperor but their admiration did not extend to the Japanese Prime Minister, 57-year-old General Hideki Tojo. A military hard-liner more adept at administration than as a field commander, Tojo's experience was with the Army and his loyalties rested there as well. He disliked the admirals and they didn't trust him. Tojo was the son of an Army general and a graduate of the military academy and of the Army staff college. In the 1930s he commanded the military police in Manchuria and was appointed Chief of Staff of the Kwantung Army there. Even after being named Prime Minister in 1941, Tojo retained his posts of army minister and a general on the active list.

Admiral Osami Nagano turned 60 in 1940. He was named Chief of Staff of the Naval General Staff in 1941 after serving as commander of the Combined Fleet during the 1930s. He was a chief advisor to the Emperor and a supporter of striking south to acquire the oil fields of the Netherlands East Indies.

Within the Imperial Japanese Navy, there were three distinct naval commands. The China Area Fleet included only a few surface warships. The command of Home and Naval Guard Stations included four bases in Japanese waters, three naval stations outside the home islands and a few smaller facilities or guard stations, but no ships. The Combined Fleet under Yamamoto was the Japanese Navy's paramount force and included command and control of most surface warships, all submarine forces, amphibious naval landing units, including Special Naval Landing Forces and all carrier and land-based aircraft.

Yamamoto was born in 1884, the son of a schoolmaster. He graduated from the Naval Academy at Etajima in 1904 and served on a cruiser at the Battle of Tsushima during the Russo-Japanese War where he suffered a leg wound and lost two fingers from his left hand. After service in the Great War, he was sent to Harvard University to study English and learn the importance of oil to a modern navy. When Yamamoto returned to Japan in 1924, he was assigned to an air station as an executive officer and, in 1926, traveled again to the United States as naval attaché in Washington. Yamamoto had great faith in carriers and naval aviation but little respect for battleships. By 1930, now a Rear Admiral, he was assigned to Japanese Naval Air Corps Headquarters where he was instrumental in developing the Navy's new carrier-borne fighter, the plane that would come to be called the Zero. By 1935 he was promoted to Vice Admiral and appointed Vice Minister of the Navy. In 1939, when his opposition to war with the western powers led to an extremist plot to assassinate him, Yamamoto was promoted to Admiral and Commander in Chief of the Combined Fleet and sent to sea.

Yamamoto knew his country could not win a lengthy war with the United States. When asked by Prince Konoye, Prime Minister before Tojo, how he viewed Japan's chances in such a war, Yamamoto replied, "We can run wild for six months, or a year, but after that I have utterly no confidence. I hope you will try to avoid war with America." Over time, however, Yamamoto became convinced of the necessity of war and that a surprise attack on the US Pacific Fleet's base at Pearl Harbor was Japan's best strategy. If Japan could indeed run wild in the Pacific, perhaps the United States would sue for peace and allow Japan to keep her conquered territories and her needed access to raw materials. By late 1941, Japan had but 18 months remaining of her supply of oil.

In theory Yamamoto's Combined Fleet included eight naval commands, some with more responsibility than others. The First, Second, Third, Fourth and Fifth Fleets included all but a few of the Imperial Japanese Navy's surface warships, troop transports and auxiliary vessels. The Sixth Fleet was assigned all the Navy's submarines.

First Fleet, based at Hashirajima on Hiroshima Bay, included the Imperial Japanese Navy's battleship force and was considered its main surface battle fleet. In December 1941 ships of the First Fleet not assigned to upcoming missions or not transferred to other fleets remained anchored in home port. They made up Combined Fleet's Main Body. Although Vice Admiral Shiro Takasu was in command, his administrative role was overshadowed whenever the 32,000-ton battleship *Nagato*, flagship of Admiral Yamamoto, was anchored at Hashirajima. And in the last month of 1941 and the first five months of 1942, *Nagato* did remain in port there along with five other battleships, two light aircraft carriers, two light cruisers and 13 destroyers.

Second Fleet, with bases at Yokosuka south of Tokyo and on Hainan

Island off China's south coast, was Combined Fleet's scouting force. By December 1941 it included more cruisers and destroyers than any other Japanese fleet. Second Fleet was commanded by Vice Admiral Nobutake Kondo, one of a few senior Japanese naval officers who believed that in the event of war, Japan could defeat the United States. Kondo was a 1907 graduate of the Naval Academy at Etajima and had traveled in Russia and in Germany. In addition to leading the Second Fleet, he would oversee all Japanese naval forces for the Malaya, Philippines and Netherlands East Indies Campaigns and, except for Yamamoto, would be responsible for more vessels and aircraft than any Pacific commander.

Third Fleet, based at Formosa (now Taiwan), was the Japanese Navy's blockade and amphibious force and included most of her transport and auxiliary vessels. In charge of Third Fleet was Commander in Chief Vice Admiral Ibo Takahashi, a 1908 graduate of the Japanese Naval Academy and a 1919 graduate of the Naval War College. He was promoted to Vice Admiral in 1939 and given his command in 1941 at age 53. His ships would deliver Japanese Army invasion forces to the Philippines and to the Netherlands East Indies.

Fourth Fleet was Japan's South Seas Force and was assigned protection of her mandate islands. Operating from the island of Truk in the Caroline Islands, the Fleet was led by Vice Admiral Shigeyoshi Inouye and was strong in cruisers and in destroyers. Inouye, also 53 years old, had studied in France and in Switzerland after the Great War and returned to Japan for additional military training. He received a naval staff appointment in the early 1920s and served as commander of a battleship. Like Yamamoto, Inouye was criticized early on for his anti-war stance and for his strong support of naval aviation and aircraft carriers over battleships. Fourth Fleet under Inouye would have responsibility for assaults on the American possessions of Guam and Wake Island.

Fifth Fleet, the Navy's Northern Force, was based at Maizuru and at Ominato on the island of Honshu. It was a small cruiser and destroyer force led by Vice Admiral Boshiro Hosogaya with responsibility for keeping shipping lanes open and secure for naval traffic.

Sixth Fleet, led by Vice Admiral Mitsumi Shimizu, included all submarines of the Imperial Japanese Navy and had its main base in the Marshall

Islands at Kwajalein Atoll. The Japanese had 11 coastal submarines, designated RO, that ranged in size from 700 to 1,000 tons standard displacement on the surface. They had 49 seagoing boats, all the I-type that displaced 1,900 to 2,180 tons. As many as 10 of the larger submarines, the seagoing *I-15* class, carried a floatplane within a hangar bay on deck. RO boats were armed with four to six 21-inch torpedo tubes, a 3-inch deck gun and carried a crew of 40 to 50 officers and men. I-type boats had six to eight 21-inch torpedo tubes, a 4- or 5-inch deck gun and a crew of 50 to 70. There were also two-man midget subs that were transported by the larger submarines and released in or near enemy territory. They displaced 80 tons or less and were armed with two to four torpedo tubes.

Japan's First Air Fleet was the Navy's primary carrier strike force and had as its nucleus Japan's six fleet carriers and 409 carrier aircraft. Fleet carriers *Akagi* and *Kaga* made up the 1st Carrier Division; *Hiryu* and *Soryu,* the 2nd Carrier Division; and *Shokaku* and *Zuikaku,* newly commissioned in autumn 1941, comprised the 5th Carrier Division. Light carriers *Hosho* and *Ryujo* made up First Air Fleet's 3rd Carrier Division and light carrier *Zuiho* with the new escort carrier *Taiyo* became the 4th Carrier Division. Together the 3rd and 4th Carrier Divisions carried just under 100 aircraft.

In July 1941 all 10 battleships of the Imperial Japanese Navy operated under First Fleet command while all six fleet carriers and the three light carriers operated under the First Air Fleet. However, as the year went on and the probability of war increased, vessels were moved among the six surface forces. Four battleships were transferred away from First Fleet, two to Scouting Force and two to the Carrier Force. The light carriers and the escort carrier were transferred from First Air Fleet, two to Scouting Force and one each to Battle Fleet and South Seas Fleet.

In the 1930s Vice Admiral Chuichi Nagumo commanded the 1st Carrier Division. Early in 1941 at age 53, he was appointed Commander in Chief of the entire First Air Fleet with *Akagi* his flagship. Nagumo was a 1908 graduate of the Naval Academy at Etajima, a destroyer man, specializing in torpedo warfare and inexperienced in naval air warfare. Serving under Nagumo was a 36-year-old junior air officer, Commander Minoru Genda. Genda earned his wings in 1929, graduating at the top of his class. As early as 1934, while an Air Corps instructor, he developed a theory on the use of aircraft carriers and their fighter planes in combat and entertained the possibility of a carrier attack on Pearl Harbor. In early 1941 Genda formulated an ambitious plan for such an attack on the US Pacific Fleet, a plan that would play significantly in Yamamoto's final blueprint. From *Akagi,* Vice Admiral Nagumo, in addition to commanding all ships in First Air Fleet, also remained in command of the 1st Carrier Division. From carrier *Hiryu,* Rear Admiral Tamon Yamaguchi led the 2nd Carrier Division and Rear Admiral Chuichi Hara, from *Zuikaku,* commanded the 5th Carrier Division.

Eleventh Air Fleet commanded by Vice Admiral Nizhizo Tsukahara included three air flotillas totaling more than 600 Navy land-based fighter, bomber and reconnaissance aircraft, eight seaplane tenders and 150 floatplanes and flying boats. Rear Admiral Takeo Tada commanded the 21st Air Flotilla based on western Formosa. Rear Admiral Sadaichi Matsunaga commanded the 22nd Air Flotilla that operated from airfields near Saigon in French Indochina and Rear Admiral Eiji Goto led the 24th Air Flotilla stationed at newly developed airfields in the Marshall Islands on Kwajalein and on Maloelap. Other aircraft were stationed in the Marianas on the island of Saipan. The Air Flotillas would support naval operations by attacking enemy targets within range of their respective bases.

China Area Fleet, under the command of Vice Admiral Mineichi Koga, was the only Japanese sea command not under Admiral Yamamoto's direct control. Based on China's east coast at Shanghai and recognized as the Navy's China Coastal Force, China Area Fleet contained a handful of surface warships. Because Koga was connected to the Japanese Imperial Household, he rose quickly through the ranks after graduating from the Naval Academy in 1906. In 1930 he was promoted to Rear Admiral and assigned to the Naval General Staff. He sided with the Navy's old-line officers in their belief in battleships over aircraft carriers and openly stated that Japan could not defeat the US Pacific Fleet. By December 1941, after falling out of favor with the General Staff, Koga commanded the smallest naval force in the Imperial Japanese Navy.

The Home Command included four large naval bases within the Japanese home islands and three facilities outside Japanese waters. The home stations included Yokosuka on Tokyo Bay, Kure south of Hiroshima, Maizuru north of Osaka and Sasebo on the west coast of Kyushu Island.

Outside of Japan the Navy maintained facilities on the east coast of Hainan Island in the China Sea, in southern Manchuria at Port Arthur and on Formosa. Other installations were built in Japan's Ryukyu Islands, at Cam Ranh Bay on the east coast of French Indochina, in the Palau Islands 500 miles east of the Philippines and at Roi-Naumur Island in the Marshall Islands.

United States Navy—Leaders and Fleets

The United States Fleet headquartered at San Diego was restructured in February 1940. Under the new arrangement, the Atlantic Squadron at Norfolk, Virginia, was renamed the Atlantic Fleet and Admiral Ernest J. King remained in charge as Commander in Chief. At Pearl Harbor on Oahu in Hawaii, Admiral James O. Richardson was replaced by Admiral Husband E. Kimmel, who now commanded the new US Pacific Fleet. An older, smaller fleet based near Manila on the Philippine island of Luzon, the US Asiatic Fleet, was under the command of Admiral Thomas C. Hart. In addition to these main facilities, US warships could also be attached to one of five naval districts. Besides being based at Pearl Harbor or attached to the 14th Naval District there, Pacific Fleet vessels might be assigned to the 11th Naval District at San Diego, the 12th at San Francisco or the 13th at Seattle. The roster of ships at the 15th Naval District in the Panama Canal Zone would generally include warships from the Atlantic Fleet but might attach vessels from the Pacific Fleet as well.

Unlike the Japanese Navy's Combined Fleet, each of the three United States fleets was thought capable of performing and completing any mission or operation without drawing vessels from other forces. Rosters of the Atlantic and Pacific Fleets included battleships, aircraft carriers, cruisers, destroyers and submarines, while the Asiatic Fleet at Manila had no battleships or carriers and only a handful of cruisers and destroyers. Because of the Allies' Defeat Germany First policy, Admiral King's Atlantic Fleet received most new warships being produced as well as vessels transferred to his command from the Pacific Fleet.

Repair facilities for US warships stationed in the Pacific were located along the west coast of the United States, on Oahu and on Luzon in the Philippines. The US had a small naval base on the island of Mindanao in the Philippines as well as facilities for ships and aircraft on Guam in the Marianas and on Wake and Midway Islands in the central Pacific. South of Hawaii there were naval bases at Johnston Island and at Palmyra near the equator. South of the equator there was a joint American-New Zealand naval facility on Samoa.

In early 1941 President Franklin Roosevelt, beginning his third term in office, and his newly appointed Secretary of the Navy, Franklin Knox, strongly supported a two-ocean US Navy. Yet the President and Knox along with their colleagues in Washington remained focused on the defeat of Nazi Germany and on war in the Atlantic theater.

The Forces Compared

Ship-based planes came into their own in the Pacific on battleships and on cruisers as well as on carriers. In planes launched with catapults and recovered with cranes, floatplane crews rescued sailors and downed pilots and collected reconnaissance data. American battleships carried three aircraft each, except for the *Iowa* class ships that carried four. Japanese battleships housed up to three aircraft and the new *Yamato* would carry five. US heavy cruisers carried as many as four floatplanes. Light cruisers of the *Omaha* class carried four planes and the *Brooklyn* class, up to eight. The Japanese *Kako* class heavy cruisers carried two floatplanes each, the *Tone* class, six, and all other heavy cruisers, four. Most Japanese light cruisers carried a single aircraft for reconnaissance.

Torpedoes would prove important weapons on American and on Japanese submarines and on the cruisers and the destroyers of both navies. The Japanese had 65 submarines available to ply the waters of the Pacific in 1941, although 21 of these were obsolete. The United States had 28 submarines assigned to the Pacific Fleet and another 29 assigned to the Asiatic Fleet. Some American light cruisers and all destroyers carried torpedoes, and all Japanese cruisers and destroyers had them. US vessels held 21-inch diameter, turbine-propelled Mark XIV torpedoes that were 20 feet long and armed with 598-pound warheads. These had an effective range of 4,500 yards, or two-and-a-quarter nautical miles, and a top speed of 46 knots. Set at a slower running speed of 30 knots per hour, the Mark XIV had a maximum effective range of 16,000 yards or eight nautical miles. The ideal range for the Mark XIV was 1,200 yards but they often performed erratically, and when successful in striking a target, they exploded only occasionally. The Japanese Navy used the Type 94 torpedo, similar in range and speed to the Mark XIV but oxygen propelled and with a larger 865-pound warhead. A second torpedo, the Type 93 Long Lance, was developed secretly by the Japanese in the 1930s. It was fast, reliable and oxygen-fueled, nearly trackless. Traveling at 49 knots, the Long Lance had a maximum effective range of 20,000 yards and delivered a half ton of explosives.

By December 1941, there were 291,000 officers and men in the Imperial Japanese Navy. The Navy had 169 surface warships in late 1941 with 21 at various stages of construction and 37 more planned. A new super battleship, *Yamato*, was scheduled for service in 1942; it would displace nearly 63,000 tons and carry nine 18.1-inch main guns. All Japanese battleships were modernized during the 1930s except *Hiei*, which was modified in 1940. Older carriers underwent various degrees of reconstruction during the 1930s but the greatest alterations occurred on carriers *Akagi* and *Kaga*, increasing standard displacements from 26,900 to 33,000 tons and from 28,000 to 35,000 tons, respectively.

The United States Navy was formidable in warship numbers and strength but weak in manpower and crew proficiency. After years of living with the country's pacifist bent, the US military had no conscription or draft. To attract recruits, most services promised young Americans a 40-hour work week. In August 1941, there were 285,000 officers and men in the United States Navy, including reservists on active duty, serving in both the Atlantic and Pacific Oceans and in the States. There were 58,000 officers and men in the US Marine Corps. By December the Navy was authorized to increase its ranks to 500,000, the Marine Corps to 104,000, primarily in response to the war in Europe. The United States Navy had a total of 229 surface warships with 120 under construction and an additional 170 planned. Although the US Navy had a third more vessels, 113 of her warships were in the Atlantic Fleet, 16 were assigned to Cavite Navy Yard at Manila with the Asiatic Fleet, and 100 were assigned to the Pacific Fleet. Of the 100, less than half were at Pearl Harbor on December 7, 1941. Eight US battleships were there and one, *Colorado*, was on the west coast. The US federal budget authorized $300 million for the years 1942 and 1943 for the Navy to augment anti-aircraft defense systems on all its battleships, carriers, cruisers and more than 100 auxiliary vessels. Additional appropriations were planned to update anti-aircraft batteries, increase deck protection and add armored shields on all 5-inch anti-aircraft guns.

By 1941 most naval officials worldwide continued to believe that naval combat consisted of battleships and battle cruisers firing online at enemy columns of similar warships. All main batteries were aimed to either port or starboard and Crossing the T in front of or behind an enemy's ship or line of ships was still considered the classic naval maneuver. It was expected that sea battles would be fought in daylight. If a surface action occurred at night or in poor visibility or at extreme range, the new and still unperfected science of radio detecting and ranging (radar) might locate the enemy. Though aircraft and the aircraft carrier were seen to influence a battle's outcome, a majority of military and political thinkers saw the carrier as a supplement to the combat effectiveness of already proven warships during surface engagements. Proponents of the battleship and proponents of carriers understandably differed on the composition and formation of a task force, a term that navies gave to a capital ship or ships surrounded and screened by cruisers and destroyers and in some cases flanked or led by submarines. The Japanese Navy often used the term strike force. To some, battleships were a navy's principal offensive weapon and formed the core of the force. Cruisers provided combat support while protecting the task force from air attack with high-volume anti-aircraft fire. Destroyers provided anti-submarine defense and additional defense against air attacks. To others, a lone carrier would be at the task force center, screened and encircled by cruisers and destroyers. Here, the battleship was considered too slow for carrier task force operations and was assigned to pre-invasion missions for fire support and bombardment.

Though both navies had their share of battleship and carrier proponents and detractors, at Pearl Harbor the Japanese would bet their nation's future on aircraft carriers and the skill of their pilots. As a weapon of war, the carrier was still a new idea. The plan being argued by the Japanese Naval General Staff and by Yamamoto and the officers of Combined Fleet to use three, perhaps as many as six carriers in one strike force was nothing less than revolutionary.

Revolutionary as it may have been, in the early hours of November 26, 1941, *Akagi, Kaga, Hiryu, Soryu, Shokaku* and *Zuikaku* and the ships of the Pearl Harbor Strike Force departed their rendezvous point amid the snow and fog of Hitokappu Bay in the Kurile Islands. Their destination—the waters of the Pacific Ocean 250 miles north of the Hawaiian Islands.

APPENDICES

Appendix A

Naval Forces
December 1941

Warship Types Ready		Imperial Japanese Navy				United States Navy			
		Laid Down	To Be Built	Total	Ready	Laid Down	To Be Built	Total	
BBs	Battleships	10	2	0	12	17	8	2	27
CVs	Fleet Carriers	6	3	1	10	6	4	8	18
CVLs	Light Carriers	4	1	0	5	0	4	4	8
CVEs	Escort Carriers	1	0	2	3	1	10	4	15
BCs	Battle Cruisers	0	0	0	0	0	0	6	6
CAs	Heavy Cruisers	18	0	0	18	18	3	5	26
CLs	Light Cruisers	20	4	1	25	19	12	20	51
CLAAs	AA Light Cruisers	0	0	0	0	0	6	2	8
DDs	Destroyers	110	11	33	154	168	73	119	360
Total Naval Forces:		169	21	37	227	229	120	170	519

United States Navy			
Warship Types	Warships Available	Atlantic Area	Pacific Area
BBs	17	8	9
CVs	6	3	3
CVLs	0	0	0
CVEs	1	1	0
BCs	0	0	0
CAs	18	5	13
CLs	19	8	11
CLAAs	0	0	0
DDs	168	88*	80**
Total Naval Forces:	229	113	116

*Atlantic Area includes 79 destroyers in the Atlantic Fleet and nine destroyers in the Canal Zone

**Pacific Area includes 54 destroyers in the Hawaiian Islands, four destroyers at San Diego, four at San Francisco, five at Seattle and 13 destroyers assigned to the Asiatic Fleet

Fleets	BBs	CVs	CVLs	CVEs	BCs	CAs	CLs	CLAAs	DDs	Totals
Japanese Navy	10	6	4	1	0	18	20	0	110	169
U.S. Asiatic Fleet	0	0	0	0	0	1	2	0	13	16
U.S. Pacific Fleet	9	3	0	0	0	12	9	0	67	100

Appendix B
Imperial Japanese Navy
December 1941
Supreme Commander in Chief: Emperor Hirohito
Chief of Naval General Staff: Admiral Osami Nagano

Combined Fleet
Commander in Chief: Admiral Isoroku Yamamoto
Chief of Staff: Rear Admiral Matome Ugaki

First Fleet (Battle Fleet—Main Body)
Commander in Chief: Vice Admiral Shiro Takasu
6 BBs:	*Fuso, Hyuga, Ise, Mutsu, Nagato, Yamashiro*
1 CVL:	*Zuiho*
1 CVE:	*Taiyo*
2 CLs:	*Kitakami, Oi*
13 DDs:	*Akatsuki, Arashi, Hagikaze, Hibiki, Hokaze, Kamikaze, Maikaze, Mikazuki, Nowaki, Shigure, Shiratsuyu, Usugumo, Yugure*

Second Fleet (Scouting Force)
Commander in Chief: Vice Admiral Nobutake Kondo
2 BBs:	*Haruna, Kongo*
2 CVLs:	*Hosho, Ryujo*
8 CAs:	*Atago, Chokai, Kumano, Maya, Mikuma, Mogami, Suzuya, Takao*
8 CLs:	*Jintsu, Kashii, Kinu, Kuma, Nagara, Naka, Sendai, Yura*
43 DDs:	*Amagiri, Amatsukaze, Arashio, Ariake, Asagiri, Asagumo, Asashio, Ayanami, Fubuki, Harusame, Hatsuharu, Hatsukaze, Hatsushimo, Hatsuyuki, Hayashio, Isonami, Kawakaze, Kuroshio, Michishio, Minegumo, Murakumo, Murasame, Natsugumo, Natsushio, Nenohi, Oshio, Oyashio, Sagiri, Samidare, Shikinami, Shinonome, Shirakumo, Shirayuki, Suzukaze, Tokitsukaze, Umikaze, Uranami, Wakaba, Yamagumo, Yamakaze, Yudachi, Yugiri, Yukikaze*

Third Fleet (Blockade and Amphibious Force)
Commander in Chief: Vice Admiral Ibo Takahashi
4 CAs: *Ashigara, Haguro, Myoko, Nachi*
1 CL: *Natori*
8 DDs: *Asakaze, Fumizuki, Harukaze, Hatakaze, Matsukaze, Minazuki, Nagatsuki, Satsuki*

Fourth Fleet (South Seas Force—Mandate Islands)
Commander in Chief: Vice Admiral Shigeyoshi Inouye
1 CVL: *Shoho*
4 CAs: *Aoba, Furutaka, Kako, Kinugasa*
4 CLs: *Kashima, Tatsuta, Tenryu, Yubari*
13 DDs: *Akebono, Asanagi, Hayate, Kikuzuki, Kisaragi, Mochizuki, Mutsuki, Oboro, Oite, Uzuki, Yayoi, Yunagi, Yuzuki*

Fifth Fleet (Northern Force—Home Waters)
Commander in Chief: Vice Admiral Boshiro Hosogaya
2 CLs: *Kiso, Tama*
14 DDs: *Akikaze, Hakaze, Hasu, Kuri, Minekaze, Namikaze, Nokaze, Numakaze, Okikaze, Sawakaze, Shiokaze, Tachikaze, Tsuga, Yukaze*

Sixth Fleet (Submarine Fleet)
Commander in Chief: Vice Admiral Mitsumi Shimizu
1 CL: *Katori*
65 Submarines

First Air Fleet (Carrier Force)
Commander in Chief: Vice Admiral Chuichi Nagumo

1st Carrier Division: Vice Admiral Chuichi Nagumo
2 CVs: *Akagi, Kaga*

2nd Carrier Division: Rear Admiral Tamon Yamaguchi
2 CVs: *Hiryu, Soryu*

5th Carrier Division: Rear Admiral Chuichi Hara

2 CVs:	*Zuikaku, Shokaku*
2 BBs:	*Hiei, Kirishima*
2 CAs:	*Chikuma, Tone*
1 CL:	*Abukuma*
11 DDs:	*Akigumo, Arare, Hamakaze, Isokaze, Kagero, Kasumi, Sazanami, Shiranuhi, Tanikaze, Urakaze, Ushio*

Eleventh Air Fleet (Land-Based Naval Aircraft)
Commander in Chief: Vice Admiral Nizhizo Tsukahara
21st Air Flotilla: Rear Admiral Takeo Tada
22nd Air Flotilla: Rear Admiral Sadaichi Matsunaga
24th Air Flotilla: Rear Admiral Eiji Goto

China Air Fleet (China Expeditionary Fleet)
Commander in Chief: Vice Admiral Mineichi Koga

1 CL:	*Isuzu*
8 DDs:	*Asagao, Fuyo, Ikazuchi, Inazuma, Karukaya, Kuretake, Sanae, Wakatake*

Appendix C
United States Navy
December 1941

Commander in Chief: Franklin D. Roosevelt
Secretary of the Navy: Colonel W. Franklin Knox
Chief of Naval Operations: Admiral Harold R. Stark

Asiatic Fleet
Commander in Chief: Admiral Thomas C. Hart

1 CA:	*Houston*
2 CLs:	*Boise, Marblehead*
13 DDs:	*Alden, Barker, Bulmer, Edsall, John D. Edwards, John D. Ford, Paul Jones, Parrott, Peary, Pillsbury, Pope, Stewart, Whipple*

Atlantic Fleet
Commander in Chief: Admiral Ernest J. King

8 BBs:	*Arkansas, Idaho, Mississippi, New Mexico, New York, North Carolina, Texas, Washington*
3 CVs:	*Ranger, Wasp, Yorktown*
1 CVE:	*Long Island*
5 CAs:	*Augusta, Quincy, Tuscaloosa, Vincennes, Wichita*
8 CLs:	*Brooklyn, Cincinnati, Memphis, Milwaukee, Nashville, Omaha, Philadelphia, Savannah*
79 DDs:	*Anderson, Babbitt, Badger, Bainbridge, Benson, Bernadou, Bristol, Broome, Buck, Cole, Dallas, Davis, Decatur, Dickerson, Dupont, Eberle, Edison, Ellis, Ericsson, Gleaves, Grayson, Greer, Gwin, Hammann, Herbert, Hughes, Charles F. Hughes, Ingraham, Hilary P. Jones, Jacob Jones, Jouett, Kearny, Lang, Lansdale, Lea, Leary, Livermore, Ludlow, MacLeish, Madison, Mayo, Mayrant, McCormick, McDougal, Meredith, Moffett, Monssen, Morris, Mustin, Niblack,*

Nicholson, O'Brien, Overton, Plunkett, Rhind, Roe, Roper, Rowan, Russell, Sampson, Schenck, Simpson, Sims, Somers, Stark, Sterett, Sturtevant, Swanson, Tarbell, Trippe, Truxtun, Upshur, Wainwright, Walke, Warrington, Wilkes, Wilson, Winslow, Woolsey

Fifteenth Naval District: Canal Zone

9 DDs: *Barney, Barry, Biddle, Blakeley, Borie, Breckinridge, Goff, J. Fred Talbot, Tattnall*

Pacific Fleet

Commander in Chief: Admiral Husband E. Kimmel

9 BBs: *Arizona, California, Colorado, Maryland, Nevada, Oklahoma, Pennsylvania, Tennessee, West Virginia*

3 CVs: *Enterprise, Lexington, Saratoga*

12 CAs: *Astoria, Chester, Chicago, Indianapolis, Louisville, Minneapolis, New Orleans, Northampton, Pensacola, Portland, Salt Lake City, San Francisco*

9 CLs: *Concord, Detroit, Helena, Honolulu, Phoenix, Raleigh, Richmond, St. Louis, Trenton*

54 DDs: *Allen*, Aylwin, Bagley, Balch, Benham, Blue, Case, Cassin, Chew*, Clark, Conyngham, Craven, Cummings, Cushing, Dale, Dent, Dewey, Downes, Drayton, Dunlap, Ellet, Fanning, Farragut, Flusser, Gridley, Helm, Henley, Hull, Jarvis, Lamson, Litchfield, Macdonough, Mahan, Maury, McCall, Monaghan, Mugford, Patterson, Perkins, Phelps, Porter, Preston, Ralph Talbot, Rathburne, Reid, Schley*, Selfridge, Shaw, Smith, Talbot, Tucker, Ward*, Waters, Worden*

*Destroyers attached 14th Naval District: Pearl Harbor

Eleventh Naval District: San Diego

4 DDs: *Crane, Crosby, Kennison, Kilty*

Twelfth Naval District: San Francisco

4 DDs:　　*Humphreys, King, Lawrence, Sands*

Thirteenth Naval District: Seattle

5 DDs:　　*Brooks, Fox, Gilmer, Hatfield, Kane*

Part Two

NOVEMBER 1941– APRIL 1942

About, about, in reel and rout,
The death-fires danced at night;
The water, like a witch's oils,
Burnt green, and blue and white.

—Samuel Taylor Coleridge, *The Rime of the Ancient Mariner* (1798)

Chapter IV

"MAY THE EMPEROR LIVE 10,000 YEARS ... BANZAI!"

Introduction

The months of August, September, October and November of 1941 in both Japan and in the United States were filled with talk of war between the two countries and with diplomatic efforts to avoid war. Liaison conferences, as well as Imperial conferences at which Emperor Hirohito was present, continued in Tokyo at a feverish pace. Japanese Prime Ministers, at first Prince Konoye, and then in mid-November, General Hideki Tojo, concurred with cabinet ministers and military Chiefs of Staff on an ongoing basis, ostensibly pressing for peace while planning for war. At a conference on September 3, Army Chief of Staff General Hajime Sugiyama introduced the idea of setting a deadline for negotiations. On September 6, at an Imperial conference, the decision was made that the Empire of Japan would go to war against the United States, Great Britain and the Netherlands unless negotiations were successful by October 10. Emperor Hirohito made it clear, however, that diplomacy would take precedence over military action. Later conferences pushed Japan's deadline for war forward to October 15 and then to early November and finally late November.

Earlier in the year, in the spring, US Secretary of State Cordell Hull put forward a four-point plan for peace that made demands on Japan to respect the territorial integrity of her neighbors. US Ambassador to Japan Joseph Grew knew though that the probability was high that Japan would wage war against the United States. In January 1941 Grew received word of rumors of an attack on the US Fleet at Pearl Harbor from the Peruvian ambassador in Tokyo and forwarded the information to Washington. However, neither the American Embassy in Tokyo nor the Department of State in Washington put much credence in the reports that, at the time, seemed incredible nor did either act on the information.

Negotiations between Japanese and US representatives were filled with mistrust and misunderstanding, racial prejudice and poor translations of documents, along with ignorance, pride and fear on both sides. Always the United States sought to buy time and always the Japanese looked toward their secret deadline. At an Imperial conference on November 5, 1941, a tentative date for military action was set for midnight November 30. In Washington on November 7, Cordell Hull received Japan's Proposal A from Ambassador Kichisaburo Nomura with wishes to resume meaningful diplomatic conversations. Hull felt that Japan's latest proposal held nothing new and that it did little to reconcile the question of Japanese aggression in China and her agreement with Germany. To placate the US and Great Britain and have trade sanctions and embargoes lifted so that oil and other essential supplies could flow, Japan would have to pull out of China and denounce the Tripartite Pact, an unlikely scenario. A week later Japanese diplomat Saburo Kurusu arrived in Washington to assist Nomura in the negotiations. A second plan, Proposal B, was put forward by the Japanese that offered to recall Japanese troops from Indochina. President Roosevelt, favorably impressed with the proposal, penciled his own four-point plan for Hull to use in talks with Nomura and Kurusu. But on Saturday, November 22, Washington intercepted a message from Tokyo to Ambassador Nomura that set November 30 (November 29 in Washington) as the final deadline for negotiations. That same day Admiral Yamamoto issued final orders for Operation Z to Vice Admiral Chuichi Nagumo and his First Air Fleet. Operation Z was the name the Japanese gave to their plan of attack on Pearl Harbor. Still hopeful that war would not come, Yamamoto included a single qualification: "In the event an agreement is reached in the negotiations with the United States, the Force will immediately return to Japan." As it was, Operation Z moved forward, along with plans for almost simultaneous Japanese attacks on several American bases in the Pacific and on British colonial strongholds.

Sinister Ballet in the Pacific

Nagumo's Pearl Harbor Strike Force began moving from Hitokappu Bay in the Kurile Islands on November 26 (November 25 in Hawaii). Hoping for cover of foul weather and avoiding normal shipping lanes, Nagumo planned to take his ships east across the International Date Line, then on a southeasterly course until about 250 miles north of the Hawaiian Islands. For the first time in history six fleet carriers sailed together for war. They sailed in two columns. Nagumo's flagship, carrier *Akagi*, led the port column and was followed by *Kaga* and *Hiryu*; carrier *Soryu* led the starboard, followed by *Shokaku* and *Zuikaku*. They were accompanied by seven oiler-supply vessels and screened by battleships *Hiei* and *Kirishima*, heavy cruisers *Chikuma* and *Tone*, light cruiser *Abukuma* and nine destroyers—*Akigumo*, *Arare*, *Hamakaze*, *Isokaze*, *Kagero*, *Kasumi*, *Shiranuhi*, *Tanikaze* and *Urakaze*. Destroyers *Sazanami* and *Ushio* and oiler *Shiriya* were assigned a separate mission; under Captain Kanano Konishi, they sailed for Midway Island.

As Nagumo's fleet left the Kurile Islands, elements of Japan's Second and Third Fleets gathered in the Pescadores Islands. This Eastern Force, the largest of the Japanese naval invasion forces, carried units of the Fourteenth Army toward the Philippines for December 10 landings on the island of Luzon. A smaller amphibious force assembled in the Palau Islands 500 miles east of the Philippines. Its mission was to secure a port at the southern tip of Mindanao Island to close the back door to the Philippines and allow no escape for American vessels retreating southward. Three days after Nagumo's force weighed anchor but before it reached the International Date Line, a convoy of troopships left Sakaide Harbor on Shikoku Island in Japan's Inland Sea and sailed to Haha Jima in the Bonin Islands. The destination of this Japanese amphibious strike force under command of Vice Admiral Arimoto Goto was the island of Guam.

Then, on December 3 (December 2 in Hawaii), a coded message, "Niitaka Yama Nobore," went from Admiral Yamamoto to Vice Admiral

Nagumo, "Climb Mt. Niitaka." It was the prearranged signal that verified a breakdown in negotiations between Japanese and American diplomats and it authorized Nagumo to proceed with the attack on the US Pacific Fleet at Pearl Harbor on the morning of December 8 (December 7 in Hawaii).

It was December 3 in Hawaii when Nagumo's warships crossed the International Date Line. At the same time a small Japanese force commanded by Rear Admiral Sadamichi Kajioka arrived at Roi-Namur on Kwajalein Atoll in the Marshall Islands. After a few days of amphibious training, it would sail a circuitous 800-mile route to the north for an attack on Wake Island. Earlier a smaller force left Kwajalein carrying the 2nd Battalion of the Maizuru Special Naval Landing Force toward Tarawa Atoll and Makin Island in the Gilbert Islands 700 miles to the southeast. And on December 5 (December 4 in Hawaii), as the Pearl Harbor Strike Force adjusted its course toward the Hawaiian Islands, Japanese troopships carrying elements of the Fifteenth Army sailed south from the island of Hainan in the South China Sea. This Malaya Strike Force rounded the tip of French Indochina and headed northwest into the Gulf of Thailand for a rendezvous with a covering force of warships. Under the overall command of Vice Admiral Nobutake Kondo, the convoy's mission was to land the Fifteenth Army on the Malay Peninsula. A British pilot spotted Kondo's Force, but British authorities mistakenly assumed the Japanese were headed for Bangkok.

On land, the Imperial Guards Division of Japan's Fifteenth Army was poised on the southwest border of French Indochina. When war started, it would cross into Thailand. Across Indochina and some 1,200 miles to the northeast, the 38th Infantry Division of Japan's Fourteenth Army was positioned near the city of Canton in China's Kwangtung Province. At the outbreak of war, the 38th Division would move south for an assault on the British island of Hong Kong.

A Majestic Sight

The island of Oahu lies in the center of the Hawaiian chain. At 40 miles from north to south and 26 miles across, it is the third largest of the Hawaiian Islands. An 1884 treaty gave the United States exclusive use of the Pearl Harbor inlet on Oahu's south shore for ship repair and as a coaling station in exchange for duty-free entry of Hawaiian sugar into the American market.

When the US annexed the Islands in 1898 after the Spanish-American War, the channel from the sea to Pearl Harbor was dredged to a depth of 35 feet. The harbor itself has a maximum depth of 60 feet and an average depth of 40 feet. Ford Island sits at its center. As early as spring 1940, the US Navy dispatched ships of the United States Fleet under Admiral J. O. Richardson to Oahu to supplement the small Hawaiian detachment there. It was believed that having this force in the mid-Pacific would discourage the Imperial Japanese Navy from advancing on the Netherlands East Indies for oil. Army and Navy forces at Oahu remained on total alert for some time that year but any concern of an attack, especially an attack on Hawaii itself, seemed remote. As time passed, the alert waned. Even in late 1941 American admirals at Pearl Harbor and in Washington expected that should the Japanese begin hostilities, they would hit the Philippines or the US possessions of Guam, Wake Island or Midway.

On the morning of December 7, 1941, the US Navy had 163 vessels stationed in and around Pearl Harbor. There were 46 of the Pacific Fleet's 100 surface warships, four of the Fleet's 28 submarines, a dozen motor-torpedo boats, 66 auxiliary vessels and 35 smaller craft. The 46 warships included eight battleships, two heavy cruisers, six light cruisers and 30 destroyers. Seven of the eight battleships were anchored east of Ford Island on Battleship Row. The eighth was across the channel at repair facilities along with two heavy cruisers.

Two of the six light cruisers were anchored on the north side of Ford Island and another was north of Battleship Row. The three remaining light cruisers were across the channel. Most of the 30 destroyers were at anchor or in dry dock undergoing repairs, but *Helm, Monaghan* and *Ward* were moving down the main channel in response to sightings of enemy submarines. Anti-aircraft guns on vessels under repair were understandably not in working order and anti-aircraft ammunition on most warships was stored in locked magazines since it was peace time.

The US Army, the Navy and the Marine Corps had less than 500 aircraft of all types and degrees of combat effectiveness assigned to seven air bases and airfields on Oahu. The Army's base at Hickam Field was just south of and adjacent to the Pearl Harbor Navy Yard and was home to 51 light, medium and heavy bombers. Wheeler Field, near the large Schofield Army

Barracks and ten miles north of Pearl Harbor, had more than 80 outdated aircraft along with 62 modern P-40 fighters. The Army's Bellows Field near Oahu's east coast housed two dozen P-40s. A small auxiliary field at Haleiwa in the north held a few P-36 and some newer P-40 fighters. The Navy had 36 PBY Catalinas along with some obsolete aircraft of various types at Kaneohe Naval Air Station on the Mokapu Peninsula as well as 70 aircraft on Ford Island. The Marine Corps Air Station at Ewa, six miles southwest of Pearl Harbor, was home to more than 50 aircraft including F3F biplane fighters and SBU Vindicator dive bombers.

When Vice Admiral Nagumo received his authorization on December 3 to "Climb Mt. Niitaka," he was further advised that as of that day, Japanese intelligence on Oahu reported no aircraft carriers at Pearl Harbor. That may or may not have been correct at the time but on the morning of December 7, the Navy's three Pacific-based carriers were indeed out of harm's way. USS *Enterprise* was on a return run to Oahu from Wake Island, USS *Lexington* was nearing Midway Island and USS *Saratoga* was at San Diego. *Enterprise* was the centerpiece of Task Force 8 that was commanded by Vice Admiral William F. Halsey. The task force included Halsey's flagship, heavy cruiser *Northampton*; two other heavy cruisers, *Chester* and *Salt Lake City*; and nine destroyers, *Balch, Benham, Craven, Dunlap, Ellet, Fanning, Gridley, Maury* and *McCall*. Task Force 8 had delivered a squadron of Marine Corps Grumman Wildcat fighters to Wake. *Lexington* and Task Force 12 commanded by Rear Admiral John Newton sortied Pearl Harbor December 5. The task force included Newton's flagship *Chicago* and two other heavy cruisers, *Astoria* and *Portland*, along with five escorting destroyers, *Drayton, Flusser, Lamson, Mahan* and *Porter*. Two days later Task Force 12 was 400 miles south of Midway Island: its mission, to launch 25 Vindicator dive bombers to reinforce Marine air units there.

In the early morning darkness of December 7, Nagumo ordered his First Air Fleet to turn into the wind and prepare to launch aircraft. At 0600 hours and still 250 miles north of the Hawaiian Islands, the six Japanese fleet carriers slowly adjusted their headings. Soon after, 10 Zero fighters took off from *Akagi*. In all, the six carriers launched 43 Zeros and saw two takeoffs aborted. Commander Mitsuo Fuchida from *Akagi* led the first wave in a Nakajima Kate level bomber; 14 Kates followed. The formation was joined by 34 level bombers from the carriers *Kaga, Hiryu* and *Soryu*. Twelve other Kates, armed with torpedoes, left from *Akagi* and were joined by 28 Kate torpedo bombers from *Kaga, Hiryu* and *Soryu*. The carriers *Shokaku* and *Zuikaku* launched 51 Aichi Val dive bombers. Immediately deck crews and plane handlers began hurried preparations to launch a second wave of aircraft.

By 0715 hours the ships of the First Air Fleet sailed closer to Oahu and launched a second wave, 170 aircraft led by Lieutenant Commander Shigekazu Shimazaki off the carrier *Zuikaku*. Carriers *Akagi, Kaga, Hiryu* and *Soryu* each launched nine Zero fighters and, together, 80 Val dive bombers. *Shokaku* and *Zuikaku* each launched 27 Kate level bombers. By 0745 a total of 353 Japanese warplanes approached Oahu. As the first wave of Japanese aircraft neared the northern tip of the island, it split into two formations for preassigned targets.

Commander Fuchida's 49 Kate level bombers flying with 40 Kate torpedo bombers made landfall at Kahuku Point. They were detected on radar at a newly constructed mobile radar shack, but the large formation was discounted as a flight of 12 B-17 Flying Fortress heavy bombers scheduled to arrive from California at Hickam Field. The second formation, 51 Val dive bombers and 43 Zero fighters, made landfall about ten miles southwest of Kahuku Point. The dive bombers, armed with either armor-piercing or general-purpose bombs, separated from the fighters over Oahu and headed toward their targets. Both Vals and Zeros flew toward Army Air Corps airfields at Hickam, Wheeler and Bellows. One group of Val dive bombers and Zero fighters headed for Ford Island. Another group flew across Oahu to the Naval Air Station at Kaneohe. Some Zeros broke away to attack the Marine Air Station at Ewa.

Fuchida's formation separated again as his own group of level bombers headed south over the sea and then east toward Pearl Harbor and the Army base at Hickam Field. Lieutenant Commander Shigemaru Murata led the rest of the Kates over land toward Pearl and Battleship Row, cruiser targets at Ford Island and other targets across the channel. Fuchida, his Kate armed with a single 800-kilogram armor-piercing bomb, led his group directly to Battleship Row. Murata's Kates, armed with 800-kilogram air torpedoes, had both battleships and cruisers as primary targets. Fuchida's level bombers began a gradual descent while Murata's group came in lower and faster. No US fighter planes challenged the Japanese; there was no anti-aircraft fire, no flak. From his Kate bomber flying at 10,000 feet, Fuchida focused his binoculars on Pearl Harbor and the ships of the US Pacific Fleet and thought it a majestic sight.

Like Tsushima, Complete Surprise

At about 0750 hours Commander Fuchida sent the Morse Code signal to the aircraft of the first wave: TO, TO, TO—ATTACK, ATTACK, ATTACK. Minutes later Zero fighters deployed and headed for Wheeler Field, dive bombers neared the naval air station at Kaneohe, level bombers descended on Hickam Field, and torpedo and dive bombers reached Pearl Harbor's Battleship Row. Fuchida radioed a second message: TORA, TORA, TORA—TIGER, TIGER, TIGER—indicating the attack at Pearl Harbor was a complete surprise. On Battleship Row, seven of America's Dreadnoughts were anchored along the east shore of Ford Island, facing south toward the harbor's main channel and the open sea. USS *California* was anchored alone. USS *Oklahoma* and USS *Maryland* were moored 1,000 feet astern of *California* with *Maryland* inboard. USS *West Virginia* and USS *Tennessee* were next with *Tennessee* inboard. USS *Arizona* was less than 100 feet astern of *Tennessee* and was inboard of the repair ship *Vestal*. The last battleship anchored on Battleship Row, USS *Nevada,* was the farthest north and behind *Arizona*. USS *Pennsylvania* was across the channel in dry dock.

For Americans, war with Japan began at 0755 hours and by 0756, Battleship USS *West Virginia* was hit by the first of a half dozen torpedoes and two bombs that would take her down. Water poured into huge holes on her port side; counterflooding corrected her list and she settled in the harbor, almost upright. An order by a quick-thinking officer brought *West Virginia*'s crew topside early in the attack and of 1,500 men on board, 105 were lost.

Arizona was only slightly protected from torpedo attack by the smaller repair ship *Vestal*. In the first minute of the attack, a torpedo missed *Vestal*, striking *Arizona* portside. At almost the same time, a single bomb penetrated *Arizona's* deck, exploding in the forward magazine. The 33,100-ton warship rose out of the water as it was torn apart by the explosion and settled so rapidly that hundreds of her crew remained trapped below. Of 1,400 officers and men on board, 1,103 went down with their ship.

USS *Oklahoma* took three torpedoes portside as her crew ran to battle stations. Water poured through gaping holes in her hull and the ship flooded quickly with no time to close compartments for counterflooding. She listed to 30 degrees. Less than five minutes into the attack, word was passed to abandon ship and by 0815, the battleship rolled over into the mud of the harbor, her propellers to the sky. *Oklahoma* had shielded *Maryland* from torpedo attack, and as *Oklahoma* began to list and then roll, some survivors climbed aboard the *Maryland* to assist that crew. Of the 1,354 officers and men aboard *Oklahoma*, 415 died. *Maryland* took two bomb hits and suffered the least damage of the anchored Dreadnoughts.

On the deck of USS *Nevada,* the 0800 hours ceremony of the hoisting of the colors was underway and a band played "The Star-Spangled Banner." As one of the Kates that torpedoed *Arizona* strafed *Nevada's* deck, her stunned crewmen ran to man her anti-aircraft guns. *Tennessee,* although shielded by *West Virginia,* took two bombs early in the attack. Most of her damage was from pieces of flaming debris thrown on her deck from the exploding *Arizona.*

Tennessee's crew fought deck fires through most of the day and she remained seaworthy. Five of her men were lost.

Across the channel in dry dock at the Navy Yard, USS *Pennsylvania* took a single bomb hit, costing the lives of 18 of her crew. Ten minutes after the first Japanese planes attacked, USS *California* was the last Dreadnought to be assaulted. At 20 years she was one of the newer battleships at Pearl Harbor. Scheduled for an Admiral's inspection the following day, *California* was completely unbuttoned, and she flooded quickly when struck by two torpedoes and a bomb that set off a magazine. Oil from her hull gushed into the harbor and created a wall of flame. Quick counterflooding kept her from capsizing and *California* settled in the harbor with the loss of 98 officers and men.

Early in the attack, Japanese aircrews sighted what they thought was an aircraft carrier on the west shore of Ford Island. It was USS *Utah,* an old, pre-Dreadnought battleship that had been converted into a target ship.

Moored with her and facing north were the light cruisers USS *Detroit* and USS *Raleigh.* Two torpedo bombers approaching from the northwest descended and launched their weapons on *Raleigh* and on *Utah.* Both ships were hit and listing to port. *Raleigh*'s forward engine room flooded and despite counterflooding, her list worsened. Astern of *Raleigh, Utah* listed heavily to port and capsized. A torpedo meant for *Detroit* passed between her and *Raleigh* and ran harmlessly aground in the mud of Ford Island. Later that morning the crew of *Raleigh* jettisoned gear and equipment from the light cruiser's deck to keep the 7,100-ton warship from capsizing. In the harbor, another light cruiser, USS *Phoenix,* was anchored alone well to the north of Battleship Row and remained undamaged.

Torpedo bombers, unable to obtain hits on the battleship *Pennsylvania* in dry dock, concentrated on substitute targets. From the north, Kates descended on two ships anchored at the dock just north of *Pennsylvania.* The outboard vessel was the old minelayer *Oglala* and the larger inboard warship, light cruiser USS *Helena.* A torpedo launched at *Oglala* traveled under the minelayer's hull and struck *Helena* starboard. A second torpedo attack on *Oglala* hit home and caused her to list heavily starboard, her flags and pennants flapping over the bridge of *Helena.* Though flooding was controlled on *Helena,* her deck, that had just been readied for Sunday morning church services, was in shambles from flying debris. Light cruiser USS *Honolulu,* flagship of Admiral Kimmel's cruiser force, was moored at the Navy Yard southeast across the channel from Ford Island. More than a dozen vessels were docked near her including light cruiser USS *St. Louis,* heavy cruisers USS *New Orleans* and USS *San Francisco,* destroyers *Bagley, Cummings,* and *Schley,* and eight auxiliary vessels. Dive bombers and low-level bombers descended on *New Orleans* and on *San Francisco,* the only heavy cruisers at Pearl. Protected from torpedoes and with huge repair cranes providing protection from bomb attacks, *New Orleans* was slightly damaged when her deck was sprayed with shrapnel from a fragmentation bomb.

Their torpedoes and bombs spent, crews of Kates and Vals along with Zero pilots raked the decks of American ships with machine gun fire. Sailors in skivvies, pajamas, aloha shirts or other unacceptable battle station attire searched for serviceable weapons of any kind. Some fired rifles and even pistols at the attacking Japanese. Witnesses reported it was nearly 10 minutes after the first torpedo hit before any defensive anti-aircraft fire was heard.

Three stalls starboard of the battleship *Pennsylvania*, a bomb penetrated the deck of the destroyer *Shaw* as she lay in dry dock. The blast exploded in the ship's forward magazine and tore off her entire bow. Dive bombers dove on *Pennsylvania* but destroyers *Cassin* and *Downes*, sharing dry dock with her, received most of the damage. Raging fires engulfed both destroyers and they were abandoned just before their magazines exploded and their torpe-does detonated. *Cassin* rolled over against *Downes,* both ships smoldering and almost unrecognizable.

As thick black smoke rose from Battleship Row and the dry dock facili-ties across the channel, Japanese planes headed back to their carriers practi-cally unscathed. Within thirty minutes of the start of the first attack, the US Navy's force of combat effective battleships in the Pacific was reduced almost to zero. Only *Nevada* remained seaworthy.

Land-based US Army, Navy and Marine Corps aircraft on Oahu were also devastated in the Japanese attack. Moments before the first air torpedoes fell on Battleship Row, the naval air station at Kaneohe was hit. Of the 36 Catalinas assigned there, three were out on patrol when a squadron of Val dive bombers struck. Japanese dive bombers and fighter planes attacked again at 0820, and at 0920 a squadron of Vals from the second wave came in to mop up. When the last attackers broke off action at 0930, 27 of the Cata-linas had been destroyed and six were damaged.

The Japanese systematically attacked US Army airfields at Bellows, Hickam and Wheeler, the naval air station at Ford Island and the Marine air station Ewa. Only the small auxiliary airfield at Haleiwa on Oahu's north coast was spared and able to launch aircraft. At Bellows Field two squadrons of Curtiss P-40 fighters were all but destroyed. The Army had six B-17s, 33 old B-18s and a dozen A-20 bombers at Hickam Field. A V-formation of Val dive bombers attacked there first. They were followed by Kate level bombers and by Zero fighters. When the last attack was over, most of the 51 bombers, parked wing to wing, were destroyed or severely damaged. The Army had 62 Curtiss P-40s at Wheeler Field. Just after 0800, 35 Val dive bombers sup-ported by Zero fighters destroyed most of them. The naval airstrip on Ford

Island was worked over by dive bombers early in the attack. Of approximately 70 aircraft there, 33 were destroyed in the first few minutes of war. The Marine Corps Air Station at Ewa was struck initially by 21 Zeros attacking at low altitude with machine gun and cannon fire. Of the 50 aircraft on the field, 30 were lost during the first attack and though Marines there fought off two subsequent fighter attacks that morning, air power at Ewa was virtually destroyed.

With the exception of a few stragglers, the first wave of Japanese aircraft broke off the attack by 0825 and returned to their carriers. By 0840 the battleship *Nevada* was underway in the channel east of Ford Island when the second wave of Japanese level and dive bombers arrived to score near-misses on her. She continued past the burning *Arizona*, the sinking *West Virginia* and the capsized *Oklahoma*. Fearing *Nevada* would sink and block the main channel, an officer gave an order to drop anchor off Hospital Point. Three Vals attacked, killing the entire anchoring detail. The only battleship to get underway during the Pearl Harbor attack, the 33,000-ton USS *Nevada* slid gently aground, having lost 50 of her crew. Later in the morning tugs towed her to the western side of Pearl where she flooded and settled in at Waipio Point.

The second wave of 170 level bombers, dive bombers and fighters deployed off the east coast of Oahu. Level bombers approached from Diamond Head in the south and dive bombers came in over Kaneohe Bay. This wave concentrated largely on Hickam Field, Ford Island, USS *Nevada* underway and on the warships hit during the first wave. Zeros strafed the floatplane base at Kaneohe and hit Wheeler, Hickam and Ford Island. The Americans met the second Japanese wave with determined resistance and strong anti-aircraft fire. The Imperial Japanese Navy lost a total of 29 planes and 55 men in both attacks. They lost five, two-man midget submarines of 50 tons each. Of the 10 Japanese sailors manning the small subs, nine perished; the tenth became the first prisoner in the Pacific War.

Aftermath

Most Americans had not heard of the Pearl Harbor Navy Yard before the morning of December 7, 1941. By the end of that day, it was the focus of their anger and their sadness, their patriotism and their resolve. Japanese attacks on the Philippines and on the Malay Peninsula would later be seen as influencing the course of war in the Pacific more profoundly, but it was the attack on Pearl Harbor that united Americans behind their President and their armed forces and officially brought the United States into the War. More heartfelt than any previous military slogan, "Remember Pearl Harbor" became the nation's battle cry.

Almost 2,500 military personnel and civilians died in the Pearl Harbor attack and well over 1,000 were injured. Over 60 percent of the military casualties occurred on two battleships, USS *Arizona* and USS *Oklahoma*. The Navy lost a total of 2,002 men with 710 wounded, more US naval combat casualties than during the Spanish-American War and the Great War combined. The Army had a total of 238 killed and 364 wounded; the Marines, 109 killed and 69 wounded. Among civilians there were 54 deaths and 35 injuries, many of those due to US Navy anti-aircraft ammunition gone astray.

The Japanese attack put all eight American battleships at Pearl Harbor out of service. *Arizona* was lost. *Oklahoma* was eventually raised and sold for scrap, but she sank in the Pacific while being towed to the mainland. *Maryland*, least damaged of all, was back in service by February 1942. *Pennsylvania* and *Tennessee* were repaired and rejoined the fleet a month later. *Nevada* was refloated, repaired and in service that December. *California* and *West Virginia* were raised, repaired and modernized; both returned to active service in 1944. The two heavy cruisers at Pearl Harbor, *New Orleans* and *San Francisco,* sustained moderate damage during the attack and were never out of service. Of the six light cruisers, *Helena, Raleigh* and *Honolulu* were moderately damaged and returned to service within a year. *Phoenix, St. Louis* and *Detroit* were unharmed. The three damaged destroyers, *Cassin, Downes* and *Shaw* were returned to service within a year.

The heavy loss of American aircraft that resulted from the attack on Oahu can be explained by the US Military's obsession with spies and with saboteurs. The Army, Navy and Marine Corps feared sabotage on the ground more than attack from the air and used armed guards to protect planes parked wing to wing in secured areas throughout the Island. Few air search and scouting missions were ordered. On the morning of December 7, less than two dozen US military aircraft were in the air over Oahu and that included the twelve B-17s arriving from California.

Although the destruction wrought at Pearl Harbor was truly significant and devastating in terms of loss of life and loss of ships and aircraft, history would record that US losses might have been considerably worse. Hindsight would illuminate mistakes the Japanese made that day that were a benefit to the United States as the war progressed. Although air commanders pressed Nagumo for a third wave by carrier-based aircraft, the Admiral declined, fearing reprisal by the American carriers. The Japanese failed to target oil storage depots on Oahu, an irony considering Japan's willingness to go to war to secure a supply of oil and considering Yamamoto's knowledge of the commodity. If the Navy's oil storage facilities had been destroyed, the US would have found it necessary to transport oil to Oahu from the mainland while avoiding enemy surface warships and submarines. Another mistake that helped the US Navy in the months after Pearl Harbor was the Japanese failure to destroy ship repair and metal-working facilities on Oahu. Had they accomplished this, the Navy Yard would have been a complete loss and US warships would have had to return to the west coast for damage repair and routine maintenance. Admiral Nagumo's decision to retire his Fleet without searching Hawaiian waters for the American aircraft carriers was another error that favored his enemy. If either or both USS *Enterprise* and USS *Lexington* had been lost or damaged, it would have taken the United States months longer to take the offensive in the Pacific.

Chapter V

THE GREATER EAST ASIA
CO-PROSPERITY SPHERE

Introduction

The Japanese attack on Pearl Harbor on December 7, 1941, the event that loomed so large in the minds of Americans, was just one component of a mammoth plan that Japanese political and military leaders began formulating almost a decade earlier. In 1932, with the establishment of the puppet state of Manchukuo in Manchuria, Japanese leaders considered their island nation's relationship to its neighbors on the Asian continent and founded the Concordia Association. It was an attempt to combine agricultural and economic objectives with concepts of racial harmony and equality but in truth it merely cemented Japan's leadership role in the occupied area. The ideals of the Association surfaced again in 1937 with the beginning of the Sino-Japanese War, the China Incident as Japan called it. And in November 1938 Japanese Prime Minister Konoye issued a proclamation aimed at removing American and European colonialism and imperialism along with the influence of communism from East Asia. This Greater East Asia Co-Prosperity Sphere at first included Japan, Manchukuo and, despite continued military resistance by China's leader Chiang Kai-shek, China as well. The Sphere was expanded in 1940 when the fall of France and the occupation of the Netherlands by Germany opened their colonies in Southeast Asia to Japanese hegemony. Eventually Japan promulgated the benefit of the Greater East Asia Co-Prosperity Sphere to all states and people of Greater East Asia as far south as Java, who, with Japan as the core, the kernel, would find their true place in the world. The move toward Asia for the Asians began in earnest with the surprise attack on Pearl Harbor and the almost simultaneous attacks on the British colonies of Malaya and Hong Kong, on the US Pacific Island possessions of Guam and Wake and on the quasi-commonwealth of the Philippine Pacific Islands.

Officers and Operations

It would be an understatement to describe the atmosphere aboard the ships of the Pearl Harbor Strike Force as jubilation. Of the 353 Japanese aircraft involved, 324 returned safely to their carriers. For Vice Admiral Chuichi Nagumo, however, there remained the decision of whether to launch a third attack on Oahu. Weighing against such a move was the fact that no American carriers were at home at Pearl and where they were and what damage they could inflict on the Japanese was unknown. So early on the afternoon of December 7, Nagumo headed his Pearl Harbor Strike Force northward at top speed. At the same time destroyers *Sazanami* and *Ushio* along with the tanker *Shiriya* were nearing their objective, the US island possession of Midway. Commanded by Captain Kanano Konishi, this Midway Neutralization Force sailed from Tokyo Bay late in November so that on the night of the Pearl Harbor attack it could shell the American air base and protect Nagumo's force from US planes based there.

Elsewhere on December 7 (Hawaiian time) in the western Pacific, other Japanese fleets and forces were poised for attack. Vice Admiral Nobutake Kondo aboard heavy cruiser *Atago* sailing between Malaya and Borneo was Commander in Chief of Southern Force, the largest number of ships under a single command in Admiral Yamamoto's Combined Fleet. Kondo's responsibility covered both the Malaya and the Philippines campaigns. The 61 surface warships of his Southern Force included two battleships, a light carrier, 11 heavy cruisers, six light cruisers and 41 destroyers.

Vice Admiral Jizaburo Ozawa commanded the part of Kondo's force that was dubbed Southern Expeditionary Fleet. At age 55, Ozawa was said to be the Japanese Navy's foremost tactician. From his flagship light cruiser *Sendai* in the Gulf of Siam, he commanded the ships that delivered Japanese land forces along the eastern shore of the Malay Peninsula, even as Pearl Harbor was under attack. General Tomoyuki Yamashita led the land forces, his Twenty-fifth Army, along with elements of Japan's Fifteenth Army.

Vice Admiral Ibo Takahashi commanded the part of Kondo's force that was called Eastern Force. On December 8 (December 7 in Hawaii), ships from Takahashi's own Third Fleet along with ships from First and Second Fleets were set to attack some of the northernmost islands in the Philippine chain.

For the United Kingdom, early December 1941 saw land units in her Asian colonial territories thinly spread and poorly trained. The Royal Navy, too, was overextended to accommodate England's worldwide holdings and the demands of war in Europe. All British ground troops on the Malay Peninsula, on the island of Singapore and at Sarawak and Brunei on Borneo were commanded by Lieutenant General Arthur E. Percival from what the British optimistically called Fortress Singapore. Singapore was charged with protecting British sea routes through the Orient and the East Indies and with guarding India from the east and Australia from the north. The 80,000 troops of Percival's Indian III Corps served in the 9th and 11th Indian Divisions, the 8th Australian Division and a Corps Reserve. About 25,000 of those officers and men were European and Australian; the others were of Indian or Malayan descent.

Royal Air Force units at airfields in Malaya and at Tengah Airfield on Singapore were commanded by Air Chief Marshal Sir Robert Brooke-Popham, Commander in Chief, Far East. At age 63, Brooke-Popham seemed an uninspiring leader and one not in tune with ideas of modern warfare. The RAF had 77 aircraft at Tengah and about the same number divided among four airfields in Malaya. The primary defensive aircraft at these airfields were fighters—Hawker Hurricanes and the slower American-built Brewster Buffaloes. Other planes there were for the most part outdated, and pilots were not assigned to combat air patrols. Rather, if Malaya were attacked from the sea, the RAF response would be to strafe landing beaches, attacking enemy ships and landing craft.

On December 2, Admiral Sir Thomas Phillips arrived at Singapore, at the anchorage the Royal Navy had used since 1919, to serve in the newly created post of Commander in Chief, Far East Fleet, formerly called the fleet of the China Station. Phillips delivered the Royal Navy's newest battleship, HMS *Prince of Wales*, and the battle cruiser HMS *Repulse* along with destroyer HMS *Electra*. These ships joined destroyers HMS *Express* and HMAS *Vampire* stationed there along with destroyers HMS *Scout*, HMS *Stronghold*, HMS *Tenedos* and HMS *Thanet* newly arrived from Hong Kong where an attack by Japanese aircraft was expected. Also at Singapore were light cruisers HMS *Danae*, HMS *Dragon* and from Australia, HMAS *Hobart*; and two submarines. A Royal Australian Navy destroyer HMAS *Vendetta*, assigned to Singapore and undergoing a refit in Singapore Harbor, was not ready for service. Phillips, age 53, was known to his seamen as Tom Thumb for his short stature. He was an officer whose competence was in question and he was concerned about the role his ships, code-named Force Z, would play in containing the Japanese.

Troops protecting the British island colony of Hong Kong in southern China were under the command of Major General Christopher M. Maltby. In early December 1941 when an invasion by the Japanese from China appeared imminent, Maltby ordered in extra supplies and sent three of his six Royal Army battalions and 16 of his 28 mobile infantry guns six miles inland on the mainland to Gin Drinkers' Line. The remaining infantry battalions and 12 mobile guns were positioned on Hong Kong. Only one Royal Navy destroyer, HMS *Thracian*, two gunboats, several British registry junks and some merchant ships were at Whampoa Docks on Kowloon Bay across from Hong Kong. The British had five obsolete aircraft at Kai Tak Airport, east of Kowloon.

Attacks on British Soil

The Malay Peninsula is 850 miles long and 200 miles wide at the broadest point. In 1941, the southern half of the peninsula, Malaya, was an assemblage of states under various levels of British protection. The northern half was part of Thailand, a country run by a pro-Japanese military dictator who had renamed it from the earlier Siam, *Thai* being the local word for free. At the peninsula's southern tip lay British Singapore, an island city separated from the mainland by the mile-wide Johore Strait. The Royal Navy's base at Singapore faced north across the strait toward the mainland. Most of the garrison's large 15-inch guns, however, faced outward to protect sea lanes. From Singapore it is less than 50 miles south across the Strait of Malacca to the island of Sumatra and to the east, less than 400 miles to Borneo. The Japanese attack on the Malay Peninsula began not at Singapore as the British expected but with landings by Southern Force's Malay Strike Force at seven beaches north along the east coast of the Malay Peninsula. For air support the Japanese Army's 3rd Air Division had available 350 aircraft and the Navy's 22nd Air Flotilla, 180 planes, at airfields in French Indochina, 300 miles across the Gulf of Siam.

By early December, the 19 troop transports of Vice Admiral Ozawa's Southern Expeditionary Fleet were gathered at the port of Samah on the large island of Hainan off the coast of Indochina. On the morning of December 4 (December 3 in Hawaii), screened by a small force of submarines, they sailed south with 40,000 men, units of Japan's Fifteenth and Twenty-fifth Armies. From the South China Sea the ships rounded the tip of French Indochina on December 6 and headed northwest into the Gulf of Siam where they were spotted by British reconnaissance aircraft. The British hopefully, but mistakenly, believed the convoy was destined for Bangkok, Thailand. Instead, the transports rendezvoused in the Gulf of Siam with 11 Japanese destroyers led by light cruiser *Kashii* and by Ozawa's flagship, light cruiser *Sendai*. The troopships and destroyers formed into smaller units and sailed toward landing beaches at Kota Bharu in Malaya and at Patani, Singora and four sites on Thailand's Kra Isthmus.

The remainder of Admiral Kondo's ships, Southern Force's Malay Cover Force, continued patrolling the waters off Malaya. This group included battleships *Haruna* and *Kongo*, seven heavy cruisers *Chokai, Kumano, Mikuma, Mogami, Suzuya, Takao* and Kondo's flagship *Atago*, and destroyers *Fubuki, Hatsuyuki* and *Shirayuki*. In the early hours of December 8 (December 7 in Hawaii), *Sendai* and four destroyers, *Ayanami, Isonami, Shikinami* and *Uranami,* bombarded the beaches at Kota Bharu from 3,500 yards offshore. It was still more than an hour before the first wave of Japanese aircraft arrived over Pearl Harbor and it was the only place the Japanese military ran into difficulty that day. The Takumi Detachment, men of the 56th Regiment of the

Twenty-fifth Army, approached the beaches in landing barges. The seas were rough. British Indian III Corps opened with artillery fire while sporadic air attacks by the British compounded the problems of the Takumi Detachment. Landing barges were capsized and sunk, a troop transport was lost and of the 5,400 men in the landing force, there were 850 Japanese casualties.

That same morning less than 100 miles north of Kota Bharu at Patani, five troop transports escorted by destroyers *Shinonome* and *Shirakumo* launched assault troops of the 5th Division. Sixty-five miles farther north at Singora, four transports protected by destroyers *Amagiri, Asagiri, Sagiri* and *Yugiri*, launched additional 5th Division amphibious assault units. Both landings were unopposed. Farther north along the Kra Isthmus, elements of the Fifteenth Army's 143rd Regiment landed at four beaches without benefit of destroyer escort and with no resistance from the British. The troops were launched near Nakhon from three transports, at Bandon from a single transport, near Jumbhorn from two troopships and at Prachab, less than 300 miles south of Bangkok, from a lone transport. Destroyer *Sagiri* served as their headquarters ship.

Before these Japanese amphibious invasion forces launched their landing craft, Japanese Army and Navy land-based air units destroyed most of the British aircraft based on the Malay Peninsula. By midnight December 8, all Japanese destroyers involved in the operation, along with destroyer *Murakumo* that had been patrolling south of Patani, and the 18 remaining troop transports were underway to rejoin Vice Admiral Ozawa's Southern Expeditionary Fleet in the Gulf of Siam. At the north end of the Gulf was the city of Bangkok, capital of nominally neutral Thailand. Earlier that day, the Imperial Guard Division of Japan's Twenty-fifth Army entered Bangkok from French Indochina. The Japanese Army moved through the city and continued west and south down the Malay Peninsula, meeting other units of the Twenty-fifth and Fifteenth Armies as invasion beaches were secured. By December 9, what little resistance Thai forces offered had ceased.

Nearly 1,400 miles northeast of Malaya on the South China coast lay the British colony of Hong Kong. The colony included the island of Hong Kong along with a 22-mile section of the mainland called the New Territories. By December 1941, Japanese troops had occupied the Chinese mainland north of Hong Kong for three years. A Japanese attack on the colony was not unexpected and Major General Maltby's orders were to hold the Gin Drinkers' Line on the mainland long enough to deny the enemy the harbor while demolition of ships and junks could be carried out. With 5,000 men, half his troops, deployed along the 10-mile stretch of Gin Drinkers' Line, Maltby felt he could hold the attackers for seven days. Four hours after the Pearl Harbor attack, the 38th Division of Japan's Fourteenth Army under Lieutenant General Taikaishi Sakai crossed the frontier into the New Territories. The force of 20,000 men included nine infantry and 17 artillery battalions along with anti-tank, field and heavy siege guns. The operation was supported by six squadrons of Army aircraft and by the Imperial Navy's Second China Expeditionary Fleet made up of light cruiser *Isuzu* and destroyers *Ikazuchi* and *Inazuma*. Japanese aircraft quickly destroyed the five Royal Air Force planes on the ground at Kai Tak airfield. Japanese bombers struck the Whampoa docks nearby while level and dive bombers repeatedly attacked British installations on the mainland and on the island. Japanese ships sank two British gunboats and some junks and captured several merchant ships at anchorage.

The old Admiralty S class destroyer HMS *Thracian* had put to sea but even as Japanese Army units began their rapid advance southward across the New Territories, the Japanese Navy controlled the waters surrounding Britain's oldest Asian colony.

As war began, a small force of two Japanese destroyers left Kwajalein Atoll in the Marshall Islands destined for the British Commonwealth's Gilbert Islands 700 miles to the southeast and just north of the equator. Early on the morning of December 10 (December 9 in Hawaii), destroyers *Asanagi* and *Yunagi* arrived off the tip of Tarawa Atoll in the Gilbert Islands carrying men of the 2nd Battalion, Maizuru Special Naval Landing Force. The 200 troops quickly and quietly overran a British outpost on tiny Betio Island. They left behind a few coast watchers and a small garrison force along with a number of construction workers and engineers to plan and build an airfield. From Betio the Japanese could monitor shipping traffic from Hawaii to Australia and to the many island chains of the South Pacific. From Tarawa the Maizuru Force sailed for Makin Atoll 120 miles to the north and again uneventfully landed a garrison force along with coast watchers as well as laborers to build a seaplane base.

Sinking Imperialism

News of Pearl Harbor reached the British at Singapore on the day of the attack. That evening they learned as well of the Japanese landings north of Singapore on the Malay Peninsula. Admiral Sir Tom Phillips's concern over how he and his Force Z might best serve against the Japanese found an outlet. In a meeting aboard his flagship HMS *Prince of Wales,* Phillips and his staff decided to take the fleet north into the South China Sea and then west toward the Thai beaches to assist British troops in turning back Japanese landing forces. *Prince of Wales* was Great Britain's newest battleship, completed that same year, modern in every respect and nicknamed HMS *Unsinkable.* Captain John C. Leach commanded her. She was joined by the old battle cruiser HMS *Repulse* under the command of Captain William Tennant. The *Repulse* was built in 1916 and although modernized over the years, she lacked the armor needed to stand up to air attack. Three Royal Navy destroyers, *Electra, Express, Tenedos,* and the Australian Navy's destroyer *Vampire* completed Force Z. The newest and one of the Royal Navy's largest aircraft carriers HMS *Indomitable* would have provided Phillips's force with air cover had she not run aground near Kingston, Jamaica, the previous month.

Force Z sortied Singapore at 1735 hours on December 8. Aboard *Repulse* Captain Tennant posted a notice, "We are going to look for trouble. I expect we shall find it." Admiral Phillips requested RAF air reconnaissance and fighter cover over Singora and hoped the element of surprise would be on his side. Early the following day Phillips learned that air support would not be forthcoming. RAF bases on the west coast of Malaya at Alor Star and at Sungei Patani and on the east coast at Kota Bharu had already been hit by enemy aircraft. The weather was with him, however, with heavy clouds, rain and mist to hide the fleet from Japanese reconnaissance planes. Furthermore, Phillips was confident the anti-aircraft defenses on *Prince of Wales* and on *Repulse,* the ships' maneuverability and the ability of his officers and men would prove decisive in battle. On the afternoon of December 9 though, Force Z was spotted by Japanese submarine *I-65.* That night a clearing sky revealed what Phillips believed to be three Japanese reconnaissance aircraft overhead. Now he was without air cover and had lost his chance for a surprise attack.

Phillips continued north for an hour and, seeing nothing of the enemy, reversed course. *Tenedos,* low on fuel, had been sent back earlier. Late that night Phillips's crew picked up a signal from Singapore: "Enemy reported landing Kuantan, latitude 3 degrees 50' North." Without breaking radio silence to announce his change in plans, Phillips turned north once again for Kuantan. About two hours after midnight on December 10, Japanese submarine *I-58* spotted the British and in fact, got off several torpedoes, all of which missed their mark. There was no Japanese landing at Kuantan. All was quiet there when Force Z arrived off the coast in early morning so at 0900 hours Phillips continued northward to investigate a ship sighting and then south again when he learned destroyer *Tenedos* was under attack by enemy aircraft.

The 22nd Air Flotilla of the Japanese Navy's Eleventh Air Fleet, with Rear Admiral Sadaichi Matsunaga in command, had been moved from Formosa to southern Indochina specifically to cover landings on the Malay Peninsula. At 1015 hours on December 10, a Nell high-level bomber from Matsunaga's Genzan Air Group based at Saigon spotted the five British warships 70 miles southeast of Kuantan. Japanese pilots had been searching for the British for hours and were ready to return to base when they got their break. Word went out to the rest of the Genzan Group and to the Nells of the Mihoro Air Group and the Bettys of the Kanoya Group—99 bombers in all. Battle cruiser *Repulse* was first to be attacked. Moving to the southwest at 25 knots, her loudspeakers ordered men to battle stations at 1107 hours with: "Enemy aircraft approaching." For most of the crew this would be their first defensive combat encounter. At 1119 hours *Repulse* opened fire with all she had. *Prince of Wales* and the three destroyers followed suit. Captain Tennant ordered evasive maneuvers. Nine Nells of the Mihoro Group descended from 12,000 feet to fly over in near perfect intervals through the barrage of metal sent up by the five ships. Eight armor-piercing bombs just missed the *Repulse.* A ninth pierced her hangar deck and exploded below. Crews contained the fire within ten minutes and the battle cruiser carried on unimpaired. Twenty minutes later at 1144 hours, Japanese planes attacked *Prince of Wales.* A Genzan division of nine Nells armed with torpedoes descended from 2,000 feet and began their approach. At 600 yards out and at 500 feet above the surface of the sea, Japanese crews released their torpedoes. Two of the nine found their mark. One of the ship's propeller shafts jammed and sliced through the hull allowing water to flood the control rooms. The battleship's steering gear, driving mechanism, radar and radio control gear were out. Several of her guns failed. She developed a 13-degree list to port and her speed fell to 15 knots. Captain Leach hoisted the "not under control" signal.

At noon aboard *Repulse* loudspeakers announced: "Standby for barrage!" Bombs exploded in the sea around her, throwing up geysers of water that drenched the seamen. Still her guns roared in unison as a division of torpedo bombers adjusted their descent from 1,700 feet and joined the level bombers in the attack. Another division of Bettys attacked. Skillfully using evasive maneuvers, Captain Tennant dodged 19 torpedoes. Seeing *Prince of Wales*'s desperate situation, Tennant radioed headquarters. It was Singapore's first notice that Force Z was under attack. Six Brewster Buffaloes took off from Tengah Airfield at 1215 hours.

Tennant slowed *Repulse* to 20 knots and moved toward *Prince of Wales* just as a division of Betty torpedo bombers of the Kanoya Air Group began their run from four miles out. *Prince of Wales* took four hits, the first of which blew a huge hole through the battleship's hull. Explosions were seen at the stern and at the bow. Her list righted temporarily, then the battleship settled in the water and began to sink at the stern. *Repulse* was hammered from all sides, taking four torpedo hits, one of which jammed her rudder. A fifth torpedo hit her boiler room. She listed 30 degrees to port. Captain Tennant ordered, "Abandon ship," and her crew headed for the oily waters. HMS *Repulse* capsized and sank at 1223 hours.

At 1246 hours, two divisions of Nell high-level bombers attacked *Prince of Wales*. One 500-kilogram bomb hit the battleship amidships. Captain Leach called destroyer *Express* alongside to take on survivors. The destroyer hung next to the battleship for 20 perilous minutes. At 1320 hours with Admiral Phillips and Captain Leach on the bridge, the Royal Navy's newest battleship slowly rolled over to port, turned on her back and sank, the first time a capital ship underway at sea was lost to enemy aircraft. The RAF Buffalo fighters from Singapore arrived in time to witness rescue operations. Of 1,309 officers and men aboard *Repulse,* 513 perished; 327 of the 1,612 men on *Prince of Wales* were lost. When Prime Minister Sir Winston Churchill heard of the loss, he was astonished. He wrote later that the sinking of

Prince of Wales and of *Repulse* was, for him, one of the greatest shocks of the war.

Assaults on American Soil

In late 1941, the Pacific islands of Guam and Wake were probably best known to Americans as refueling points along the route of the famous flying Clipper Ships of the Pan American Airways system. Clipper flights from San Francisco and Los Angeles put military observers, foreign correspondents and US government agents within six days travel of Manila. Guam was the sole US possession, or for that matter, the only foreign possession within the huge Pacific Mandate accorded Japan by the League of Nations after the Great War. Guam's capital city of Agana, with a naval radio station and a trans-Pacific cable station, was a focal point of the Pacific communication network. An American possession since 1899, Wake Island was a threat to Japan because of its proximity to her mid-Pacific Island territories and because it, too, served in the line of communication and supply between the United States and the Philippines.

During the Washington Naval Conference of 1922, the United States and Japan agreed not to fortify their holdings in the central Pacific but the treaty covering this decision lapsed in 1936. By December 1941, there was talk in the press and within the US Navy of fortifying Guam while a military buildup on Wake was in its early stages. The Japanese saw the invasion and takeover of both islands as essential to establishing their defense perimeter in the Pacific and their push toward the Greater East Asia Co-Prosperity Sphere. Vice Admiral Shigeyoshi Inouye of Japan's Fourth Fleet stationed at Truk in the Caroline Islands was charged with both operations. Guam was a push-over; Wake was another story.

Guam lies 1,500 miles east of Manila and 3,000 miles west of Hawaii. On the morning of the Pearl Harbor attack, there were less than 700 combatants stationed there—153 US Marines, a 245-man native insular force and naval personnel totaling about 270. On hand were three patrol craft, an old oiler and USS *Penguin*, a minesweeper. Japanese intelligence incorrectly estimated US strength on Guam at 2,000 men along with anti-aircraft guns and heavy coastal-defense guns. As it was, the heaviest weapon on the 20-mile-long island was the Browning .30-caliber light machine gun. Radio operators on Guam received word at 0600 hours on the morning of December 8 (December 7, 1100 hours in Hawaii) that Pearl Harbor had been attacked. They proceeded with orders to destroy all records and communication equipment. Within hours Japanese naval bombers arrived from Saipan 100 miles to the north. They bombed the dock area and hit *Penguin*. Raids continued with planes from the Fourth Fleet stationed at Truk and from the floatplane unit of seaplane tender *Kiyokawa Maru*. Just after midnight on December 10, Rear Admiral Arimoto Goto's invasion force arrived offshore. Minelayer *Tsugaru* and destroyers *Kikuzuki, Oboro, Uzuki* and *Yuzuki* accompanied transport ships carrying 5,000 men of the Japanese Army's South Seas Detached Force and the Yokosuka Special Naval Landing Force. Within hours, the Japanese were on the beach and had advanced into the capital, Agana. Captain G. J. McMillan, the senior officer on Guam, learned of landings on other parts of the island and sounded a car horn to signal a US ceasefire. Offshore Admiral Goto's heavy cruisers *Aoba, Furutaka, Kako* and *Kinugasa* hadn't fired a shot. The Japanese lost ten men, the Americans seventeen. Captured Americans spent the duration of the war at a prison camp in the Japanese home islands.

Japan's capture of Wake Island was more costly. The US suspected it would be one of Japan's first targets in the event of war and began fortifying Wake in August 1941. By November, 388 Marines, 68 sailors, five soldiers from Army communications, 70 employees of the Pan American Air Service and 1,146 civilian construction workers were based there. Crews specialized in the development and construction of island airfields and submarine bases had just completed a 5,000-foot-long runway and were completing shorter cross sections by early December. Wake is a complex of three islands, a low-grade atoll in the shape of a reversed C with Wake in the center, Peale Island to the north and Wilkes Island to the south. The atoll lies about 2,200 miles west of Hawaii and covers less than three square miles in territory. A US airfield on Wake was a significant threat to Japanese bases in the Marshall Islands, 600 miles to the south. Wake was fortified with six 5-inch shore batteries, a dozen 3-inch anti-aircraft batteries, 24 .50-caliber heavy machine guns and some .30-caliber light machine guns. On December 4 with the arrival of Admiral Halsey's Task Force 8 from Pearl Harbor, Wake Island gained Marine Fighter Squadron VMF-211, a dozen Grumman F4F Wildcats brought in aboard USS *Enterprise*, with fighter pilots, crews and a command staff—59 in all. Halsey's task force, carrier *Enterprise*, three heavy cruisers and nine destroyers, was back within 200 miles of Hawaii on the morning of the Pearl Harbor attack. There were no warships at Wake, she remained short on troops and without radar, without barbed wire or mines on the beaches and no revetments for the newly arrived Wildcats.

The Japanese too had been making their plans for Wake Island. On December 3, the 6th Destroyer Flotilla reinforced with Cruiser Division 18 arrived in the Marshall Islands from Fourth Fleet's anchorage at Truk in the Carolines. This force of nine warships was joined by two submarines and four troop transports. Dubbed the Wake Island Strike Force, the ships left from Kwajalein in the Marshalls on December 8 (December 7 in Hawaii) commanded by Rear Admiral Sadamichi Kajioka aboard his flagship light cruiser *Yubari*.

On Wake, Marine Major James Devereux, Navy Commander Winfield Cunningham and Major Paul Putnam, in command of the Wildcat squadron, received word of the attack on Pearl Harbor four hours after it took place. Four of the Marine Wildcats were off on morning patrol. A Pan Am Clipper that had lifted off from the lagoon a half hour earlier bound for Guam returned on orders from Cunningham. Marines and construction workers readied the atoll and searched the skies for Japanese planes. Just before noon on December 8 (December 7, 1400 hours in Hawaii), 36 Betty bombers of the 24th Air Flotilla based on Kwajalein arrived in a rain squall. Dropping their bombs from 2,000 feet, they destroyed eight of the recently arrived Wildcats still on the ground. The new airstrip was cratered and the Pan Am seaplane facility on Peale Island was destroyed. Three of the six 5-inch coastal defense guns were wiped out along with their ammunition. The Japanese lost no aircraft that day and their Bettys returned at noon the next day and the next day again. With some help from civilian workers, the Marines were better prepared for the subsequent attacks and shot down two of the bombers and damaged a third. Proud and exhausted, the Americans on Wake waited for reinforcements and for what they believed would be an inevitable attack from the sea. The Pan Am Clipper, bullet holes plugged, left that afternoon for Midway.

Ships of the Wake Island Strike Force were spotted to the south very early on the morning of December 11. They were the oldest light cruisers in the Japanese Navy, *Tatsuta* and *Tenryu*, followed by six destroyers. Two destroyer-transports sailed to the starboard side of the column and two Maru troopships to port. Shortly after 0500 hours, with the sea running high, Admiral Kajioka turned his flagship *Yubari* to port. The others followed. On shore, Major Devereux's men were under orders not to fire until the Japanese were drawn within range of the 5-inch coastal defense guns still in service. Now moving west and parallel to Wake, just before 0530 hours, the Japanese opened fire from 6,000 yards. Structures on Wilkes and on Wake were hit and oil storage tanks on Wake were set ablaze. Two of the Japanese troop transports, each with 225 amphibious assault troops, dropped anchor and prepared to launch landing craft. Still there was no fire from the shore. Kajioka assumed his three days of bombing raids had destroyed American defenses. The nine warships continued firing and reversed course to the east. They were 4,500 yards offshore. It was 0600 hours and the Marines, their batteries trained on the Japanese, were getting angry and anxious. At 0610 Devereux gave the order to commence firing. Battery A on Wake fired on *Yubari* and then on one of the destroyer-transports. The transport was hit and went dead in the water. Realizing he had moved in too closely, Kajioka turned his flagship to the southwest and escorted the other destroyer-transport away on a zigzag course. The remaining troopships, the converted Marus carrying the garrison troops, came under fire from L Battery on the western tip of Wilkes Island. One ship was hit. Destroyers *Hayate*, *Mochizuki* and *Oite* maneuvered to fire back. *Hayate* was hit straight on, exploded and sank with no survivors. She was the first Japanese surface warship sunk in the war. *Oite* took a solid hit with a 5-inch shell and turned away with nineteen wounded. She and *Mochizuki* retired to the southwest. At about 0630 hours destroyers *Kisaragi*, *Mutsuki* and *Yayoi* supported by light cruisers *Tatsuta* and *Tenryu* formed a column west of Wake and commenced firing on B Battery at the western tip of Peale Island. The Marines returned fire and hit *Yayoi*, killing one, wounding seventeen. The remaining Japanese ships made smoke and at 0700 hours retired.

At 0730 hours, patrolling Marine Wildcats spotted the Japanese in retreat about 30 miles southwest of Wake. They went after the enemy in steep dives through heavy flak. A .50-caliber machine gun round struck a depth charge on *Kisaragi*, causing an explosion that lifted her out of the water and crashed her back into the sea with all men on board. Admiral Kajioka headed his force south and back to Kwajalein in the Marshall Islands. He'd be back.

Aftermath

Stunned by the news of the Japanese attack on Pearl Harbor, Americans listened intently to a radio address by their president on Monday evening, December 8. In his fireside chat, Franklin Roosevelt accepted the challenge of the Japanese on behalf of all Americans and their Congress: "We are now in this war. We are all in it all the way. So far, the news has been all bad. We have suffered a serious setback in Hawaii. Our forces in the Philippines are taking punishment but are defending themselves vigorously. The reports from Guam and Wake and Midway Islands are still confused but we must be prepared for the announcement that all these outposts have been seized." Americans would soon learn just how fast and how far Japanese Army, Navy and Air Force units had advanced on December 7 and in the three days following.

The island of Guam was in the hands of the enemy and the Wake Atoll was under continuous attack, severing supply routes between Hawaii and the Philippines. The only capital ships of the British Royal Navy in the Pacific, HMS *Prince of Wales* and HMS *Repulse*, were sunk with the loss of 840 men. On the Malay Peninsula, the Japanese established beachheads as British, Australian and Indian units withdrew to the south toward Singapore. Japanese infantry units rolled over the flanks of Commonwealth troops, negotiating swampy wetlands and thick jungle terrain previously considered impassable. All British aircraft and ships at Hong Kong were destroyed and the British garrison there was outnumbered two to one by the advancing enemy.

In the United States, some Americans, particularly those on the west coast, were in a state of near panic. There were reports of an imminent invasion of Oregon and of Washington state and reports that Japanese planes were approaching San Francisco. Some communities in southern California were evacuated. Inland cities were ordered blacked out in anticipation of Luftwaffe London-style bombing raids. Some government buildings were sandbagged. The racing season at Santa Anita was canceled and the 1942

Rose Bowl Game was moved to the stadium at Duke University in North Carolina.

By December 11, Germany and Italy formally declared war on the United States in accordance with their Tripartite Alliance with the Japanese. And Japan with less than 2,000 human casualties, the loss of four ships and less than 50 aircraft owned most of the Pacific along a 5,000-mile front from Malaya in the west to the International Date Line in the east. She established a defense perimeter that even her most optimistic military strategists thought impossible in so little time. Her advance toward the Greater East Asia Co-Prosperity Sphere was well underway.

Chapter V

APPENDIX D

United Kingdom Commonwealth Forces
Commonwealth Forces in Pacific—December 1941 to December 1942

6 BBs: *Prince of Wales, Ramillies, Resolution, Revenge, Royal Sovereign, Warspite*

2 CVs: *Formidable, Indomitable*

1 CVL: *Hermes*

1 BC: *Repulse*

5 CAs: *Cornwall, Dorsetshire, Exeter, Australia (RAN), Canberra (RAN)*

8 CLs: *Caledon, Danae, Dragon, Emerald, Enterprise, Adelaide (RAN), Hobart (RAN), Perth (RAN)*

26 DDs: *Arrow, Decoy, Electra, Encounter, Express, Fortune, Foxhound, Griffin, Hotspur, Jupiter, Scout, Stronghold, Tenedos, Thanet, Thracian, Napier (RAN), Nepal (RAN), Nestor (RAN), Nizam (RAN), Norman (RAN), Pakenham (RAN), Paladin (RAN), Panther (RAN), Vampire (RAN), Vendetta (RAN), Voyager (RAN)*

Far East Fleet (China Station)
Based at Singapore—December 1941 to February 1942

Commander in Chief: Vice Admiral Tom Phillips

1 BB: *Prince of Wales*

1 BC: *Repulse*

1 CA: *Exeter*

3 CLs: *Danae, Dragon, Hobart (RAN)*

9 DDs: *Electra, Express, Scout*, Stronghold*, Tenedos*, Thanet*, Vampire (RAN), Vendetta (RAN), Voyager (RAN)*

*Destroyers previously stationed at Hong Kong's Victoria Harbor

Eastern Fleet
Based at Ceylon—February to December 1942

Commander in Chief: Admiral Sir James Somerville

5 BBs: *Ramillies, Resolution, Revenge, Royal Sovereign, Warspite*

2 CVs: *Formidable, Indomitable*

1 CVL: *Hermes*

2 CAs: *Cornwall, Dorsetshire*

6 CLs: *Caledon, Danae, Dragon, Emerald, Enterprise, Adelaide (RAN)*

19 DDs: *Arrow, Decoy, Express, Fortune, Foxhound, Griffin, Hotspur, Scout, Tenedos, Napier (RAN), Nepal (RAN), Nestor (RAN), Nizam (RAN), Norman (RAN), Pakenham (RAN), Paladin (RAN), Panther (RAN), Vampire (RAN), Issac Sweers (RNN)*

Chapter VI

THE PHILIPPINES INVADED

Introduction

To say that the geographic scope of Japan's December 1941 onslaught in the Pacific was huge would be an understatement. That a country roughly the size of the state of California was able to launch coordinated naval, air and land assaults in diverse corners of the Pacific seemed inconceivable despite the war planning underway in Allied military circles. Even as Pearl Harbor came under attack from Japanese carrier-based aircraft, amphibious assault troops of the Japanese Army landed on the Malay Peninsula, 6,500 miles west of the Hawaiian Islands. Within three hours of the Pearl Harbor attack, Japanese carrier-based aircraft attacked the US naval base at Davao on the Philippine Island of Mindanao, over 5,500 miles west of Pearl Harbor. Within six hours of the attack, Japanese land-based aircraft bombed US air bases on the island of Luzon in the Philippines and raided the US island possessions of Guam and Wake. On the night of December 7, Japanese surface warships bombarded Midway Island, 1,500 miles west of Pearl Harbor. Off the Chinese Mainland, the island of Hong Kong, Great Britain's oldest colony, was attacked by land-based bombers as units of Japan's Sixteenth Army threatened from the north.

The following day, Japanese land-based aircraft raided Cavite Naval Yard on Manila Bay and struck nearby airfields a second time. A day later, Japanese amphibious troops came ashore on the island of Guam in the Marianas and within an hour, Guam's defenders surrendered. Only at Wake Island did the Japanese meet stiff resistance. Here on December 11 (December 10 in Hawaii), they were forced to abandon an amphibious troop landing—Japan's first unsuccessful assault of the three-day-old war. But even as US Marines on Wake Island repelled the enemy, Japan's Army was solidly entrenched on the Malay Peninsula, her Navy controlled the surrounding waters and her aircraft freely roamed the skies. Off the east coast of Malaya, the last Royal Navy capital ships in the region were sunk by Japanese land-based torpedo and level bomber aircraft. This loss of HMS *Price of Wales* together with American losses at Pearl Harbor meant the Allies had no serviceable battleships in the Pacific. And on a small island north of the Philippine Island of Luzon and on Luzon itself, Japanese amphibious landings were underway.

The Philippines lay north of the equator, 800 miles across the South China Sea from present-day Vietnam. Formed from over 7,000 islands and islets, the country covers a distance from north to south of nearly 1,200 miles. Its population in 1941 was 17 million with Luzon the most populous island and site of the capital city of Manila. The United States purchased the Philippines from Spain in 1898 and by the 1920s, Manila Bay was home port to ships of the US Navy's Asiatic Fleet. A smaller US naval facility was located on the southernmost island of Mindanao. In December 1941, ships on the active roster of the US Asiatic Fleet included a single heavy cruiser, two light cruisers, 13 destroyers, 40 small craft and auxiliary vessels and 29 submarines. The submarines represented some of the US Navy's newer boats while the 16 surface warships were some of the oldest vessels the Navy had in service.

Unlike the rubber rich Malay Peninsula, there were no natural resources of interest to Japan in the Philippines. It was the location of the island chain just 600 miles from the Japanese home island of Okinawa that made it an essential holding to reinforce the western flank of Japan's defense perimeter. Further, a presence in the Philippines would protect the Japanese military's Malaya and Hong Kong operations and provide anchorage and naval staging areas for Japan's planned Netherlands East Indies Campaign.

Officers and Operations

Admiral Thomas C. Hart was 64 years old in late 1941, an 1897 graduate of the United States Naval Academy. In more than 40 years in the Navy he had served in the Spanish-American War and as a commander of a submarine division in the Great War, as Superintendent of the Naval Academy as well as in several high-ranking positions in the US Navy. Hart took command of the old US Asiatic Fleet in 1939 when it was based at Shanghai for the protection of American interests in China. In fall 1940, as Japanese aggression in the Far East increased, Hart transferred the Fleet from Shanghai to Manila Bay in the Philippines to work more closely with the Army there. By November 1941 when an attack by the Japanese seemed imminent and without carrier support to protect his vessels, Hart began transferring ships under his command away from Manila and the Philippines. He dispatched light cruiser *Marblehead* and nine destroyers to patrol duty off the east coast of Dutch Borneo. The Fleet's one heavy cruiser, its flagship *Houston,* along with light cruiser *Boise* sailed south on December 4, leaving four destroyers, some submarines and a few auxiliary craft at Cavite Navy Base on Manila Bay. Seaplane tender USS *William B. Preston* remained the only military craft at the Davao facility at Malalag Bay on Mindanao.

Although US naval forces in the Philippines were sparse, the number of ground troops for defense of the islands seemed adequate. Troops in the US Army's Far East Command under Lieutenant General Douglas MacArthur included infantry and air units totaling 140,000 officers and men. Active Filipino units accounted for 110,000 of those while the US Army contributed the remaining 30,000 ground and air troops. MacArthur had resigned from the US Army in 1935 and only recently rejoined when appointed Field Marshal of the Philippine Army. In July 1941, at age 61, he was recalled to active duty by President Roosevelt and reinstated with the rank of Lieutenant General. MacArthur hoped to increase his troop strength to 200,000 men by April 1942, the window in which he expected the Japanese would attack the Philippines.

Major General Jonathan M. Wainwright commanded MacArthur's North Luzon Force, responsible for the island's defense from Manila northward. Wainwright, at age 58, led 60,000 men in four infantry divisions and one cavalry division, the largest concentration of troops in the Philippines.

Brigadier General George M. Parker Jr. and later, Brigadier General Albert M. Jones, commanded South Luzon Force. Brigadier General William F. Sharp led Visayan-Mindanao Force, three Philippine divisions in defense of islands from Mindoro southward. MacArthur's battle plan in the event of a Japanese invasion of the Philippines was to defend the beaches. A radiogram from US Army Chief of Staff General George C. Marshall on the afternoon of the Pearl Harbor attack assured MacArthur he had the complete confidence of the War Department and that he could expect every possible assistance within its power. But MacArthur and the Philippines received no help, no reinforcements. That very day a convoy bound for Manila with planes and men was diverted to Fiji and four large troopships had already been ordered back to San Francisco. US strategy in the Far East would be strictly defensive and it is believed MacArthur might not have been privy to the British/American agreement to defeat Germany first before taking an offensive stance against the Empire of Japan.

MacArthur's Far East Command provided most of the air power in the Philippines with many of the Army's modern planes concentrated at Clark Field north of Manila and at Nichols and Nielsen Fields just east of the city. Aircraft were also stationed at the grassy Iba auxiliary field northwest of Clark and at small airstrips at Baguio and at Tuguegarao farther north. US Army air power in the Philippines amounted to just under 300 planes, all stationed on Luzon. There were 35 new Boeing B-17 Flying Fortress heavy bombers stationed at Clark Field, 107 Curtiss Warhawk P-40 fighters at Clark and Nichols Fields and another 100 US Army aircraft at these and other airstrips. In addition, the US Navy had 32 Consolidated Catalinas, four Grumman Ducks and five Vought Kingfishers, all seaplanes, in Manila Bay and at Davao on the island of Mindanao.

For the Imperial Japanese Navy in the Philippines Campaign, the responsibility for bombing, invading and securing objectives went to Vice Admiral Ibo Takahashi. Takahashi was Commander in Chief of Japan's Third Fleet and Commander in Chief of Eastern Force, the Philippine Support Force. He reported to Vice Admiral Nobutake Kondo of Japan's Southern Force. Takahashi's force included nearly 200 vessels: 36 surface warships, some 50 auxiliary vessels and more than 100 transports. These were assigned to various strike, attack or cover forces in numbers from three to 29 vessels and these forces themselves were often renamed depending on the geographic areas in which they served.

Rear Admiral Raizo Tanaka, age 49, was a specialist in destroyer and torpedo warfare and commanded the only Japanese carrier in the Philippines campaign, light carrier *Ryujo*. Operating from the Palau Islands east of Mindanao, he personally led the ships designated Davao Attack Force, while under him, Rear Admiral Kuyuji Kubo led Legaspi Strike Force. These forces were charged with attacking sites on the eastern shores of Mindanao and Luzon and with controlling the surrounding waters. Commander-in-Chief of the Fourteenth Army, Lieutenant-General Masaharu Homma, age 54, was leader of all Japanese ground forces charged with invasion of the Philippines. Homma would ultimately be responsible for the handling, movement and actions of more than 60,000 Japanese troops. Although Japan's Navy anticipated stiff opposition from the US Navy in the Philippines, Japan's Army expected General Homma to secure surrender there within 50 days of its first landings on Luzon.

Japanese Air Strikes on Mindanao and Luzon

None of Japan's six fleet carriers were available for her initial attacks on the Philippines since carriers *Akagi*, *Hiryu*, *Kaga*, *Shokaku*, *Soryu* and *Zuikaku* were on their way back to Japan's Inland Sea from the Pearl Harbor attack. Only light carrier *Ryujo* and three seaplane tenders, *Chitose*, *Mizuho* and *Sanuki Maru*, were in Philippine waters for sea-based air support. *Ryujo* could launch up to 37 planes while the seaplane tenders carried a total of 30 floatplanes, all ready on the morning of the Pearl Harbor attack to carry out Japan's initial air assault on the Philippines. It came on the island of Mindanao at Malalag Bay anchorage on Davao Gulf, 600 miles south of Manila. There, seaplane tender USS *William B. Preston* picked up a clear radio message from Fleet Headquarter in Manila warning that Japan had commenced hostilities and Allied forces were to govern themselves accordingly. With Davao just 500 miles west of a Japanese naval base in the Palau Islands, the crew of *Preston* expected trouble. The last US vessel at Malalag, *Preston* launched two of her four Catalinas to search the southern Philippine waters. Within hours, nine Claude fixed-wheel fighters and 13 Val dive bombers off light carrier *Ryujo* arrived over Davao. The Claudes strafed the two floating

Catalinas, setting them ablaze. *Preston,* underway for open waters, zigzagged across the bay, skillfully avoiding bombs from the Vals. After the attack, she returned to pick up survivors and late on December 8, she was dispatched away from Davao and eventually away from the Philippines, part of a vast US retreat southward toward Borneo and Australia.

Four hundred miles north of the Philippines lay the island of Formosa. It had been ceded to Japan by China in 1895 in the peace treaty that ended the Sino-Japanese War. The Japanese had air bases on Formosa at Taichu, Tainan, Takao and Takai. On December 8 (December 7 in Hawaii), the Japanese Navy's Eleventh Air Fleet had over 200 land-based aircraft at those bases, poised for a predawn launch on Mindanao. The Japanese Army's 5th Air Division, also on Formosa, could provide more than 100 additional aircraft. The Japanese fully expected American air attacks on their Formosan bases once news of Pearl Harbor reached Manila, but those attacks were not forthcoming. Although General MacArthur's office reportedly received word of the attack at 0330 hours Manila time, misunderstandings and miscommunications were blamed for a lack of an immediate response by the Americans. Far East Air Chief Major General Lewis Brereton, despite two requests, could not secure MacArthur's permission to send his B-17 bombers out from Clark Field.

On Formosa, once some heavy early morning fog lifted, the first of 32 Japanese Army Mitsubishi Sally medium bombers took off for Luzon and its northern airfields at Baguio and at Tuguegarao. Within two hours, 192 aircraft of the Imperial Navy's Eleventh Air Fleet—84 Zero fighters escorting 108 Betty and Nell bombers—headed south for US air bases at Clark and Nichols Fields and for the small field at Iba. At Clark Field, with few US planes in the air and all B-17 heavy bombers parked wing-to-wing in the open, the Zeros, Bettys and Nells found an inviting target. Of the 35 B-17s of the US Army Air Corps' 19th Bombardment Group, 15 were destroyed and five severely damaged along with machine shops, hangars and barracks. The raid lasted less than fifteen minutes. Between Clark and Nichols Fields, 56 of the P-40 Warhawk fighters were lost. Another 30 US aircraft of various types were destroyed at these fields and at Nielsen and at Iba. Human casualties on the ground totaled 230. The Japanese lost seven Zeros that day.

On December 9 (December 8 in Hawaii), some of the undamaged B-17

bombers at Clark Field were transferred south for Australia along with bombers from Nichols Field. The P-40 Warhawks that survived the initial attacks
were caught by Japanese bombers later that day. The next day, 52 Zero fighters flew over Luzon's air bases, destroying any US aircraft climbing to meet
them. Eighty high-level Japanese bombers attacked Cavite Navy Yard on
Manila Bay against light anti-aircraft fire. The yard, its warehouses, barracks, radio station and torpedo storage were left ablaze. The raid killed or
injured 500 men. Japanese fighters and bombers left Nichols and Nielsen
Fields inoperable. By evening, US air power in the Philippines was reduced
to less than three squadrons. With air bases destroyed, the few remaining
planes on Luzon were dispersed to smaller airstrips in the islands or, if range
permitted, to the Netherlands East Indies or to Australia. Japan controlled
the Philippine skies and US vessels in the area sailed under constant threat of
enemy air attack.

Only four US destroyers remained at Cavite on December 10: USS *John
D. Ford,* USS *Peary,* USS *Pillsbury* and USS *Pope.* In a Japanese attack that
day, *Peary* took a bomb hit that damaged her forward stack and superstructure. She was towed away from a burning wharf and an exploding stash of
torpedoes by the minesweeper *Whippoorwill* assisted by *Pillsbury.* Eight of
Peary's crew were lost. USS *Sealion,* a submarine in for repairs, was sunk.
That afternoon, Admiral Hart released most of the remaining ships at Cavite
southward and by late December, the four destroyers along with an assortment of auxiliary vessels were headed south as well. At the end of 1941, small
craft and a few motor torpedo boats were all that remained of the US Asiatic
Fleet at its home base.

When Japanese attacks on the Philippines began, heavy cruiser *Houston*
and light cruiser *Boise* were in the central Philippines off the island of Cebu
and heading south. Destroyers *Barker, Bulmer, Parrott, Paul Jones* and *Stewart* supported by light cruiser *Marblehead* were stationed off the east coast of
Borneo at Tarakan. Destroyers *Alden, Edsall, John D. Edwards* and *Whipple*
and seaplane tender *Blackhawk* were 400 miles further south at Balikpapan
also on Borneo's east coast. US military authorities at Manila knew hours in
advance to expect Japanese raids on the Philippines at any time. With few
exceptions, no preparations were made. The two major US naval facilities
there were lost. Most US Army Air Corps planes were destroyed. Air bases

were severely damaged. And US air power in the Pacific offered no danger to Japanese airfields on Formosa and little threat to Japanese naval strike forces as they began their invasion of the Philippines at several strategic locations.

Initial Amphibious Landings

By November 25, 1941, the vessels of Admiral Takahashi's Eastern Force were assembling at four staging areas. Most were near the Pescadores west of Formosa. Others gathered off Formosa's east coast. Some were in the Ryukyu Islands south of Japan and others still in the Palau Islands east of the Philippines. Their initial invasion targets included five sites in the Philippines where landings were timed to coincide with or follow closely upon the attack at Pearl Harbor. Later there would be two major amphibious invasions, one on the west coast of Luzon at Lingayen Gulf and another from the east at Lamon Bay. Batan, a small island 120 miles north of Luzon, not to be confused with the Bataan Peninsula west of Manila, was the first Japanese invasion site. On the morning of December 8 as bombers of Japan's Eleventh Air Fleet waited on Formosa for the early morning fog to lift, Rear Admiral Sueto Hirose's Third Surprise Attack Force arrived off Batan. Also called Northern Island Strike Force, it included two Maru transports supported by destroyer *Yamagumo*. The transports (converted merchant ships) carrying 490 Army and Navy assault troops flawlessly disembarked a portion of their men who quickly garrisoned the island. The landings met no resistance and there were no casualties. Two days later, the remaining troops of the force went ashore on the island of Camiguin in the Babuyan Channel 40 miles north of Luzon. Again, there was no resistance.

At Apari on Luzon's north coast on December 10, the Japanese First Surprise Attack Force was not so fortunate. Poor weather and rough seas added to Rear Admiral Kenzaburo Hara's problems with poorly designed landing craft. Hara's force of 25 vessels included his flagship, light cruiser *Natori*, six destroyers, a variety of minesweepers and anti-submarine craft, and six Maru transports carrying men of the Army's Tanaka Detachment. The debarkation was slow and costly, contested by a few US aircraft whose crews fought the assault aggressively. As destroyers *Fumizuki, Harukaze, Hatakaze, Minazuki, Nagatsuki* and *Satsuki* attempted to protect their charges, a Japanese minesweeper took a bomb hit and was sunk. Destroyer *Harukaze* was hit and damaged and *Natori* saw several near misses. With much of the 2,000-man assault force ashore, Admiral Hara suspended the landing and ordered remaining supplies thrown overboard in the hope that troops on shore could retrieve them.

Vigan, 100 miles from Apari on Luzon's west coast, was also scheduled for an amphibious assault on December 10. However, the Second Surprise Attack Force under Rear Admiral Shoji Nishimura met with poor weather and with US Army Air Corps planes in the area. Nishimura postponed the landing a day and moved the operation to landing beaches further south. The force had staged in the Pescadores and included Nishimura's flagship, light cruiser *Naka*, seven destroyers, six minesweepers, nine anti-submarine vessels and six transports.

The destroyers were *Asagumo, Harusame, Minegumo, Murasame, Natsu-gumo, Samidare* and *Yudachi*. The transports carried elements of the Four-teenth Army's Kanno Detachment, a force of over 2,000 men. US Army fighters appeared over Vigan again on December 11 as the Kanno Detach-ment loaded into landing craft. *Naka* was strafed with the loss of three men. Two transports were bombed and beached with 25 assault troops injured. One minesweeper was bombed and sunk with the loss of most of its 100-man crew. When the fighters departed, the landings continued with little resistance ashore.

The attacks by US Army Air Corps fighter planes and bombers during the first four days of the war were one of the few positive notes for Americans in the Philippines Campaign. US airmen showed incredible determination and authorities in Manila often enhanced any success story for the benefit of an American public hungry for good news. One story reported was of a young B-17 pilot, US Army Captain Colin Kelly. On December 10, Kelly radioed from a position over the South China Sea that his crew had bombed and set afire a Japanese *Kongo-* class battleship. Manila enhanced the report saying that Kelly's crew had badly damaged the battleship *Haruna*. Later reports indicated the battleship was sunk. Actually, *Haruna* was over a thou-sand miles away, part of Vice Admiral Nobutake Kondo's Southern Force covering the Malaya Invasion. Kelly's B-17 had attacked a Japanese warship, but it was most likely the heavy cruiser *Ashigara*, flagship of Admiral Taka-hashi. The ship was not sunk nor was it damaged. Captain Kelly and his plane did not survive the mission although many of his crew bailed out and were rescued. Nonetheless early newspaper and magazine reports gave Americans cause to be proud of their fighting men in the Philippines and especially proud of their airmen. One question couldn't help being asked, however, "Where was our Navy?"

Legaspi and Davao

While the US Navy became increasingly absent in the Philippines, the Imperial Japanese Navy proceeded on schedule with its plan for taking the island nation. Its next target was Legaspi on southern Luzon. Rear Admiral Raizo Tanaka was in tactical command of a force of 38 vessels that operated from the Palau Islands. By December 10, much of this Legaspi Cover Force was on station off the island of Samar in the Philippine Sea. It included *Ryujo,* her escort destroyer *Shiokaze,* heavy cruisers *Haguro, Myoko,* and *Nachi,* Tanaka's flagship, light cruiser *Jintsu,* and destroyers *Amatsukaze, Hatsukaze, Hayashio, Kuroshio, Natsushio* and *Oyashio.* Under Tanaka, Rear Admiral Kuyuji Kubo led the Fourth Surprise Attack Force from his flagship light cruiser *Nagara.* The force included destroyers *Kawakaze, Suzukaze, Tokitsukaze, Umikaze, Yamakaze* and *Yukikaze,* seaplane tenders *Chitose* and *Mizuho,* two minesweepers, two patrol craft and a convoy of seven transports carrying over 3,000 assault troops. The troops were charged with securing and neutralizing enemy airfields on southern Luzon in preparation for a major assault later at Lamon Bay. On the night of December 11, the transports began the transfer of 2,500 men of the Army's Kimura Detachment and 575 Special Naval Landing Force assault troops of the 1st Kure Battalion into landing barges. Early the following morning, the troops went ashore at Legaspi against light resistance from Filipino troops. There was little pre-invasion support required from the fighters and bombers of *Ryujo* or from the seaplanes off the tenders. By evening on December 12, much of southeastern Luzon was firmly in Japanese hands. Two days later, five US B-17 bombers arrived from Australia over the harbor at Legaspi. Admiral Kubo's vessels should have made easy targets for the Americans but even with Japanese crews off guard, only one minesweeper was strafed in the attack and no Japanese ships were damaged. Tanaka's Cover Force and the transports were ordered back to Palau.

By December 17, Tanaka's force, now refueled and renamed Davao Attack Force, sortied Palau with 12 transports carrying 3,500 men of the Army's Sakaguchi Detachment, 1,500 men of the Miura Detachment and a small force of Special Naval Landing Force assault troops from the 2nd Kure Battalion. Their destination was the US Naval base on Davao Gulf, the spot where aircraft from *Ryujo* attacked USS *William B. Preston* and two Catalinas on the first day of the war. The convoy entered a quiet Malalag Bay before dawn on December 20: Tanaka's flagship *Jintsu*, destroyers *Amatsukaze, Hatsukaze, Hayashio, Kuroshio, Natsushio,* and *Oyashio*, and the Maru transports. A small landing party from *Amatsukaze* met some resistance on the pier with the loss of one seaman. The destroyer fired on shore, dispersing Filipino troops and setting oil supplies afire. Japanese residents of Davao, some of whom had been rounded up and imprisoned at the start of the war, were evacuated. Within days of the invasion, a half dozen US B-17s raided Japanese ships anchored in the harbor. Only the destroyer *Kuroshio* sustained damage with four of her crew wounded. The American bombers returned to Australia.

From Davao, Admiral Tanaka dispatched another strike force south and west to the island of Jolo in the Celebes Sea between Mindanao and British North Borneo. On the morning of December 24, ten vessels reached Jolo. Light carrier *Ryujo* and destroyer *Shiokaze* were joined by seaplane tender *Chitose.* The three vessels distanced themselves from Jolo as four destroyers, *Hatsukaze, Hayashio, Natsushio* and *Oyashio,* escorted three transports toward the island. Within an hour of transferring a battalion of 500 assault troops of the Army's Sakaguchi Detachment and 200 men of the 2nd Kure Battalion from transports to landing barges, the Japanese secured the island. There was no opposition and there were no combat casualties. Japan now controlled an island only 200 miles from British North Borneo.

The Main Blow, the Pincers Clinch

By December 20, there were 13,000 Japanese troops on the ground in the Philippines. Japan's primary purpose in these initial landings was to secure advanced air bases to cover later major invasions at Lingayen Gulf northwest of Manila and at Lamon Bay southeast of Manila that began in earnest on December 22. During the first weeks of war, most troop transports of Admiral Takahashi's Eastern Force remained anchored off Formosa. Now with a foothold established, a convoy of more than 70 troopships sailed south from the Pescadores with 43,000 assault troops of General Homma's Fourteenth Army. Moving toward the invasion sites in Lingayen Gulf, they joined cruisers and destroyers from Rear Admiral Kenzaburo Hara's Apari Strike Force, from Rear Admiral Nishimura's Vigan Strike Force, and from Rear Admiral Kubo's Legaspi Strike Force. Admiral Nobutake Kondo and elements of his Southern Force moved north into the South China Sea, bringing battleships *Haruna* and *Kongo* and 10 other warships including Kondo's flagship, heavy cruiser *Atago*. *Haruna* and *Kongo* had been the only capital ships supporting Japanese landings on the Malay Peninsula where they stood by to counter movement by *Prince of Wales* and *Repulse*. Kondo's ships, newly renamed Distant Support Force, were assigned heavy pre-invasion bombardment of the Lingayen Gulf beaches. Takahashi's warships, now called Philippine Support Force, took up station west of Luzon. Kondo's force positioned itself south of Takahashi.

Japanese bombers and fighters flying from Formosa had been attacking US and Filipino defense positions along the coast of Lingayen Gulf since December 18. Just after midnight on December 22, the largest Japanese amphibious operation of the two-week-old Pacific war began. US submarine *Stingray* sighted the Japanese force the day before the landing and alerted General MacArthur who expected an attack at the south end of Lingayen Gulf. It was not to be. Based on earlier intelligence information, the Japanese moved their main landing 30 miles to the north where there were few coastal defenses. The weather was foul as Kondo's battleships and Takahashi's cruisers fired their heavy guns in an early morning bombardment. A few remaining US fighters harassed the enemy. Destroyer *Nagatsuki* was strafed. Four B-17s attacked the convoy with 100-lb bombs but failed to score any hits. Although most US Asiatic Fleet submarines ordered to Lingayen Gulf arrived too late to disrupt the amphibious operation, one small Japanese transport was torpedoed and sunk as the invasion began and a second transport was lost the following day. Merchant seaplane tender *Sanuki Maru* was slightly damaged by a shell from a coastal defense gun and some landing craft were overturned in rough seas but for the most part, the first of General Homma's assault troops landed on the beaches of Lingayen Gulf to little resistance. By evening on December 22, three of the four Japanese infantry regiments were ashore and moving inland while two armored regiments prepared to disembark. Two days later, reconnaissance units were 10 miles inland and heading south toward Manila. Troops of the 48th Division's 9th Regiment linked up near San Fernando with the Tanaka Detachment that arrived at Apari on December 10.

On December 23 with Japanese units moving rapidly toward Manila from both north and south, and with the failure of his plan to defend the beaches, MacArthur was forced to fall back on an old plan for defense of the Philippines, WPO-3, War Plan Orange-3. It called for the withdrawal of Filipino and American troops to the Bataan Peninsula where they would hold out until reinforcements arrived. The peninsula formed the western shore of Manila Bay. It was 30 miles long from north to south and between 15 and 20 miles wide—mountainous jungle in the west, ravine and marsh in the east.

That night, December 23, ships of the Lamon Bay Strike Force sailing from the Ryukyu Islands arrived off the east coast of Luzon 60 miles southeast of Manila. The force was commanded by Vice Admiral Kuyuji Kubo aboard light cruiser *Nagara* and included the same destroyers that delivered troops at Legaspi on December 12. At Lamon Bay, 24 transports disembarked over 7,000 men of the Fourteenth Army's 16th Division. By mid-morning on Christmas Eve the troops were on the march toward Manila. The Kimura Detachment moving up from Legaspi would link up with them. Southern Luzon was under Japanese control. The giant pincer movement the Japanese Army envisioned was underway.

In Manila that morning, General MacArthur gave instructions for the transfer of his headquarters to Corregidor Island in the mouth of Manila Bay. The steamer *Don Esteban* carried him, his staff, his wife and child 30 miles across the bay that night. Filipino and US troops in the city were ordered to Bataan. Admiral Hart arranged to remove the headquarters of the Asiatic Fleet from Manila. At Malacanan Palace, Philippine President Manuel Quezon was convinced to declare Manila an open city in the hope it would not be destroyed by the Japanese, then he and his Vice President left to join MacArthur on Corregidor.

Aftermath

In his address on December 8, President Roosevelt told the American public that US forces in the Philippines were taking punishment but defending themselves vigorously. Punishment yes, but the vigorous defense was not the case then nor did it become more of a reality as the month of December wore on. The heavy loss of aircraft on the ground in the first days of war, the early retreat of warships to Borneo and Australia, the failure to take offensive action against Japanese airfields, submarines in the wrong place at the wrong time and with torpedoes that often failed, a lack of communication, or was it a lack of cooperation, among officers—on and on went the list of reasons, or excuses, why the Philippines succumbed so quickly. Loss of the American protectorate must have caused not only despair in Washington but a good amount of embarrassment as well.

Filipino and American troops outnumbered the Japanese invaders two to one, three to one in some of the early landings. Yet Filipino troops were poorly trained and poorly equipped. They spoke in various dialects. They had no armor. The well-trained 48th Division of General Homma's Fourteenth Army included three infantry regiments, a reconnaissance regiment and two armored regiments. By the time of the Lingayen Gulf landings, it was anticipated that as many as 20 percent of Filipino ground troops on Luzon fled into the jungle. By the end of December 1941, all US air bases in the Philippines were lost to the Japanese or destroyed and the entire US Asiatic Fleet had fled south. The attack on Pearl Harbor was deemed a surprise and yet, Admiral Kimmel as Commander in Chief of the Pacific Fleet and General Short as head of US Army forces in Hawaii were accused of incompetence, failure to maintain a state of military readiness and poor judgment. Kimmel was relieved of his command and both he and Short retired from the military in early 1942. Kimmel continued a relentless pursuit of his and of the Navy's innocence. In 1944 his case and Short's were heard before Naval Department and War Department courts of inquiry, respectively.

In contrast to Kimmel's and Short's humiliation, General MacArthur was honored in spite of the strategic errors he made in the early days of the war. He seemed reluctant or unable to admit a Japanese attack on the Philippines was imminent despite signs and planning to the contrary. Even after learning of the attack on Pearl Harbor, MacArthur failed to be convinced by his subordinates to order US bombers over Japanese air bases on Formosa. And after the Japanese were on Philippine soil, the General did not transfer plentiful supplies to Corregidor from bases on Luzon. Yet, MacArthur was not censured. Instead, he received his fourth star late in 1941, and in 1942 was awarded the Congressional Medal of Honor.

Chapter VII

JAPANESE CONQUESTS CONTINUE— BORNEO, WAKE ISLAND, HONG KONG

Introduction

In the first week of war, Japanese generals and admirals were euphoric with victory fever. Except for the assault on Wake Island, all their operations were successful as Japanese forces advanced rapidly on targets across the Pacific. Japanese naval officers joined in the optimism after their earlier disagreement with Combined Fleet's plans for the Pearl Harbor attack and for campaigns on the Malay Peninsula, at Hong Kong and in the Philippines. Just a month earlier, for Japan to wage war against the United States of America and the British Commonwealth, said to have the two most powerful navies in the world, was sheer madness to many. By December 15, however, with the Japanese Navy virtually unstoppable at objectives throughout the Pacific, her senior officers understandably contracted victory fever as well.

For American and British naval leaders there was no such exhilarating malady. Not a single Allied battleship remained in service in the Pacific. British warships were sequestered in port at Singapore and the US Asiatic Fleet was in retreat. The carriers of the US Pacific Fleet, for the most part, remained within the area of the Hawaiian Triangle, the area from Midway Island in the west to Johnston Island in the south and back to Hawaii.

Officers and Operations

Vice Admiral Jizaburo Ozawa, operating from Cam Rahn Bay in French Indochina, was responsible for all Japanese naval operations in the South China Sea and commanded the Malaya Strike Force in its amphibious landings during the opening hours of the war. Ozawa's next assignment, mid-December landings on northern Borneo, was considered merely a subsidiary operation to the Malaya attacks and he anticipated a weak response from the British there. Units of the British Royal Army on Borneo served under General Arthur E. Percival's Malaya Command that was headquartered at Singapore. These troops of battalion strength garrisoned settlements, air bases, oil fields and refineries along the northwest coast at British North Borneo, Brunei and Sarawak.

Across the Pacific 3,500 miles to the northeast lay the tiny atoll Americans called Wake Island. The Japanese wanted Wake so that the US could not use it as an air base from which to attack the Marshall Islands and because it was in the US line of supply and communication to the Philippines. Wake was also essential to the establishment of the Japanese defense perimeter in the Pacific. The man with overall responsibility for securing Wake Island and Guam in the Marianas chain was Vice Admiral Shigeyoshi Inouye, headquartered with the Japanese Fourth Fleet on Truk in the Caroline Islands. With the failure of Admiral Sadamichi Kajioka's Wake Island Strike Force on December 11, Inouye called for a beefed-up second attack there. Kajioka's force was reinforced with Rear Admiral Aritomo Goto's 6th Cruiser Squadron of the Guam Invasion Force. In addition, the 2nd Carrier Division under Rear Admiral Tamon Yamaguchi was diverted toward Wake from its return to Japan after the Pearl Harbor attack.

Yamaguchi had held a variety of posts since his graduation from the Naval Academy at Etajima in 1912. Beginning in 1921 he studied at Princeton for two years and later served on the Japanese Naval General Staff and as naval attaché in Washington. In 1941 at age 49 he was promoted to Rear Admiral and given command of the First Air Fleet's 2nd Carrier Division that included carriers *Hiryu* and *Soryu*.

The US plan to reinforce the Marine garrison on Wake Island and keep the atoll in American hands included carrier USS *Saratoga* but the US Navy's determination to defend Wake was not as strong as the Japanese Navy's determination to take it. On December 8 *Saratoga* left San Diego for Pearl Harbor carrying a squadron of Marine Brewster Buffalo fighter planes that were previously authorized for Midway Island. *Saratoga's* destroyer escort included three old four-stackers—USS *Dent,* USS *Talbot* and USS *Waters.* Once at Pearl Harbor *Saratoga* would serve as the core of Task Force 14 with Rear Admiral Frank Jack Fletcher in command. Over the course of the war, Fletcher would develop a reputation for being an overly cautious commander.

On Hong Kong, Major General C. M. Maltby led 10,000 British, Indian and Canadian troops in the defense of an island that had no raw materials and no real strategic value although British honor and emotions were involved. Lt. General Taikaishi Sakai led a force of 20,000 Japanese artillery and infantry troops against Hong Kong. He was supported by Army aircraft and by the Imperial Navy's Second China Expeditionary Fleet.

Landings on British Borneo

The British colonies of Sarawak, Brunei and British North Borneo held rich oil fields and established refining facilities. A military presence on the island of Borneo would give the Japanese control of the area's main sea routes and begin the erosion of Britain's Malay Barrier. Borneo is the world's third largest island covering 260,000 square miles and in 1941, it was home to three million people, most of them living in small settlements along the coastline. Sarawak, Brunei and British North Borneo lay on the north and northwestern third of the island. Dutch Borneo covered the southern two-thirds.

Before dawn on the morning of December 13, a Japanese naval force weighed anchor from Cam Rahn Bay. Destroyers *Murakumo, Shinonome* and *Shirakumo,* supported by a submarine chaser, escorted 10 troop transports 700 miles south across the South China Sea. The transports carried units of the Fifteenth Army's 18th Infantry Division and elements of the 2nd Battalion of the Yokosuka Special Naval Landing Force. The ships were joined soon afterward by light cruiser *Yura* and seaplane tender *Kamikawa Maru* and later in the morning by heavy cruisers *Kumano* and *Suzuya* and destroyers *Fubuki* and *Sagiri.*

By the night of December 15, the transports were anchored off the northwest coast of Borneo and early the following morning, more than 1,000 Japanese Army and SNLF assault troops went ashore at Miri in Sarawak and at Seria in Brunei. By that time British Royal Army troops had sabotaged oil fields at both sites and set demolition charges at the Lutong oil refinery. The Japanese met only minor resistance from the defenders who withdrew inland. Attacks by the few remaining British aircraft operating from Singapore and from airfields in Sarawak together with Dutch aircraft flying from Dutch Borneo did little to delay the amphibious landings.

Japanese vessels remained off the coast of Sarawak and Brunei for several days after the invasion with only slow floatplanes from tender *Kamikawa Maru* for combat air patrol. They were vulnerable without carrier air support, and they were at the far range of Japanese land-based aircraft on French Indochina. On the morning of December 18, Japanese destroyer *Shinonome,* patrolling the Bornean coastline 10 miles north of Miri, exploded and sank with her entire crew of 228 officers and men. The Dutch Air Force took responsibility, but it was likely a torpedo from a Dutch submarine that took the *Shinonome* down.

Cruisers *Yura, Kumano* and *Suzuya* along with the *Kamikawa Maru* remained in the area while the four destroyers and the subchaser escorted transports south to Kuching in southwestern Sarawak. On the morning of December 24, elements of the Japanese Army and Naval assault units disembarked near a British airfield under construction. British construction workers along with a reinforced battalion of about 1,000 Royal Army troops in the area had moved inland and did not oppose the landing. The Japanese lost two transports, one to Dutch aircraft and another to a Dutch submarine. Three more transports suffered torpedo damage, and the Japanese destroyer *Sagiri* took two torpedo hits and sank with the loss of 121 of her crew.

Three days later, destroyers *Murakumo, Shirakumo* and *Fubuki* led the remaining transports 100 miles south to the undefended Dutch Bornean settlement of Permangkal. On the morning of December 27, 500 Japanese Army and Navy assault troops went ashore there and by year's end, Japanese forces controlled the beaches, oil refineries and airfields in the British colonies of Sarawak and Brunei. Only North Borneo remained in British control but by the second week of 1942, it too would fall to the Japanese with little opposition.

A Second Assault on Wake

By December 20, 1941, the 1,700 US marines, sailors, soldiers and civilians on Wake Atoll had endured over a week of bombings since holding off an invasion by Admiral Kajioka's Wake Island Strike Force. Almost every day at roughly 1100 hours, Wake was attacked by twin-engine Betty bombers of the Japanese Navy's 24th Air Flotilla flying from the Marshall Islands. Some evenings Kawanishi Mavis flying boats took a turn, dropping their bombs on one or more of the three islands that make up the atoll. With runways and structures damaged and most shore defenses knocked out, Wake's exhausted defenders looked east for reinforcements in what Marine Corps Major James Devereaux called the period when time stood still.

Since war began, discussions had been underway in Washington and at Pearl Harbor on how best to reinforce Wake, America's stronghold in the Pacific. US intelligence was uncertain of how many Japanese carriers participated at Pearl Harbor and could only guess at the total number of carriers in Japan's Combined Fleet. Any US naval force sent in relief of Wake, 2,500 miles from Hawaii and near the Japanese mandate islands, might easily fall into an ambush. Nevertheless, when *Saratoga* arrived at Pearl Harbor on December 15, Pacific Fleet Commander-in-Chief Husband E. Kimmel quickly assigned her as the core of the new Task Force 14 charged with the relief of Wake Island. By the next day, the force was underway with Vice Admiral Frank Jack Fletcher in command, his flag on heavy cruiser USS *Astoria*. TF 14 included heavy cruisers *Minneapolis* and *San Francisco*, destroyers *Blue, Dunlap, Fanning, Helm, Henley, Jarvis, Mugford, Patterson* and *Ralph Talbot*, and fleet oiler USS *Neches*. They would rendezvous with USS *Tangier*, a seaplane tender-transport carrying equipment, supplies and 200 Marines, to reinforce the garrison on Wake, hopefully before a second Japanese attack.

Meanwhile destroyers *Oite* and *Yayoi* and other damaged vessels of Admiral Kajioka's Wake Island Strike Force were under repair in the Marshall Islands in preparation for just such a second assault. Light cruisers *Tatsuta* and *Tenryu* and destroyers *Mochizuki* and *Mutsuki* remained with the force.

Destroyers *Asanagi* and *Yunagi* replaced the destroyers lost in the first attack and light cruiser *Yubari* continued as Kajioka's flagship. The new, stronger naval unit included two converted destroyer transports, three Maru transports, a minelayer and a troop-carrying seaplane tender, *Chitose*, with 28 seaplanes. Some of the 2,000 assault troops in the force were of the 2nd Battalion, Maizuru Special Naval Landing Force transferred from Saipan. Others were Special Naval Landing Force amphibious troops of the 2nd Battalion, Yokosuka Regiment, who served in the invasion of Guam.

In the Pacific north of Wake, Rear Admiral Tamon Yamaguchi commanded the 2nd Carrier Division, a force of six ships that broke away from Admiral Nagumo's First Air Fleet after the attack on Pearl Harbor. It included heavy cruisers *Chikuma* and *Tone*, destroyers *Tanikaze* and *Urakaze* along with carriers *Hiryu* and *Soryu* that would launch 108 aircraft toward Wake from a distance of 200 miles. A third Japanese force commanded by Vice Admiral Arimoto Goto approached Wake from the southeast. It included the Fourth Fleet's bombardment unit of heavy cruisers that took part in the assault on Guam, Goto's flagship *Aoba,* along with *Furutaka, Kako* and *Kinugasa.*

By December 17, in Washington and at Pearl Harbor, there was turmoil among the Navy brass. Admiral Kimmel was relieved as Commander-in-Chief, Pacific Fleet. His replacement, Admiral Chester W. Nimitz, was not scheduled to arrive at Pearl Harbor for another week. Vice Admiral William S. Pye, as interim Commander-in-Chief, was in a difficult position. Without time to develop his own strategy or appoint his own staff, he decided simply to wait for the reinforcement of Wake Island. *Saratoga* and Task Force 14 steamed slowly west, hindered by rough seas and the need to refuel destroyers from the slow fleet oiler *Neches*. Nevertheless, on December 20, the early morning arrival on Wake of a Navy PBY patrol plane brought a reassuring dispatch. It spelled out when the relief expedition would arrive—the 24th—and it listed the planes and troops it carried. Next morning shortly after the PBY took off for its return to Midway Island, however, the mood on Wake changed again. Twenty-nine Vals and 18 Zeros swept down from the clouds to bomb and strafe the atoll once again, the first wave off *Hiryu* and *Soryu.* They did little damage but this evidence that Japanese carriers were in the area quelled any optimism among Wake's defenders. When reports of the enemy carriers reached Pearl Harbor and Admiral Fletcher, whose ships were over 600 miles distant, a series of communications resulted eventually in the recall of Task Force 14. By then Rear Admiral Kajioka's Wake Island Strike Force was once again approaching the atoll from the south.

On Wake on the morning of December 22, only two of the 12 Grumman F4F Wildcats delivered earlier in the month were still in service. Marine Second Lieutenant Carl Davidson and Marine Captain Herbert Freuler went up on morning patrol. While scouting to the north at 12,000 feet, Davidson sighted a half dozen Zero fighters at his altitude and two squadrons of Val dive bombers at 18,000 feet. Davidson radioed Freuler just airborne to the south of Wake who turned north to attack the Zeros while Davidson climbed toward a formation of Vals. Freuler sent one Zero into a steep dive and hit a second that exploded close enough for a piece of the plane to hit his Wildcat. As Freuler fought to control his aircraft, a Zero on his tail raked his plane with machine gun and 20-millimeter cannon fire, injuring him in the back and shoulder and sending him into a dive. Freuler nursed his F4F back to crash land on Wake. The Zeros and Vals arrived over the atoll within minutes and concentrated on shore batteries, gun emplacements and anything that moved. Davidson never returned.

Late on the dark, rainy night of December 22, and in the first hours of the 23rd, amphibious assault troops of the Wake Island Strike Force transferred to landing barges at two miles out. They came ashore on Wilkes Island and at points along the four-and-a-half mile south stretch of Wake Island while two Japanese transports beached on the coral reef near the air strip. Wake's defenders fired their first shots at 0230 hours. By 0300 hours Major Devereux lost communication with his men on Wilkes Island and with other units as well. Fighting was fierce, hand to hand. Lines held and fell. Unlike in the first attack on Wake, civilian construction workers fought beside military men. One machine gun section took down wave after wave of attackers but soon sensed that the supply of Japanese troops would never end. A lieutenant and three men held out all night near the landing strip with two submachine guns, three pistols and two boxes of hand grenades. Commander Cunningham remembered that Admiral Pye had asked to be kept informed of the situation on Wake and about 0500 hours, he sent this dispatch to Pearl Harbor: "Enemy on island. Issue in doubt." He said it was a phrase he had

read years before in the book *Revolt of the Angels* by Anatole France in which
the angels were victorious over Satan's legions. It signified hope for him, but
at dawn Japanese planes arrived and the Japanese ground forces continued
their advance. Cunningham at his command post on Peale Island conferred
with Devereux who was near the air strip on Wake. About 0730 hours, the
Commander gave the Major permission to surrender. Shortly after 0900
hours, knowing there were Japanese carriers in the area and fearing the loss
of the *Saratoga,* Admiral Pye recalled the Task Force.

Hong Kong Falls

The island of Hong Kong became a British colony in 1842. Over time Great
Britain acquired additional territory on the Chinese mainland up to the
Sham Chun River. It was here that Lieutenant General Sakai's troops crossed
the frontier on December 8. In the next two days, Japanese infantry and
artillery battalions advanced fifteen miles over rough, hilly terrain to take an
important redoubt on the Gin Drinkers' Line. Royal Scots troops on the line
were ordered not to counterattack and within a day, Major General C. M.
Maltby called for evacuation of the mainland. Heavy fighting during the
retreat resulted in high casualties among the Royal Scots and lighter casualties among Punjabi and Rajput Indian battalions. On the sixth day, destroyer
HMS *Thracian* that had gone to sea early in the Japanese advance returned
and, with the ferry boat *Victoria*, carried British troops and materiel across
Lei Yue Mun Strait. That same day, December 14, Hong Kong Governor Sir
Mark Young rejected a Japanese call for surrender.

While the obvious threat of a Japanese invasion came from the mainland
to the north and east, British, Canadian and Indian troops manned a system
of forts and pillboxes that circled the entire island and covered the beaches.
The Hong Kong Volunteer Defense Corps was stationed at the west of the
island. Japanese artillery fire continued heavily and accurately. Two nights
after the British withdrawal from the mainland, Hong Kong's defenders
managed to hold off an advance across the straits by two companies of Japanese infantry in rubber boats.

A second demand for surrender was received on December 17 and again
Governor Young refused. The Japanese proceeded with plans for a full-scale
invasion that began on the night of December 18. They crossed Lei Yue Mun

Strait in sampans, junks and rubber boats and captured two British garrisons without a shot. Over the next few days, heavy fighting continued with the British holding Wong Nai Chung pass at the center of the island and the Japanese advancing around the south. Japanese Army Sally bombers operating from bases on the Chinese mainland and from French Indochina raided the colony almost daily. By December 22 most of the island's water reservoirs were lost to the Japanese. On Christmas morning, the Hong Kong Defense Council continued to reject surrender and Maltby planned a counterattack. By that afternoon, though, the General told Governor Young that further fighting meant only the slaughter of the garrison. After eighteen days of bitter struggle, Governor Young surrendered Great Britain's oldest colony to Lieutenant General Taikaishi Sakai. It was Christmas day.

New War Plans, Old Strategies

By the New Year 1942, Japanese naval leaders were able to count off a significant number of victories in the first phase of their country's war to establish the Great East Asia Co-Prosperity Sphere. In January, therefore, as the campaign against the Netherlands East Indies was getting underway, Admiral Isoroku Yamamoto asked Combined Fleet Headquarters to begin planning for a Second Phase of Naval Operations to be implemented after Japan's initial war objectives were met. The planning fell to Yamamoto's Chief of Staff Rear Admiral Matome Ugaki and required the approval of the Navy's General Staff under Admiral Osami Nagano. Plans that involved ground troops would have to be agreed upon by Army leaders.

An early plan by Ugaki to invade Midway, Johnston and Palmyra Islands followed by an invasion of the Hawaiian Islands was rejected out of hand by most admirals as too ambitious. A counterproposal by Admiral Nagano for an amphibious invasion of Allied facilities at Darwin, Australia, was turned down by the Army but naval leaders agreed that an air attack on Darwin by planes of Admiral Nagumo's First Air Fleet would be strategically sound. In March Ugaki proposed a plan for amphibious landings in India and on Ceylon (now Sri Lanka) to prevent British interference in the Japanese takeover of Burma. Japanese Army leaders rejected that, citing the need for 10 Army divisions just to take Ceylon at a time when German offensives against Russia in the west would open a front for the Japanese Army in the north.

Instead, the Navy's First Air Fleet planned carrier-based air attacks on the British Eastern Fleet in the Indian Ocean for April.

Naval General Staff planners next proposed a strategy that would isolate Australia from the United States by seizing Port Moresby on the south coast of New Guinea. Though the idea had been scrubbed earlier when US carriers were sighted in the area in early March, General Staff recommended that troops sailing from Rabaul take Port Moresby and from there secure Allied holdings on New Hebrides, New Caledonia, Fiji and Samoa. With lines of communication severed between the US, Australia and New Zealand, the Japanese could invade Hawaii and force the US Pacific Fleet to retreat to the mainland. Yamamoto rejected the plan, citing the difficulty of sending his ships so far from a friendly anchorage and into the range of enemy long-range bombers.

By April, Rear Admiral Ugaki modified one of his earlier plans to suggest landings at targets in the Aleutian Islands and on Midway Island. The attack on the Aleutians would be a feint intended to draw out the American carriers and possession of Midway would give the Japanese a site from which to monitor and attack US planes and ships in the Hawaiian Triangle. Yamamoto favored the Midway plan. It was called Operation MI and was scheduled for early June. Almost as an afterthought, Combined Fleet and General Staff agreed on an operation first proposed four years earlier to invade Port Moresby. The new plan added landings on Tulagi, an island in the Solomon chain, to establish a seaplane base from which to monitor Allied activity in the Coral Sea. An invasion force would strike Port Moresby within days of the Tulagi operation and Allied ships responding to the Tulagi landings would be caught between the two Japanese forces. This plan was named Operation MO and was scheduled for early May. Some admirals were not impressed.

Aftermath

Japanese amphibious assaults on Borneo continued into the New Year and were met with only a weak response by Great Britain's Royal Army. British and Dutch air crews also did little to oppose Japanese landings or slow the enemy advance. The most robust resistance to the Japanese came from Dutch submarines that accounted for the sinking of two Japanese destroyers, at least one troop transport and damage to three more transports. On January 8, 1942, Japanese transports deployed Army troops at Jesselton, North Borneo, 150 miles northeast of Seria. On January 17, Japanese Army troops landed at Sandakan, and within two days, British authorities on North Borneo surrendered to the Japanese.

For the Americans, the loss of Wake Island to the Japanese might have been avoided. The US Navy had three carriers available, *Enterprise, Lexington* and *Saratoga,* while the Imperial Japanese Navy had two, *Hiryu* and *Soryu.* Other Japanese carriers were far out of range. In addition to the American carriers, Wake Island itself provided an airstrip. The United States had 225 carrier-based aircraft to the 108 on the Japanese carriers. But after the losses at Pearl Harbor, no US naval officer would take responsibility for risking US Pacific Fleet carriers. Forty-nine Marines, three sailors and 70 civilians were killed in the battle for Wake and buried there. One hundred construction workers remained on the atoll to work for the Japanese and were executed there in October 1943. Other Americans, military and civilian, who survived the capture of Wake were transferred to prison and work camps in China and in Japan for the duration of the war, Commander Cunningham and Major Devereux among them. Japanese losses in the taking of Wake were estimated at 820 dead and over 1,100 wounded with another 1,800 lost to bombing, illness and starvation during the occupation, 20 times the number of Americans lost.

Almost 4,500 British, Canadian and Indian soldiers were killed in the defense of Hong Kong. Another 6,000 plus spent the duration of the war in prison camps. Among the Japanese, there were 2,750 casualties. HMS *Thracian,* the British destroyer that had ferried troops from the mainland to Hong Kong, ran aground on Christmas Day 1942. She was scuttled and later captured by the Japanese Army, repaired at Yokosuka, and in November 1943 commissioned in the Japanese Navy as Patrol Vessel 101.

Chapter VIII

ATTACKING THE NETHERLANDS EAST INDIES

Introduction

The great crown jewel of Japan's expansionist aspirations lay in the islands of the Netherlands East Indies: Dutch Borneo, Sumatra, Java, Celebes, Dutch New Guinea, Timor and thousands of other islands spread across a stretch of ocean as wide from west to east as the distance from the United States to Europe. The consolidation of these territories into the Greater East Asia Co-Prosperity Sphere would provide Japan the geographic and economic hegemony the Empire needed for the world leadership role it sought. Most immediately, the area would give Japan a supply of oil estimated at 60 million barrels a year. In addition, the islands offered rubber, tin, bauxite, coal, some gold and diamonds, as well as agricultural products.

At the time of the outbreak of World War II in Europe, the Netherlands East Indies had been a Dutch colony for almost 150 years, going back to the dissolution of the Dutch East India Company in 1799. The colony's population in 1940 was estimated at 70.5 million, including one million Chinese and 250,000 Dutch nationals. Its capital Batavia (now Jakarta) was located on the northwestern shore of the island of Java. After the German occupation of the Netherlands in May 1940, the People's Council in Batavia, although loyal to the Dutch government in exile, became for the most part autonomous. It protested when a Japanese official referred to the Netherlands East Indies as part of the Greater East Asia Co-Prosperity Sphere and it refused Japanese demands for more local foodstuffs, fishing and prospecting rights and for unrestricted access to its ports. In August 1941, the People's Council, this time on orders from the Dutch government in exile, refused further oil sales to Japan. Within hours of the attack on Pearl Harbor, the Dutch declared war on Japan. But it was not until January 11, 1942, when the Japanese made their initial attacks on Dutch Borneo and on Celebes, that Japan declared war on the Netherlands East Indies. Optimistic members of the Japanese General Staff estimated it would take four months to conquer the colony.

Officers and Operations

At a conference code-named Arcadia held in Washington, DC, from December 22, 1941, to January 14, 1942, Franklin Roosevelt and Winston Churchill and their military advisors met to coordinate war strategy for the US and the Commonwealth nations. One plan arrived at during the meetings was an attempt to combine the forces of American, British, Dutch and Australian military units involved in the defense of Allied territories in the South Pacific. It was called ABDA Command. Charged with defense of the Malay Barrier, elements of the ABDA included ABDAAIR using American, Commonwealth and Dutch planes; ABDAARM with British Army forces and the Netherlands East Indian Army and ABDAFLOAT, the Command's naval force. British Field Marshal Sir Archibald Wavell was appointed head of ABDA with headquarters on Java. Born in 1883, Wavell served in the Boer War and in the First World War, in which he lost an eye at the Battle of Ypres. Early in World War II, he led most of the Western Desert campaigns against Germany and Italy in North Africa and then served as Commander-in-Chief, India.

US Admiral Thomas Hart, who commanded the US Asiatic Fleet when it withdrew from the Philippines in December, was named the first commander of ABDAFLOAT. Hart continued in command of the Asiatic Fleet until February 4, 1942, when he was replaced by Rear Admiral W. A. Glassford, who previously commanded the Fleet's strike force. Hart was pessimistic about the ability of Combined Command to save the Netherlands East Indies and considered their defense a lost cause. On February 12, 1942, Hart was relieved as head of ABDAFLOAT as well, ostensibly on grounds of ill health, and returned to the United States. He was replaced by Dutch Admiral Conrad Helfrich, 55 years of age, whose previous title was Commander-in-Chief of the Royal Netherlands Navy in the Netherlands East Indies and who held the optimistic belief that the Japanese could indeed be defeated on the seas. Second to Helfrich and in tactical command of ABDA's strike force was Dutch Rear Admiral Karel Doorman, his flag on HNLMS *De Ruyter*. At age 53, he was known for his tenacity and clear thinking but a man who had never engaged in surface naval combat.

Major General Lewis H. Brereton, US Army, who formerly commanded the Far East Air Force established by General MacArthur in the Philippines, now commanded ABDAAIR. It included 200 obsolete Dutch aircraft and any remaining serviceable US bombers and fighters previously stationed in the Philippines, along with Royal Air Force planes that fled from Singapore and the Malay Peninsula. For ABDAARM, Dutch Lt. General Hein ter Poorten commanded numerous small, mixed land units totaling 100,000 men stationed throughout the Netherlands East Indies. These were made up of Dutch, British and Australian ground commands, three-fourths of whom were stationed on Java, and 25,000 assigned to garrison small bases, towns and settlements on islands across the huge chain.

Vice Admiral Ibo Takahashi, who earlier commanded all Japanese naval operations in the invasion of the Philippines, was assigned tactical command of two major forces assigned to the Netherlands East Indies Campaign, Central Force and Eastern Force. Under Takahashi, Vice Admiral Sueto Hirose commanded Central Force and its advance echelon, while Rear Admiral Shoji Nishimura commanded the escort destroyers. Their first objective was Dutch Borneo. Eastern Force was commanded by Rear Admiral Takeo Takagi. Takagi, a 1912 graduate of the Japanese Naval Academy, was a specialist in torpedo warfare and submarines but had also commanded surface ships. Under Takagi, Rear Admiral Raizo Tanaka led Eastern Force's escort group and Rear Admiral Kuyuji Kubo led the invasion forces. Early targets assigned to Eastern Force included sites on Celebes (now Sulawesi) and on Ambon Island and, later, on Bali.

Vice Admiral Jizaburo Ozawa, who successfully landed amphibious troops along the east coast of the Malay Peninsula in the first hours of the Pacific War, was now in command of Western Force. From his newly assigned flagship, heavy cruiser *Chokai,* Ozawa was in command of a force that carried troops of the Japanese Sixteenth Army from Indochina toward Sumatra just as Singapore was about to fall on February 15. Vice Admiral Chuichi Nagumo, who led the attack on Pearl Harbor, continued in command of First Air Fleet that included the Imperial Navy's six fleet carriers. Nagumo was also in tactical command of the 1st Carrier Division within the fleet, carriers *Akagi* and *Kaga.* Rear Admiral Tamon Yamaguchi led the 2nd Carrier Division with *Hiryu* and *Soryu.* After Pearl Harbor and the attack on Wake Island on December 23, the 2nd Carrier Division returned to Japan. Vice Admiral Chuichi Hara led the 5th Carrier Division with *Shokaku* and *Zuikaku.* Except for a raid on Darwin, Australia, on February 19, 1942, the Japanese carriers played a somewhat peripheral role in the campaign to isolate Java. Senior commanders of all Japanese forces in the South Pacific reported to Vice Admiral Nobutake Kondo based at Cam Ranh Bay, and ultimately, all fleet commanders reported to Admiral Isoroku Yamamoto, Commander in Chief, Combined Fleet.

Staging at Davao

With the retreat of USS *Preston* from Malalag anchorage on the island of Mindanao in the Philippines in early December, Davao Gulf would serve as the staging base for Central Force and for Eastern Force in the Japanese advance on the Netherlands East Indies. Allied Catalinas flying patrols over the area had been warning of a large buildup of Japanese ships at Davao ever since the Japanese took over the US Asiatic Fleet base there on December 20. By early January 1942, the anchorage was home to 42 surface warships, four seaplane tenders and numerous other auxiliary vessels and troop transports. The ships anchored at Malalag included light carrier *Zuiho,* heavy cruisers *Ashigara, Haguro, Maya, Myoko, Nachi,* light cruisers *Jintsu, Nagara, Naka* and 33 destroyers including *Akebono, Amatsukaze, Arashio, Ariake, Asagumo, Asashio, Harusame, Hatsuharu, Hatsukaze, Hatsushimo, Hayashio, Ikazuchi,*

Inazuma, Kawakaze, Kuroshio, Michishio, Minegumo, Murasame, Natsugumo, Natsushio, Nenohi, Oshio, Oyashio, Samidare, Sazanami, Suzukaze, Tokitsukaze, Umikaze, Ushio, Wakaba, Yamakaze, Yudachi, and *Yukikaze* and seaplane tenders *Chitose, Mizuho, Sanuki Maru* and *Sanyo Maru*. On the morning of January 4, 10 US Army B-17 heavy bombers flying from Java appeared over the harbor at 30,000 feet. The Flying Fortresses released their 250-lb bombs, one of which scored a direct hit on the No. 2 turret of heavy cruiser *Myoko*, killing 35 of her crew and injuring 29. Fragments from the explosion damaged four Mitsubishi floatplanes on seaplane tender *Chitose* and bomb fragments struck *Nachi*, Takagi's flagship. *Nachi* remained with the fleet, but *Myoko* was forced to return to Sasebo, Japan, for repairs.

Central Force

On January 7, Vice Admiral Sueto Hirose led the advance echelon of Central Force south and west from Davao Gulf for Dutch Borneo and invasion sites there at Tarakan Island, at Balikpapan and at Banjarmasin. The force included seaplane tenders *Sanuki Maru* and *Sanyo Maru*, three minelayers, four minesweepers and a convoy of 16 troop transports carrying the Sakaguchi Detachment of the Sixteenth Army's 56th Regiment and 780 Special Naval Landing Force assault troops of the Kure 2nd Battalion. Rear Admiral Nishimura aboard *Naka* led the destroyers—*Asagumo, Harusame, Minegumo, Natsugumo, Samidare, Suzukaze, Umikaze* and *Yudachi*. On the morning of January 11, warships of Nishimura's squadron supported amphibious landings at two sites on Tarakan. The 1,300 men of the Royal Netherlands Army who garrisoned the island's oil port were able to sabotage an oil field on the mainland and destroy some airfield facilities before surrendering. Within a week, an air flotilla of the Japanese Navy's Eleventh Air Fleet was headquartered at Tarakan and an occupation force gathered there to secure the next objective, Balikpapan, 400 miles to the south.

On January 21, Nishimura's destroyers escorted a convoy of 15 troop transports south through Macassar Strait where they were sighted by patrolling Catalinas. To disrupt the Japanese invasion, Admiral Hart on Java ordered Rear Admiral Glassford aboard USS *Boise* to lead a force of two light cruisers and eight destroyers from Timor to Balikpapan. They were to refuel on the way at Surabaya. As it happened, cruisers *Marblehead* and *Boise* were forced to retire, the former due to engine trouble and the *Boise* with her keel damaged on a shoal. Some destroyers of the division were on convoy and escort duty; others were in repair. That left four old four-stackers for the mission, USS *John D. Ford*, USS *Parrott*, USS *Paul Jones* and USS *Pope* with Commander P. H. Talbot aboard the *Ford* in command. The four arrived off Balikpapan in the first hours of January 24 to a night sky lit by the fire of oil refineries the Dutch had blown up on the mainland. Earlier, B-17s flying from Java hit and damaged two of the troop transports, *Tatsugami Maru* and *Nana Maru*. Around midnight, a Dutch submarine torpedoed another transport, *Tsuruga Maru*, causing it to explode and sink. Amidst heavy smoke, the American destroyers arrived undetected at about 0300 hours and launched 10 torpedoes toward transports anchored outside the harbor. Every torpedo missed its mark. Nishimura, unaware this was an attack by surface vessels, led his destroyers out from the harbor in search of submarines. Captain Talbot led his column into the anchorage and in a second series of torpedo attacks beginning at about 0330 hours, the Americans torpedoed and sank three transports, *Sumanoura Maru*, *Kuretake Maru* and the damaged *Tatsugami Maru*. Their torpedoes spent, the Americans opened fire with 4-inch main batteries and sank a patrol boat. By dawn, the four destroyers retired to the south and formed up with *Marblehead* north of Java for their return to Surabaya. The Battle of Balikpapan went down as a bright spot for the US Navy, its first surface action of the Pacific War, the first surface action fought by American naval forces since the Spanish-American War. Undeterred, Japanese troops went ashore that morning at Balikpapan and within five days, a Japanese air flotilla was operating there.

From Balikpapan, troops of the Sakaguchi Detachment marched in column on Banjarmasin, 200 miles southwest, after the Japanese discounted an amphibious landing there. Other troops arrived by barge at Laut Island and marched in from the east. Nishimura aboard *Naka* remained off Balikpapan with destroyers *Harusame*, *Samidare* and *Yudachi* to protect anchored transports and barges moving along the coastline, while five of his destroyers sailed for Makassar on the southern tip of Celebes to assist Eastern Force in protecting amphibious landings there. A Dutch Army company of 200 men defended oil fields near Banjarmasin and an airfield 16 miles inland at Ulim. The Japanese secured the area on February 10 and by late in the month had the Ulim airfield in operation. Japanese air and naval forces were now within 300 miles of the Allied airfield and harbor at Surabaya on the north coast of Java.

Eastern Force

On January 9, 1942, two days after Central Force sailed from Davao for Tarakan, Admiral Takahashi watched the equally impressive departure of the vessels of Eastern Force sortie the harbor for Celebes. The island of Celebes lies just east of Borneo and consists of four long peninsulas separated by three gulfs. Not rich in oil or other natural resources, the island was of strategic importance to the Japanese for its border on the Molucca Sea and for its fine airfield at Kendari and deepwater anchorage at nearby Staring Bay.

Eastern Force included a Main Body under Rear Admiral Takeo Takagi. In it were light carrier *Zuiho*; heavy cruisers *Haguro* and *Nachi*, Takagi's flagship; destroyers *Akebono*, *Ikazuchi*, *Inazuma*, *Kawakaze* and *Yamakaze*; and seaplane tenders *Chitose* and *Mizuho*, each carrying 12 aircraft. The escort group was commanded by Rear Admiral Raizo Tanaka from his flagship, light cruiser *Jintsu*, and included destroyers *Amatsukaze*, *Hatsukaze*, *Hayashio*, *Kuroshio*, *Natsushio*, *Oyashio*, *Tokitsukaze*, and *Yukikaze* and 11 transports. In an attack set to coincide with the January 11 assault by Central Force at Tarakan, Tanaka debarked his transports that same day at Menado on the northern tip of Celebes. A few Allied bombers attacked the Japanese ships without success. A drop of over 300 Japanese paratroopers of the 1st Yokosuka Battalion flown in from Davao, the first use of Japanese paratroopers in the Pacific War, confused the invasion more than it helped. The Dutch garrison of 1,500 men, only 400 of them regular army, was quickly overwhelmed and within weeks, Menado airfield was home to elements of the Japanese Navy's 21st Air Flotilla. Nearby Kema and Bangka Roads were also secured. Staging from Menado on January 21, Tanaka led his destroyers and troop transports further south through the Molucca Sea toward Kendari, a distance of 300 miles. On the morning of January 24, Tanaka's force was spotted off Kendari by American seaplane tender *Childs*. *Childs* avoided the Japanese in a rain squall at first and later escaped damage during an attack by Japanese bombers. Dutch military in the area offered little resistance against the Japanese and that night, Kendari fell to troops of the Sasebo

Special Naval Landing Force. The air base there, perhaps the best air facility in the Netherlands East Indies, was in immediate use by Betty and Nell bombers of the 21st Air Flotilla that could handily reach targets on Java and on Timor and that were also in range of Australia.

East from Celebes across the Molucca Sea, Ambon Island was garrisoned with 3,500 Australian, British and Dutch troops. The installation posed a threat to the Japanese on Celebes and to their planned advance on Timor. On January 23, more than 50 fighter and bomber aircraft from carriers *Hiryu* and *Soryu* arrived over Ambon to soften up the Allies. A Royal Australian Air Force squadron of 13 Lockheed Hudsons withdrew, leaving ABDAARM troops without air defense. In the week that followed, planes from *Hiryu* and *Soryu* operating from Kendari as land-based aircraft and floatplanes from tenders *Chitose* and *Mizuho* flew protective cover for 11 transports involved in the amphibious landings that began at Ambon on January 31. A surface support force included heavy cruiser *Maya* and destroyers *Ariake, Sazanami* and *Ushio*. The eight destroyers of Rear Admiral Tanaka and flagship *Jintsu* were joined at Ambon by destroyers *Arashio, Asashio, Michishio* and *Oshio* that arrived from Davao. ABDA troops, some fighting from fortified positions, offered fierce resistance but were forced to surrender on February 3, after which Japanese forces occupied Amboina airfield.

Yanks, Brits, Some Dutchmen, and a Few Lads from Down Under

The idea of a force like ABDA Command was first considered in early April 1941 at a conference in Singapore that included representatives of the United States, Great Britian, the Netherlands, Australia and New Zealand. The meetings produced no useful conclusions. After the attack on Pearl Harbor, and with Roosevelt's and Churchill's Arcadia Conference, however, plans for such a Command went forward. Although Sir Archibald Wavell set up the ABDA Command Headquarters on Java in mid-January 1942, the initial ABDAFLOAT strike force formed on February 2. It would be the first time in history that naval, air and ground forces of several nations operated together under a single leadership. By that time, the total number of cruisers and destroyers available to ABDA numbered 37 and the number of submarines was 46. The US Navy contingent included the heavy cruiser *Houston*, light cruisers *Boise* and *Marblehead* and destroyers *Alden, Barker, Bulmer, Edsall, John D. Edwards, John D. Ford, Paul Jones, Parrott, Peary, Pillsbury, Pope, Stewart,* and *Whipple* and 22 modern submarines and six older S-Type subs.

The US surface warships and submarines of ABDAFLOAT had all served in the United States Asiatic Fleet based in the Philippines. The auxiliary vessels of the old Asiatic Fleet were at Port Darwin, Australia, the major Allied service and supply base in the South Pacific. Surface warships of the British Royal Navy contingent included heavy cruiser *Exeter*, light cruisers *Danae* and *Dragon* and destroyers *Electra, Encounter, Jupiter, Scout, Strong-hold,* and *Tenedos.* Naval forces of the Royal Navy also supplied two modern submarines. The Royal Australian Navy offered light cruisers *Hobart* and *Perth*.

Some of the British ships joining ABDA were those that left Hong Kong before December 7 to join other ships attached to China Force at Singapore. After the sinking of *Prince of Wales* and *Repulse*, the ships of China Force retreated to Java and to Sumatra. After Pearl Harbor, HMS *Exeter* was transferred from duty in the Atlantic to Singapore and then to ABDA. HMAS *Hobart*, that had been on transport duty in the Mediterranean, arrived at Singapore in late December 1941 as part of a troop convoy and then went into ABDA. The ships of the Royal Netherlands Navy contingent included light cruisers *De Ruyter, Java, Tromp*, destroyers *Banckert, Evertsen, Korten-aer, Piet Hein, Van Ghent, Van Nes,* and *Witte de With* and 12 K-type and four O-type submarines. Four of the destroyers were commissioned in 1928, three others in 1930. At the time Holland fell to the Germans in May 1940, the Royal Netherlands Navy had five light cruisers, eight destroyers, 24 submarines and several minesweepers, small torpedo boats and auxiliary vessels. It had neither battleships nor heavy cruisers nor aircraft carriers. Three of her light cruisers, *De Ruyter, Java* and *Tromp* were already serving in the Netherlands East Indies. In addition to its main naval base at Darwin, ABDA-FLOAT had anchorages at Tanjong Priok off Batavia and at Bunda Roads off Surabaya, both on the north coast of Java, and at smaller facilities on Java's south coast at Tjilatjap and on Timor at Koepang.

Makassar Mission

In the first days of February, Allied reconnaissance spotted Japanese vessels near Staring Bay south of Kendari on Celebes and in the Makassar Strait west of Celebes. ABDA Command believed that either Banjarmasin on Borneo's southern shore or Makassar City on Celebes was the next targeted invasion site. The Japanese force was reported to include three cruisers and several destroyers escorting convoys of troopships. To counter this movement, an ABDA naval force of roughly the same size commanded by Rear Admiral Karel Doorman sortied Bunda Roads just after midnight February 4, the first time that ships of ABDAFLOAT sailed together. Doorman's fleet included his flagship, light cruiser HMNS *De Ruyter*, the US Navy's heavy cruiser *Houston*, light cruisers HMNS *Tromp* and USS *Marblehead*, destroyers HMNS *Banckert*, HMNS *Piet Hein*, HMNS *Van Ghent*, USS *Barker*, USS *Bulmer*, USS *John D. Ford* and USS *Stewart*. Doorman's goal was to meet the Japanese in a night action; however, such a plan required a run in daylight across the Java Sea, putting his force under high risk of attack. Just before 1000 hours, a lookout aboard *De Ruyter* spotted a flight of Japanese aircraft. More than 30 twin-engine Mitsubishi Nell bombers flying from Kendari for a planned strike on Surabaya came upon the ABDA force and attacked it instead, concentrating on the cruisers. *Houston* took a bomb hit on her aft gun turret, knocking out three of her nine 8-inch guns. The blast killed 48 of her crew and injured more than 50. *De Ruyter* was attacked but came through without serious damage. Several plates on *Marblehead*'s bow were heavily damaged in the concussion of a near miss and one bomb smashed through her deck, wrecking her steering gear and setting fuel storage afire. Another bomb damaged her wardroom and sick bay. Four Catalina flying boats showed up only to be shot down by the Nells. The destroyers and *De Ruyter* circled *Marblehead* after damage control straightened her rudder somewhat for retreat to Tjilatjap. *Houston* retreated to Port Darwin. Allied anti-aircraft fire took down one Japanese bomber.

Although Doorman's force never saw the enemy ships it hunted, the Japanese were in the area, approaching Makassar from Kendari. Rear Admiral Kubo aboard flagship *Nagara* led 11 destroyers from Eastern Force: *Arashio*, *Hatsuharu*, *Hatsushimo*, *Hayashio*, *Kawakaze*, *Kuroshio*, *Michishio*, *Natsushio*, *Nenohi*, *Oshio* and *Oyashio*, and five from Central Force, *Asagumo*, *Mine-*

gumo, Natsugumo, Suzukaze and *Umikaze.* Kubo's ships escorted a convoy of transports carrying units of the Sasebo Regiment's Special Naval Landing Force assault troops. By February 8, the 400 Dutch troops defending Makassar City had endured days of air bombardment and the area fell quickly. Although casualties in the amphibious invasion were light among Japanese land forces, Kubo's Makassar Occupation Force did not arrive unscathed. Destroyer *Suzukaze* was torpedoed by a submarine with the loss of nine lives and destroyer *Natsushio* was hit by a torpedo from a US submarine and suffered eight dead and two wounded. Destroyer *Kuroshio* rescued the remaining crew and *Natsushio* sank 20 miles from Makassar while under tow.

Bali-Lombok—ABDA's First Surface Action

With the taking of Banjarmasin and Makassar during the second week of February, the Japanese had Java isolated from the north. The Allies expected the next assault would be on Timor, the half-Dutch, half-Portuguese island farther to the east. To counter such an attack, a troop convoy of ABDAARM units escorted by heavy cruiser USS *Houston* sortied Port Darwin, Australia, on February 15. Five hundred miles out of port, the convoy was attacked by Japanese aircraft and forced to return to Darwin. Allied intelligence was incorrect, though. The Japanese had set not Timor but Bali as their next target since occupation of that island's airfield would put their planes within 100 miles of the Allied naval base at Surabaya. The small, volcanic island of Bali lies just east of Java, separated from the larger island by Bali Strait. A very small island, Nusa Besar, lies 15 miles east of Bali with Badung Strait separating the two. East of Nusa Besar is Lombok Island, and between them, Lombok Strait.

Early on February 18, surface warships of Eastern Force led by Rear Admiral Kuyuji Kubo aboard his flagship, light cruiser *Nagara*, sailed from Makassar for Bali, 400 miles to the south. The force included destroyers *Arashio, Asashio, Hatsushimo, Michishio, Nenohi, Oshio* and *Wakaba*, escorting transports *Sagani Maru* and *Sasago Maru* with assault troops of the Fourteenth Army's 48th Division. Rear Admiral Doorman, stationed at Tjilatjap, was notified of the enemy force and by nightfall was on his way with orders to intercept it. Doorman, too, had 400 miles to cover. His force included light cruisers *Java* and his flagship *De Ruyter*, destroyers *Piet Hein, John D.*

Ford and *Pope*. A fourth destroyer, *Kortenaer,* ran aground in Tjilatjap's narrow harbor and was left behind. A second ABDA force sortied the harbor at Surabaya to meet the Japanese. Led by Commander T. H. Binford, it included destroyers *John D. Edwards, Pillsbury, Stewart* and Binford's flagship, *Parrott,* and Dutch light cruiser *Tromp*. Following Binford's ships on the same heading was a third and smaller force of nine motor torpedo boats. Admiral Doorman's plan was to use these forces in three waves to attack the Japanese ships and transports in Badung Strait before troops could go ashore on Bali.

Kubo's ships arrived at Sanur Roads off Bali's southeast coast at 2200 hours on February 18 and, without pre-invasion bombardment, transferred assault troops to landing barges and put them ashore with no opposition. Kubo's goal was to get his ships in and out of enemy territory quickly. Light cruiser *Nagara* and destroyers *Hatsushimo, Nenohi,* and *Wakaba* sortied to the northeast, but sporadic raids the next day by US B-17 bombers from ABDAAIR seriously damaged transport *Sagani Maru*. She sailed north escorted by destroyers *Arashio* and *Michishio*. On February 19, transport *Sasago Maru* with destroyers *Asashio* and *Oshio* weighed anchor at 2300 hours just as Doorman's force arrived, too late by a full day to prevent the invasion.

The Japanese destroyers illuminated the area with searchlights and star shells while Doorman's warships closed the distance. *Asashio* and *Oshio* sailing east were in a position of crossing the T of light cruiser *Java* sailing north behind *De Ruyter*. At a range of under 2,500 yards, *Java* fired her forward-facing 5.9-inch main guns on *Asashio*. *De Ruyter* fired on *Oshio*. The Japanese returned fire with their 5-inch guns and turned south. No hits were recorded on either side. *Pope, John D. Ford* and *Piet Hein* continued north astern of *Java* by 5,000 yards with *Piet Hein* making smoke that obscured both US and Japanese destroyers. At 2305 hours, *Piet Hein* reversed course and fired torpedoes and her four 4.7-inch main guns on *Asashio*, which returned similar fire. *Piet Hein* was struck by a single torpedo, went dead in the water and sank quickly with her crew of 120 officers and men.

Next, *Pope* and *Ford* turned south and parallel to *Asashio*. After an exchange of fire and torpedoes, the US ships circled, attempting to exit Badung Strait to the north according to Admiral Doorman's original plan, but screened by smoke, they turned to the southeast. The Japanese, it was later learned, mistakenly fired on each other without effect and returned north to *Sasago Maru*, the transport. About this time, the four US destroyers of the second wave, *Parrott, Edwards, Pillsbury* and *Stewart* followed by Dutch light cruiser *Tromp* arrived at the southern entrance of Badung Strait. Commander Binford and his skippers became confused by several flashing lights, possibly signal lights. They fired a total of 15 torpedoes at the retiring Japanese ships; none found its target. Again, *Asashio* and *Oshio* turned to face the Allies. *Stewart* began firing at 0215 hours and *Edwards* was able to launch only two torpedoes. The Japanese fired back, hitting *Stewart* and knocking out her steering engine room. *Edwards* almost collided with *Parrott* and as they and *Stewart* sailed to the northeast, the three were separated from *Pillsbury* and *Tromp* by the Japanese destroyers. At 0241 hours, *Tromp* was hit by gunfire from *Asashio*, but the damaged cruiser avoided torpedoes from *Oshio* and managed to hit the attacker with her 5.9-inch guns. As *Asashio* and *Oshio* broke off action and returned to their transport, destroyers *Arashio* and *Michishio* steamed into the fray with *Edwards* and *Stewart* on their starboard side and *Pillsbury* to port. *Michishio* was assaulted from both sides and went dead in the water, 13 of her men lost and 83 wounded. The Battle of Bali-Lombok ended as the ABDA ships continued north. Of the nine Allied motor torpedo boats, only four arrived in Badung Strait and they neither searched the area nor used their weapons. The first surface action of ABDA-FLOAT went down as a failure. Japanese troops landed safely, and Japanese planes were received at Bali airfield the following day. *Michishio* was returned to service. For the Allies, *Piet Hein* and her crew were lost, and *Tromp* was sent to Sydney for repair.

Attack on Australia

Allied defenses had disintegrated and with the Battle of Bali-Lombok, only a few southern islands in the Netherlands East Indies remained under Dutch control. One of these islands, Timor, contained a major Dutch anchorage at Koepang and was the principal air station and staging area for Allied aircraft shuttled as reinforcements from Darwin to Java's airfields at Surabaya, Batavia and Tjilatjap. Scheduled for a Japanese attack on February 20, once Timor capitulated, the nearest Allied air station and full-service naval base in the South Pacific would be at Darwin, Australia, 500 miles to the southeast.

If Darwin were neutralized, the nearest major Allied anchorage in the South Pacific was at Fremantle, near Perth, more than 2,000 ocean miles to the southwest. To attack Darwin, the Japanese Army and Navy General Staff both considered and then rejected a plan for an amphibious invasion along Australia's northern coastline. With a strong force of Admiral Kondo's warships patrolling in the Indian Ocean, searching for enemy vessels fleeing south from the Netherlands East Indies, Combined Fleet ordered First Air Fleet and its carriers to strike at Darwin and surrounding installations. For the attack, Admiral Yamaguchi's 2nd Carrier Division, *Hiryu* and *Soryu,* rendezvoused with 1st Carrier Division's *Akagi* and *Kaga* in the Palau Islands on February 15. The four Japanese carriers sailed southward without battleship support but escorted by heavy cruisers *Chikuma, Tone,* light cruiser *Abukuma* and destroyers *Ariake, Hamakaze, Isokaze, Kasumi, Shiranuhi, Tanikaze* and *Urakaze.* A few hours after ABDA naval forces broke off action during the Battle of Bali-Lombok and headed for Surabaya, Admiral Nagumo's strike force of 14 ships reached their launch-point in the Banda Sea 220 miles north of Darwin.

By dawn on February 19, from carrier *Akagi,* Commander Fuchida led a total of 187 Kate level bombers, Val dive bombers and Zero fighters south to Port Darwin. From air bases at Kendari and Ambon, 54 high-level land-based bombers and a squadron of four-engine flying boats were also on their way. More than 250 Japanese aircraft reached the target where aircrews destroyed 11 vessels, harbor facilities, over 20 aircraft, airfield installations and a cluster of oil tanks. In a second attack, Zero fighters strafed the city of Darwin where old and dry wooden structures burned out of control. Over 230 persons, military and civilian, were lost. Anti-aircraft fire was heavy but ineffective and no Japanese planes were lost. By afternoon, the 14 surface warships of Nagumo's First Air Fleet headed north toward Celebes and Staring Bay where they remained briefly before taking part with the main body of Vice Admiral Nobutake Kondo's Southern Force in the Isolation of Java.

Chapter IX

ISOLATING JAVA

Introduction

In January 1942, as the Japanese Navy's Eastern and Center Forces sortied Malalag Bay on Mindanao in the Philippines, few Japanese admirals expected Allied forces would fold so quickly. With the major Allied base at Darwin destroyed, with anchorages and air bases on Borneo and Celebes in Japanese hands and with Japanese troops landed on Sumatra just across the narrow Sunda Strait from Java, their sights were set on the last Allied bases remaining in the Netherlands East Indies, Java and the small island of Timor that was divided between Dutch and Portuguese control.

Timor—The Romp of Eastern Force Continues

The assault on Timor began on February 20, 1942. The island was strategically important to the Japanese because of its proximity to Australia and because it was from Timor that Allied aircraft from Australia were ferried on to Java, especially the shorter-range fighters. The capital of Dutch Timor was in the southwest at Koepang. The Portuguese capital, Dili, was in the north. A mixed ABDAARM regiment defended the Dutch half of the island while a battalion of 600 troops were stationed in the Portuguese sector.

Rear Admiral Raizo Tanaka led the Timor Invasion Force that included his flagship, light cruiser *Jintsu*, destroyers *Amatsukaze, Hatsukaze, Hayashio, Kuroshio, Oyashio, Tokitsukaze,* and *Yukikaze* and 14 transports carrying the Sixteenth Army's 38th Regiment. Tanaka's force sailed south from the island of Ambon and included some limited air cover by floatplanes from seaplane tender *Mizuho*. On the morning of the invasion, some Japanese Army units landed near Dili and secured its airfield, allowing access by land-based transport aircraft flying from Kendari on Celebes. Other troop ships continued south for an amphibious assault at Koepang where paratroopers of the 3rd Battalion of the Special Naval Landing Force Yokosuka Regiment were dropped. No Allied aircraft or surface warships opposed the invasion of Timor. ABDA ground forces battled the enemy for four days before they surrendered and the island was lost to the Japanese.

Western Force

After commanding Southern Expeditionary Fleet that delivered Japanese forces along the Malay Peninsula in early December 1941, Vice Admiral Jizaburo Ozawa's naval force returned to Cam Ranh Bay in Indochina. For the next two months, Japanese Army troops advanced southward down the peninsula toward Singapore as Commonwealth troops repeatedly gave up ground. By January 21, 1942, believing the British were still firmly entrenched near the settlement of Mersing 60 miles north of Singapore, the Japanese landed amphibious troops of the Twenty-fifth Army's 55th Regiment 20 miles north of Mersing at Endau. A few RAF aircraft were dispatched to the area from Singapore and from Sumatra but they did nothing to slow the assault. On January 26, Japanese ships were spotted north of Endau and RAF planes were again launched to attack enemy land and naval targets. It was here off the coast of the Malay Peninsula that the British lost their battleship *Prince of Wales* and battle cruiser *Repulse* in the first days of the war. Now they sent the last two surface warships at Singapore, destroyers HMS *Thanet* and HMAS *Vampire,* to attempt to disrupt yet another Japanese landing. *Vampire* was armed with six torpedoes, *Thanet* with four. The Japanese mistook the World War I vintage destroyers for light cruisers and sent their light cruiser *Sendai* and destroyers *Amagiri, Fubuki, Hatsuyuki, Shirayuki* and *Yugiri* to intercept them. The unequal forces met off Endau in the early hours of January 27. *Thanet* was hit, set afire, hit again and sunk by accurate fire from the 5-inch guns of *Amagiri* and *Hatsuyuki*. Of her crew of 98 officers and men, 57 survived the oily waters to be taken prisoner. *Vampire* retreated safely to Singapore and then to Batavia.

Within days, Japanese land troops reached Johore Strait that narrowly separates Singapore from the Malay Peninsula as civilians escaping Singapore found transport away from her crowded docks aboard any craft that appeared seaworthy and many that did not. Dozens of vessels, large and small, headed toward Sumatra and Java; some tried for Australia but great numbers of civilians perished at sea at Japanese hands.

By late January, awaiting the imminent fall of Singapore, the ships of Western Force gathered at Cam Rahn Bay in Indochina, prepared to play their part in Japan's Isolation of Java. The force included battleships *Haruna, Kongo* and light carrier *Ryujo*. A force of seven heavy cruisers, *Atago, Chokai, Kumano, Mikuma, Mogami, Suzuya* and *Takao*, was bolstered by an eighth heavy cruiser, *Maya*, which transferred from Eastern Force.

Also gathering at Cam Rahn Bay were four light cruisers and 26 destroyers that would sail with Western Force. These warships included light cruisers *Kashii, Natori, Sendai, Yura* and destroyers *Akatsuki, Amagiri, Arashi, Asagiri, Asakaze, Ayanami, Fubuki, Fumizuki, Hagikaze, Harukaze, Hatakaze, Hatsuyuki, Hibiki, Isonami, Matsukaze, Minazuki, Murakumo, Nagatsuki, Nowaki, Satsuki, Shikinami, Shirakumo, Shirayuki, Uranami, Yugiri* and *Hatsuharu* which had transferred from Eastern Force. Also from Eastern Force were seaplane tenders *Chitose* and *Mizuho* and numerous auxiliary vessels and troop transports.

By the first week of February 1942, Vice Admiral Nobutake Kondo's Western Cover Force had sortied the anchorage, his flag on *Atago*. It included the two battleships, heavy cruisers *Maya* and *Takao* and destroyers *Akatsuki, Arashi, Hagikaze, Hatakaze, Hibiki* and *Nowaki*. Light cruisers *Kashii* and *Sendai* and destroyers *Amagiri, Asagiri, Uranami* and *Yugiri* departed as well.

On February 9, a convoy of nine Japanese troop ships sortied Cam Ranh Bay carrying elements of the 229th Regiment of the Sixteenth Army's 38th Division. Vice Admiral Jizaburo Ozawa followed the next day aboard his flagship *Chokai*, leading ships of the Western Java Invasion Support Force: heavy cruisers *Kumano, Mikuma, Mogami* and *Suzuya* and destroyers *Ayan-*

ami, Hatsuyuki, Isonami, Murakumo, Shirakumo and *Shirayuki.* The force included light carrier *Ryujo* for air cover and her escort destroyer *Shikinami.* On February 11, Rear Admiral Shintaro Hashimoto aboard light cruiser *Yura* left Cam Ranh Bay with another convoy of 12 transports carrying additional elements of the 229th Regiment. To protect the transports, the force included destroyers *Asakaze, Fubuki, Hatsuharu,* and *Matsukaze.* Later, destroyers *Hatsuyuki, Murakumo, Shirakumo* and *Shirayuki* along with seaplane tenders *Chitose* and *Mizuho* would support the force as it moved toward Java.

Debarkation point for the officers and men of the 229th Regiment was the island of Bangka off southeastern Sumatra and due north by 250 miles of the city of Batavia on Java. Nearly 140 miles long and 65 miles wide, Bangka at the time held 10 percent of the world's supply of tin.

A week later, on February 18, a more formidable assault force left Cam Ranh Bay. Destined for Java, it included 56 transports carrying the 230th Regiment of the Sixteenth Army's 38th Division, along with the Sixteenth Army's 2nd Division that had been based on Formosa and on Okinawa. It was covered by Third Escort Force: light cruiser *Natori* and destroyers *Fumizuki, Harukaze, Minazuki, Nagatsuki* and *Satsuki* and reinforced later by *Akatsuki, Hatakaze* and *Hibiki.*

ABDA intelligence reports of this massive Japanese advance toward the islands of Banka, Sumatra and Java meant one thing for certain to General Wavell. The great oil refinery at Palembang on Sumatra and the surrounding oil fields would be an early Japanese target. Wavell ordered Admiral Doorman's force, now south of Bali, to sail for Sunda Strait between Sumatra and Java, a 600-mile journey, to try to save Palembang. Doorman arrived on February 14 with an ABDAFLOAT force of five cruisers and 10 destroyers. He had HMS *Exeter,* a heavy cruiser, and light cruisers HMNS *Java,* HMNS *Tromp,* HMAS *Hobart* and his flagship, *De Ruyter.* For the mission, the combined ABDA destroyer force included HMNS *Banckert,* HMNS *Kortenaer,* HMNS *Van Ghent,* HMNS *Van Nes* and US destroyers *Barker, Bulmer, John D. Ford, Parrott, Pope* and *Stewart.* Almost immediately Dutch destroyer *Van Ghent* hit a reef off Bangka and sank; a second destroyer, *Banckert,* was released to rescue survivors. The following day, continuous bombing by aircraft from *Ryujo* and by Japanese land-based planes caused only slight damage to the ABDA ships but the usually indomitable Doorman retired reluctantly in the face of Admiral Ozawa's powerful force.

Banka and Palembang fell quickly to units of the Sixteenth Army and to paratroopers of Special Naval Landing Force's 1st Battalion of the Yokosuka Regiment flown in from Malaysia. In addition, ABDA lost Dutch destroyer *Van Nes*, sunk off Banka on February 17 while picking up escapees from Singapore.

Checkmate on Java

The ABDA Combined Command established on January 15, 1942, was dissolved by General Sir Archibald Wavell on February 25. Three days before, in a message to Winston Churchill, Wavell expressed his belief that the defense of Java would not last long and that he saw little further usefulness for his headquarters. Wavell was reassigned to India and the Dutch Governor General on Java assumed command of all remaining Allied forces. Major General Lewis Brereton, US Army, left for Australia, replaced by Dutch Lieutenant General L. H. van Oyen as Air Chief. Most US planes salvaged from the Philippines went with Brereton. Two weeks earlier, at the request of the Dutch, Admiral Hart had been relieved as head of ABDAFLOAT by Dutch Admiral Conrad Helfrich who was headquartered inland on Java at Bandung. Under Helfrich, Rear Admiral Karel Doorman remained in command of the ships that had constituted ABDAFLOAT, now the naval strike force charged with defending Java against the imminent Japanese invasion. Dutch officers were in charge of all remaining armed forces. For Helfrich, Doorman and the others, the fight had come down to a defense of their homeland and their families and their tenacity would never be in question.

Doorman had 15 serviceable warships operating out of the harbor at Surabaya: his flagship *De Ruyter*, Dutch light cruiser *Java* and destroyers *Kortenaer* and *Witte de With*. He had six US warships: heavy cruiser *Houston* and destroyers *Alden, John D. Edwards, John D. Ford, Paul Jones* and *Pope* and five Commonwealth ships: heavy cruiser *Exeter* and destroyers *Electra, Encounter* and *Jupiter*, along with the Australian light cruiser *Perth*. At Batavia's Tanjong Priok Harbor, Doorman had eight warships: British light cruisers *Danae* and *Dragon* and destroyers *Express, Scout, Stronghold* and *Tenedos*, Australian destroyer *Vampire* and Dutch destroyer *Evertsen*.

South of Java in the waters of the Indian Ocean, the 1st and 2nd Divisions of Vice Admiral Nagumo's First Air Fleet with carriers *Akagi, Kaga, Hiryu* and *Soryu* stood by, ready to cut off Allied reinforcements from Australia or from India and to prevent an Allied retreat from Java. The force included battleships *Hiei* and *Kirishima*, heavy cruisers *Chikuma* and *Tone*, light cruiser *Abukuma*, and destroyers *Ariake, Hamakaze, Isokaze, Kasumi, Shiranuhi, Tanikaze* and *Urakaze*. The Main Body of Admiral Kondo's Distant Cover Force was also south of Java and included the 29,000-ton battleships *Haruna* and *Kongo*, heavy cruisers *Maya, Takao* and Kondo's flagship, *Atago*. Supporting the Main Body were destroyers *Arashi, Hagikaze, Hatakaze* and *Nowaki*, along with *Akatsuki* and *Hibiki* that would shortly return to Western Force and action in Sunda Strait.

To the northwest of Java, Allied reconnaissance aircraft had been monitoring the movement of the Japanese convoys as they approached near Gaspar Strait. This was Western Force under Admiral Ozawa. Helfrich hoped to challenge it with the warships stationed near Batavia, but actually, the Japanese continued their approach without Allied opposition.

Six hundred miles to the east, ships of Central Force and of Eastern Force prepared to rendezvous for an advance on the north coast of Java and amphibious landings west and east of Surabaya. After its success on Borneo and at Makassar, Central Force under Rear Admiral Shoji Nishimura returned to the southern Philippine island of Jolo. On February 19, Nishimura left Jolo aboard his flagship *Naka* with eight destroyers, *Asagumo, Harusame, Minegumo, Murasame, Natsugumo, Samidare, Yamakaze* and *Yudachi*. Now dubbed First Escort Force, the ships escorted a convoy of 41 transports that carried units of the Fourteenth Army's 48th Division. By February 23, they were southbound off the east coast of Borneo and two days later, Nishimura's force rendezvoused in the Java Sea with the ships of Eastern Force under Rear Admirals Takagi and Tanaka. Takagi led heavy cruisers *Nachi* and *Haguro* with destroyers *Akebono, Ikazuchi, Inazuma, Kawakaze* and *Yamakaze*. Tanaka aboard light cruiser *Jintsu* had nine destroyers: *Amatsukaze, Hatsukaze, Hayashio, Kuroshio, Oyashio, Sazanami, Tokitsukaze, Ushio* and *Yukikaze*.

Allied fighters and bombers lacked the range to attack these Japanese forces while still at a distance and Allied warships lacked air cover and were subject to constant air attacks, so Vice Admiral Helfrich decided to wait until the enemy drew closer. Doorman's ships had been making sweeps of the north coast of Java for days. On the night of February 26, they ventured 80 miles north of Surabaya toward Bawean Island, and in a stroke of bad luck, they just missed a Japanese landing there. The next day, as Doorman returned to Surabaya, Helfrich ordered him to seek out and attack the enemy convoy approaching from the northeast. The Dutch continued to believe the Japanese could be stopped at sea but should that strategy fail, at least Doorman's force was to slow the enemy invasion by destroying what warships and troop transports he could. The coming confrontation would be Japan's first major naval battle since Tsushima in 1905 and the world's greatest sea battle since the 1916 Battle of Jutland.

The Battle of the Java Sea

Doorman's force sortied Surabaya to the northwest at 1500 hours on February 27. It included his flagship *De Ruyter* and destroyers HMS *Electra,* HMS *Encounter* and HMS *Jupiter,* leading the column. Astern of the flagship were heavy cruisers HMS *Exeter* and USS *Houston* and light cruisers HMAS *Perth* and HMNS *Java.* Dutch destroyers *Kortenaer* and *Witte de With* sailed to port of the cruisers. Trailing the Dutch ships were four old US four-stackers, *Alden, Edwards, Ford* and *Paul Jones.* A request by Doorman for air cover was denied and Doorman himself had left all his floatplanes ashore the previous day since he anticipated a night action. He would be blind until contact was made and once action began, he had no spotting aircraft to direct, correct or adjust his ships' surface fire. On the other hand, Japanese floatplanes had reported Doorman's location and direction to Rear Admiral Takagi who ordered the 41 troop transports heading for landing beaches on the Java coast to reverse course to the north.

About 1600 hours, sailing south of Bawean Island on a southerly course, a lookout aboard *Jintsu* spotted mastheads on the horizon at 17 miles out. Within minutes, heavy cruiser *Haguro* confirmed the sighting. At the same time, lookouts on *Electra* spotted *Jintsu* and her destroyers but failed to see *Nachi* and *Haguro* and light cruiser *Naka* and their destroyer squadrons several miles astern. The Japanese warships in three columns corrected their headings to the southwest to cross in front of the Allied ships. When Doorman realized the attempt to cross his T, he ordered an increase to flank speed that caused his columns to become strung out and separated. By 1615, the two forces were running on nearly parallel westerly headings. Takagi placed Nishimura's ships, flagship *Naka* with destroyers *Asagumo, Harusame, Minegumo, Natsugumo, Samidare* and *Yudachi,* to the south. North of Nishimura, Tanaka aboard *Jintsu* led destroyers *Amatsukaze, Hatsukaze, Hayashio, Kuroshio, Oyashio, Tokitsukaze* and *Yukikaze.* From a range of 16 miles and still north of Nishimura, heavy cruisers *Nachi* and *Haguro* opened fire, each with ten 8-inch guns. Their targets responded in an unequal match—heavy cruiser *Exeter* with six 8-inch guns and *Houston* with the six of her nine guns still in operation. In the early part of the battle, *Naka* and her destroyers fired several series of long lance torpedoes, all failing to find their targets. HMS *Exeter* was set afire early in the fight by a direct hit from *Nachi.* The ensuing blast severed steam lines, causing the loss of six of her eight boilers. Reduced to five knots, *Exeter* maneuvered to avoid a collision with *Houston* and in the process confused the Dutch cruisers. Doorman turned his ships to port and as he tried to reform them, *Kortenaer* was hit by a torpedo, probably from *Haguro.* She went dead in the water, rolled over to port, broke in half and sank. The US destroyers were not yet engaged due to their distance.

Knowing he had to restore order to his force, Doorman signaled, ALL SHIPS FOLLOW ME. Out of the confusion, the Allied ships formed two columns with *Houston, De Ruyter, Perth* and *Java* sailing to the southeast screened by the four destroyers, and *Exeter* screened by *Witte de With, Jupiter, Encounter* and *Electra* sailing south by southeast. After 1700 hours, *Haguro* and *Nachi* fired on *De Ruyter's* column and *Nachi* launched torpedoes at *Exeter's* column. *Naka* and her destroyers fired on *Exeter* and her screen and launched a second series of torpedoes; again all missed their targets. *Houston* returned *Naka's* fire, and *Electra* commenced firing with her four 4.7-inch main guns. One shell struck *Jintsu*, killing one man and wounding four. The air was heavy from ships making smoke and from the fires on *Exeter.* Takagi ordered the transports to turn south again toward Java and formed his warships for a new attack.

Nachi and *Haguro* were farthest to the north, 10 miles from Doorman's ships, their twenty 8-inch guns still engaged in a long-distance barrage. They launched more torpedoes just before 1730 hours and ceased fire as they retired to the west. The *Jintsu* and *Naka* columns fired torpedoes from eight miles and from 10 miles, respectively, and reversed course to the northwest. Four of *Naka*'s destroyers launched torpedoes from five miles while two destroyers, *Asagumo* and *Minegumo,* closed in further and launched torpedoes from just under four miles. In the meantime, *Encounter* and *Electra* separated from *Exeter, Jupiter* and *Witte de With* to counter the torpedo attack. *Encounter* engaged *Minegumo* in a surface attack; *Electra* engaged *Asagumo*, making a direct hit from about three miles that cost the loss of four of the Japanese destroyer's crew. *Asagumo* at the same time scored at least two hits on *Electra*. *Electra* carried on slowly with her crew at their battle stations until an abandon ship order was passed and she went down. Doorman ordered *Exeter* escorted by *Witte de With* back to Surabaya and, realizing most of the Japanese were retiring, took the *De Ruyter* column once again after the transports. The US destroyers hunted the transports as well but before long, the exhausted Allies reversed course away to the southeast. This might have signaled the end of the battle.

After 1800 hours, though, with a new formation of four cruisers, *De Ruyter, Java, Houston* and *Perth,* and five destroyers, *Jupiter* and the four US destroyers, Doorman came out of the smoke and spotted *Nachi* and *Haguro* on a parallel northbound course, nine miles to the northwest. *Jintsu* and her destroyers were 10 miles off Doorman's port beam. Doorman wanted the transports. The Japanese heavy cruisers turned toward the Allies and fired on *Houston*; she was hit by two 8-inch shells, both duds. *Houston* fired back with her forward turrets, both out of ammunition and being supplied with shells brought forward from her disabled rear turret. *Nachi* and *Haguro* followed with a torpedo attack that forced Doorman to visually order all his ships south. However, Commander Binford aboard *John D. Edwards* read a flashing signal from *De Ruyter* as Counterattack and led the four American destroyers toward the Japanese. From five miles and parallel to the heavy cruisers, Binford's ships fired their starboard torpedo tubes. Reversing course, they fired their port tubes. No hits were scored and their torpedoes spent, the Americans still continued north. Takagi headed the transports toward Java for a night landing and a few hours passed without further engagement. Low on fuel, Binford's destroyers turned south for Surabaya. Doorman's column continued its search for the transports, sailing near to the Java coast and into a minefield newly laid by the Dutch west of Surabaya. At 2125 hours, British destroyer *Jupiter* at the rear of the column suffered a huge explosion, most likely from a floating Dutch mine that broke loose. She sank within four hours.

Reduced to his cruisers, Doorman continued to search to the north with *De Ruyter, Perth, Houston* and *Java* while *Encounter* retired to rescue survivors in the water, men from *Kortenaer* that went down hours before. *De Ruyter* opened fire on the Japanese heavy cruisers, and the main guns of *Perth, Houston* and *Java* joined in. Then silence. Just before 2300 hours at a range of five miles, *Nachi* launched eight torpedoes and *Haguro,* four. Fifteen minutes later, Doorman's flagship burst into flames, every flare and rocket in the Dutch cruiser's pyrotechnic locker ignited. Within minutes, as *De Ruyter* went down, there was a tremendous explosion at the rear of the column. *Java* was engulfed in flames, settled at her stern and slid under as 500 of her crew struggled in the water, some shouting three cheers for the Dutch Queen. Of *De Ruyter's* crew, 366 officers and men were lost. Following Doorman's earlier order to leave survivors to the mercy of the enemy and go to Batavia, Captain Hector Waller of HMAS *Perth* took command and ordered USS *Houston* to follow to the southeast. The enemy cruisers followed until Waller turned southwest toward Batavia. By the next morning, Takagi escorted the transports of Eastern Invasion Force back toward Java after a delay of less than a day. Losses for the Japanese included only destroyer *Asagumo* seriously damaged. The Allies lost three destroyers, *Kortenaer, Electra* and *Jupiter*; two light cruisers, *De Ruyter* and *Java*; and their intrepid Rear Admiral Karel Doorman.

Commander Binford at Surabaya with 700 men aboard the four old American destroyers asked headquarters at Bandung for permission to try to escape to Australia. Low on fuel and without torpedoes, *Alden, John D. Edwards, John D. Ford* and *Paul Jones* slipped safely through Bali Strait on the night of February 28. But Allied losses in the Java Sea continued. That same night, the damaged British heavy cruiser *Exeter,* escorted by *Encounter* and *Pope,* sortied Surabaya with orders to try to reach Ceylon by sailing first toward Borneo and then making a run the next night for Sunda Strait. It was not to be. The next morning, March 1, they were spotted by Japanese aircraft and met by Admiral Takagi with *Nachi* and *Haguro* and destroyers *Kawakaze* and *Yamakaze*. Vice Admiral Ibo Takahashi, Commander in Chief of Third Fleet and head of Central and Eastern Invasion Forces, arrived west of the Allied ships with heavy cruisers *Ashigara* and *Myoko*. Destroyers *Akebono* and *Ikazuchi* were also in the area.

Just before 1000 hours, the Allies fired on *Akebono* and *Ikazuchi* before making smoke and attempting escape to the east. The Japanese returned fire and launched torpedoes continuously and moved in closer on the slow-moving *Exeter* while *Encounter* and *Pope* at first tried to distract the Japanese but soon raced east, trying to save themselves. An 8-inch shell knocked out *Exeter's* last functioning steam pipe and her crew began to open sea valves in preparation for flooding and scuttling the ship. Finally, a single torpedo caused her to explode amidships and plunge into the sea. Ten miles to the east, the crew of *Encounter* prepared to abandon their sinking ship that had been damaged while running a gauntlet between the Japanese cruisers and destroyers. *Pope* continued east in a rain squall for half an hour but by 1230 hours, six Val dive bombers from light carrier *Ryujo* arrived overhead. A concussion from one bomb knocked one of *Pope's* propeller shafts out of line and ripped a hole in her hull below the water line. Next, six Kate level bombers attacked but though no hits were recorded, the order was given to abandon ship. At about 1300 hours, a final salvo from Takagi's heavy cruisers hit *Pope*. She sank quickly from the stern, the last Allied warship in the Java Sea.

Battle of Sunda Strait

The 14-mile-wide strait separating the southern tip of Sumatra from western Java was filling up with the 56 transports and early units of Admiral Ozawa's Western Force by the last day of February 1942. The convoy carrying the Japanese Sixteenth Army's 2nd Division had dropped anchor off St. Nicholas Point on the Java coast covered by heavy cruisers *Kumano*, *Mikuma*, *Mogami* and *Suzuya* and escorted by destroyers *Ayanami*, *Hatsuyuki*, *Isonami*, *Murakumo*, *Shirakumo* and *Shirayuki*. A second force and escort group included light cruiser *Natori* and destroyers *Akatsuki*, *Asakaze*, *Fubuki*, *Hatsuharu*, *Hibiki* and *Matsukaze*. It was a formidable force of perhaps as many as 100 vessels.

This was the scene as heavy cruiser *Houston* and light cruiser *Perth* entered Sunda Strait late on the night of February 28, hoping for safe port at Tjilatjap on Java's south coast. Apparently at first, neither the Japanese nor the Allies were aware of each other's presence. Once the officers and men aboard the cruisers saw what they were up against, and almost certainly sensing their ships were doomed, their response was characteristically heroic. Both ships opened fire on the transports anchored in Bantam Bay. By 2300 hours, Japanese cruisers and destroyers appeared from every direction. Long lance torpedoes launched from destroyer *Fubuki* at less than two miles missed *Houston* and *Perth* and struck two of the anchored transports instead. Heavy cruisers *Mikuma* and *Mogami* fired on *Perth*. She went dead in the water but continued firing on the Japanese with all she had for another half hour. Finally, her forward engine room was struck by a torpedo, causing an explosion that lifted the 7,000-ton warship out of the water. She sank at just about midnight, taking most of her crew of 550 officers and men with her.

USS *Houston* took a salvo of 8-inch shells in her aft engine room that knocked out all her steam lines and killed her entire engine room crew. Within seconds, more men were lost as a shell exploded on deck. Of her two remaining three-gun turrets, Number One turret was out of ammunition and the 8-inch ammunition in Number Two was nearly gone. A torpedo knocked out her main battery plot room so that *Houston*'s remaining guns had to be fired locally. The heavy cruiser was burning and listing badly. Her captain, after giving the order to abandon ship, was killed by an exploding shell as he came down from the bridge. *Houston* took three torpedoes in her starboard side, rolled over and sank just before 0100 hours on March 1. Some survivors managed to swim to Java while many were killed as Japanese fired into the oily sea. Japanese soldiers and sailors, too, struggled in the water. One transport was sunk, three were beached and destroyers *Shirakumo* and *Harukaze* received some battle damage.

Aftermath

On March 1, 1942, assault troops of the Imperial Japanese Navy's Eastern and Western Invasion Forces came ashore on Java almost unopposed. Japanese troops landed in northern Sumatra on March 8 and by the end of the month held the entire island. That same day, the Dutch East Indies Government on Java surrendered unconditionally and 93,000 men of the Royal Netherlands East Indies Army, along with other Allied troops, surrendered to the Japanese. In the ensuing occupation, Sumatra, Java and several other islands were administered by the Japanese Army while the Navy controlled Celebes and the British and Dutch areas on Borneo. On Java, 30,000 Dutch nationals were held in internment camps and on Sumatra 1,500 civilians who had fled Singapore were detained. Throughout the Dutch East Indies, clusters of Japanese compounds would eventually hold tens of thousands of prisoners from Australian soldiers to Dutch nuns, from British colonial administrators to American ex-patriots and their families and of course, Dutch colonials from all walks of life.

With the taking of the Malay Barrier, Japan became almost self-sufficient in terms of oil, rubber, minerals and food production. Her control of the straits between the islands of the huge Netherlands East Indies chain meant that her ships had free access to the Indian Ocean and movement toward India and Australia. The geographic dimensions of the Greater East Asia Co-Prosperity Sphere were practically complete with only Burma to the west and New Guinea to the east left to conquer. In the campaign, the Japanese Navy lost only one of the more than 40 warships that had staged at Davao— destroyer *Natsushio*, sunk while under tow after being torpedoed by a US submarine at Makassar, the first Japanese surface warship sunk by an American submarine.

For the Allies, for the ABDA Command that formed in early February, 20 of 37 warships were lost in the attempt to delay or prevent a Japanese invasion. The US Navy lost six of 16 ships: heavy cruiser *Houston* at Sunda Strait, destroyers *Edsall* south of Java, *Peary* in the Darwin raid, *Pillsbury* south of Bali, and *Pope* at the Battle of the Java Sea. Destroyer *Stewart* was damaged at Bali-Lombok and returned to Surabaya where she was confiscated and repaired by the Japanese. The fate of destroyer *Edsall* remains a mystery. She was ordered out of Darwin in late February 1942 as an escort for aircraft tender USS *Langley* that was carrying aircraft and flyers to Tjilatjap but failed to rendezvous and was never heard from again. The two US light cruisers survived the campaign. *Boise* was sent back to the States after running aground on the way to Balikpapan and *Marblehead*, after being struck by two bombs at Makassar, was sent to Ceylon and then to South Africa for extensive repairs. Destroyers *Alden, John D. Edwards, John D. Ford* and *Paul Jones* survived the Battle of the Java Sea and made it safely to Australia. *Barker* and *Bulmer* were attacked in mid-January while in port at Surabaya and although damaged, both managed to reach Australia. *Parrott* and *Whipple* survived the Netherlands East Indies Campaign and retreated to Australia.

The Commonwealth navies lost five of their 11 warships in the Combined Command. The British Royal Navy saw heavy cruiser *Exeter* and destroyers *Electra, Encounter* and *Jupiter* sunk in the Battle of the Java Sea. *Exeter* is remembered for her brave fight against *Graf Spee* in the 1939 Battle of the River Platte. Destroyer *Stronghold* was sunk south of Java in early March. British light cruisers *Danae* and *Dragon* escaped to Ceylon as did destroyers *Scout* and *Tenedos*. The Royal Australian Navy's light cruiser *Perth* was sunk in the Battle of Sunda Strait. Light cruiser *Hobart* took minor damage in an air attack while refueling at Batavia in late February and prevented from taking part in the Battle of the Java Sea; she transferred to Australia.

The Royal Netherlands Navy lost all but one of her Combined Command ships. Light cruiser *Tromp*, damaged at Bali, was returned to Surabaya and sent on to Sydney for repairs. Light cruisers *De Ruyter* and *Java* were sunk in the Battle of the Java Sea along with destroyer *Kortenaer*. Destroyer *Banckert*, undergoing repairs at Surabaya at the time of the Battle, was scuttled by the Dutch and refloated by the Japanese. *Piet Hein* was sunk in the ABDA attempt to stop Japanese landings on Bali and *Van Nes* was sunk by Japanese land-based aircraft in Banka Strait. *Van Ghent* ran aground and wrecked at Tjilatjap before the Battle of Bali-Lombok and was never repaired. *Witte de With* survived the Battle of the Java Sea only to be scuttled afterward at Surabaya. *Evertsen*, while trying to join *Houston* and *Perth* for the escape south through Sunda Strait, took heavy damage from Japanese destroyers and was beached by her crew the following day.

It is said that Churchill referred to "The forlorn battles of the ships and men of ABDA." The reasons for their defeat were many. The forces of the American, British, Dutch and Australian navies had little or no chance to exercise together as the Combined Command. They lacked air cover. There was the language difference and the lack of a unified code or signaling system. And the Defeat Germany First policy left Allied forces in the South Pacific short on supplies and manpower as it did throughout the Pacific. Yet, the four nationalities kept faith in battle and cheered each other on, even in times of devastating defeat. The defense of the Netherlands East Indies may have been hopeless as Sir Archibald Wavell believed early on, but it was not without heroism.

The four-month estimate the Japanese General Staff gave its Navy and Army for the isolation and conquest of Java was double the actual time required. The battles lasted just two months, January 11 to March 8, 1942.

Chapter X

OPERATION C AND THE BRITISH FAR EAST FLEET

Introduction

By March 1942, three months into the Pacific War, the Army and the Navy of the Empire of Japan were unstoppable. American possessions Guam and Wake Island had fallen and the situation in the Philippines was deteriorating rapidly. Japanese troops landed in the Gilbert Islands. British territories on North Borneo, Brunei and Sarawak were in enemy hands. The island of Hong Kong, the Malay Peninsula, and Singapore, Britain's Gibraltar of the Pacific, capitulated.

Troopships carried Japanese Army units toward Rangoon on the Bay of Bengal while other units moved over land from Thailand into Burma. The last major Allied naval repair facility in the South Pacific at Darwin was destroyed and Japanese assault troops had landed in the Bismarck Archipelago. The exiled Dutch Government lost the islands of the Netherlands East Indies and collectively, the Allies had hundreds of thousands of military personnel and civilians, including women and children, imprisoned within Japan's ever growing defense perimeter.

While Japanese assault troops enveloped the island of Java from both the east and the west, the carriers of Vice Admiral Chuichi Nagumo's First Air Fleet and the battleships and heavy cruisers of Vice Admiral Nobutake Kondo's Southern Force were on station south of Java in the Indian Ocean. Their mission: to attack and neutralize Allied bases and other military targets on Java's southern coast. On March 3, 1942, carriers *Akagi, Kaga, Hiryu* and *Soryu* turned into the wind and began launching aircraft—Val dive bombers and Kate level bombers with Zero fighters for protection—180 planes in all. The Allied naval base at Tjilatjap and other targets on Java were destroyed. At sea, Kondo's surface force claimed three Allied destroyers, 17 transports and countless smaller craft. Java and the Netherlands East Indies surrendered to the Japanese on March 8. Nagumo's First Air Fleet headed east, back to base at Staring Bay on Celebes and fleet carrier *Kaga* returned to Japan for engine repairs.

Admiral Nagumo in the Indian Ocean

A Japanese presence in the Bay of Bengal and in the Indian Ocean was essential to an extension of the defense perimeter and to the protection of units of the Japanese Fifteenth Army moving into Burma over land and to amphibious units landing south of Rangoon. Presenting a serious deterrent to this Japanese advance was the British Royal Navy that operated from naval bases and airfields on Ceylon (now Sri Lanka) and that was charged with control of India's coastlines and ports and the defense of sea lanes over which merchant and military ships carried metals, oil and other critical cargo. Although Japanese Army generals held that an occupation of Ceylon would require an overextension of supply lines, Japanese naval officials believed that destruction of the British Fleet at Ceylon would convince the Army otherwise.

Vice Admiral Sir Geoffrey Layton commanded naval bases on Ceylon at Colombo and at Trincomalee as well as the island's airfields. His immediate superior, Admiral Sir James Somerville, became Commander in Chief of Eastern Fleet, all British Royal Navy vessels in the Indian Ocean, on March 26, 1942, his flag on battleship HMS *Warspite.* Somerville fully expected that a Japanese attack was imminent and was concerned his reconnaissance data on Japanese ships might be inaccurate. In addition, he was told by the

Admiralty to avoid unnecessary risks. Churchill would later call the Japanese raid in the Indian Ocean the most dangerous moment of the War.

In the southeast Sea of Bengal, the Andaman Islands and the Nicobar Islands were administered by India. Commonwealth troops garrisoned there had already been withdrawn. Undefended, both groups fell quickly to the Japanese.

Operation C

Admiral Kondo, Commander in Chief of all Japanese naval forces in Southeast Asia, appointed Nagumo's First Air Fleet to lead the upcoming Indian Ocean operation. The main thrust of this campaign, Operation C, would be aimed at British Commonwealth naval bases on Ceylon. Kondo ordered the carriers of Rear Admiral Chuichi Hara's 5th Carrier Division, *Shokaku* and *Zuikaku*, to join Admiral Nagumo and First Air Fleet, including *Hiryu* and *Soryu,* at Staring Bay. With their arrival on Celebes, Nagumo commanded the same ships, except for *Kaga,* that made up the Pearl Harbor Strike Force. To further increase First Air Fleet's surface fire power, Kondo released the battleships *Haruna* and *Kongo* to Nagumo, joining *Hiei* and *Kirishima.*

On the morning of March 26, with five aircraft carriers, four battleships, two heavy cruisers, a light cruiser and nine destroyers all fueled and resupplied, First Air Fleet sortied Staring Bay. From the carrier *Akagi,* Admiral Nagumo charted a course west through the Java Sea, Sunda Strait and northwest toward Ceylon. Operation C, or C-Day, was set to begin on April 5. As Nagumo's carrier planes prepared to raid Ceylon's naval and air bases, a second force led by Vice Admiral Jizaburo Ozawa sortied the southern Burmese port of Margui on the Kra Isthmus. It included two light carriers, five heavy cruisers and a number of destroyers with orders to attack India's coastline from Madras to Calcutta, striking bases, harbors and the Commonwealth's merchant shipping.

The Commonwealth surface warship force consisted of five old battleships, *Warspite, Ramillies, Resolution, Revenge* and the *Royal Sovereign.* The old light carrier *Hermes* and the Royal Navy's newest fleet carriers, the 23,000-ton *Formidable* and *Indomitable,* provided Admiral Somerville's carrier strength. The Fleet's cruiser force consisted of two heavy cruisers, HMS *Cornwall* and HMS *Dorsetshire,* light cruisers HMS *Caledon,* HMS *Emerald,*

HMS *Enterprise* and Australian light cruiser HMAS *Adelaide*. Destroyers *Arrow, Decoy, Encounter, Fortune, Foxhound* and *Hotspur* of the British Royal Navy, Australian destroyers *Napier, Nestor, Nizam, Norman, Pakenham, Paladin, Panther* and *Vampire* and the Dutch destroyer *Isaac Sweers* made up Eastern Fleet's destroyer force—more ships than Japanese reconnaissance had reported. Somerville divided his ships into Force A, the newer, faster vessels, and Force B, the older, slower ones.

For air power, most of Eastern Fleet's 50 fighters were Hawker Hurricanes. Admiral Somerville's 57 carrier-based bombers included Fairey Swordfish and Albacore open-cockpit biplanes. A squadron of Fairey Fulmar fighter-reconnaissance aircraft was based on light carrier *Hermes* and Ceylon's land-based aircraft included a dozen twin-engine Bristol Blenheim light bombers from a Canadian squadron. With slightly more than 130 old, outdated aircraft, Great Britain's pilots would go up against 350 modern Japanese carrier-based planes, all flown by seasoned pilots. Recalling the fate of HMS *Prince of Wales* and HMS *Repulse,* Somerville knew his aircraft were no match for the Japanese, but he hoped to locate the enemy force first and launch his Swordfish and Albacore biplanes in a surprise night torpedo attack. Before Admiral Nagumo reached the Indian Ocean, British Intelligence intercepted and deciphered Admiral Yamamoto's orders for Operation C. Knowing of the Japanese plan, Admiral Somerville, by March 30, ordered most of his ships away from the naval bases at Colombo and Trincomalee for a small British base on Addu Atoll in the Maldive Islands, 600 miles southwest of the southern tip of India. Other ships were sent out on patrol.

On April 4, 1942, as the Imperial Japanese Navy's First Air Fleet approached the island of Ceylon from the southeast, Nagumo's force was spotted by a British PBY Catalina reconnaissance aircraft. Though Zeros flying Combat Air Patrol shot the floatplane down, the Catalina pilot was able to alert Ceylon of the approaching enemy force. Before dawn the next morning, Nagumo's warships were 200 miles south of Ceylon and after turning into the wind, the five Japanese carriers began launching 36 Zero fighters, 54 Val dive bombers and 30 Kate level bombers. By daybreak, 120 aircraft were airborne on a northerly heading toward the Royal Navy base at Colombo. Leading the first air strike on Ceylon in a Kate level bomber was

Commander Mitsuo Fuchida, the officer who led the first wave of the attack on Pearl Harbor.

Admiral Layton ordered heavy cruisers *Cornwall* and *Dorsetshire* to clear port and join the warships at Addu Atoll. He ordered light carrier *Hermes,* that had returned to Ceylon to pick up 12 fighter-reconnaissance aircraft, back to sea without her aircraft. As Nagumo's strike force approached, with his search aircraft unable to locate the Commonwealth fleet and dissatisfied with a lack of solid intelligence, he chose to keep his ships south of Ceylon. Japanese carrier planes, however, had launched, formed up and were heading north toward Colombo when they spotted a dozen British Swordfish in formation below. These aircraft had apparently taken off from Trincomalee and were headed southwest to reinforce Colombo. Unseen by the British, half the Zeros turned and dove on the unsuspecting open-cockpit biplanes and on the first pass, destroyed all but two of the slow-moving Swordfish.

Commander Fuchida ordered his group to circle wide around Colombo to come in from the north in the event the enemy had been alerted. Over the base, Fuchida saw no British fighters in the skies and no aircraft parked along the runways at the airfield east of the city. Peeling off and dropping out of formation, some of the Kates and Zeros attacked the airfield as remaining level bombers, Val dive bombers and Zero fighters continued toward shipping and installation targets at Colombo Harbor. With no warships as targets, the Japanese did considerable damage to cargo vessels and harbor installations and faced little resistance from ground troops.

As Commander Fuchida reformed aircraft for return to the carriers for refueling and rearming, he received a message relayed from one of Nagumo's scouting floatplanes that two British heavy cruisers had been sighted south of Ceylon. These were HMS *Cornwall* and HMS *Dorsetshire*. In addition, Fuchida's group spotted 18 Hurricanes and six Fulmar fighters directly ahead, approaching from the south. Most of the Hurricanes went after some Vals that were still looking for targets over the harbor and shot down or damaged a dozen of the Japanese dive bombers. When the Zeros did enter the dogfight, they took down 20 British aircraft within minutes with the loss of only a single Zero fighter. Admiral Nagumo sent 53 Aichi Val dive bombers against the cruisers; planes that survived the Colombo raid refueled and rearmed. With no Combat Air Patrol for protection, *Dorsetshire* and *Cornwall* were sighted by the Japanese southwest of Ceylon and both sent to the bottom within 20 minutes on the morning of April 4. Over 400 British sailors and Marines were lost while over a thousand survivors spent 30 hours in the water before being rescued.

After leaving Trincomalee on April 8 with none of her planes, the old carrier HMS *Hermes* was taken down along with HMAS *Vampire* and auxiliary ships by at least 32 Aichi Vals with Zero escorts. *Hermes* was laid down in 1918 and commissioned in 1923, the first ship purpose-built as an aircraft carrier. She had served worldwide and well and went down with over 300 men. *Vampire's* captain was lost along with seven crewmen.

Aftermath

Admiral Sir James Somerville could have lost more in what was a humiliating retreat. His assignment to the British Far East Fleet came just as the Japanese prepared to attack. He had served honorably in WWI at Gallipoli and was involved in the evacuation of Dunkirk. In June 1940, Churchill gave him the unenviable task of neutralizing the main element of the French battle fleet and he took part in the sinking of the *Bismarck*. After his losses in the Indian Ocean and to keep from risking his carriers, Somerville moved Eastern Fleet's newer ships, Force A, to East Africa and the older ships of Force B to Bombay.

Operation C was Japan's only foray into the Indian Ocean and many Japanese military, including Commander Fuchida, thought it a strategic mistake.

Part Three

MAY 1942– DECEMBER 1942

They will live a long time, these men of the South Pacific. They had an American quality. They, like their victories, will be remembered as long as our generation lives. After that, like men of the confederacy, they will become strangers. Longer and longer shadows will obscure them, until their Guadalcanal sounds distant on the ear like Shiloh or Valley Forge.

—James Michener, *Tales of the South Pacific* (1946)

Chapter XI

THE UNITED STATES NAVY GOES ON
THE OFFENSIVE

Introduction

In the early months of war, the aircraft carriers of the US Pacific Fleet, the only real impediment to Admiral Nagumo's advance, were conspicuous by their absence. With little exception, *Enterprise, Lexington* and *Saratoga* remained within the Hawaiian Triangle. In mid-December 1941, there was a plan to send *Lexington* and Task Force 11 to attack Japanese installations at Wotje Atoll in the Marshall Islands. That did not happen. Later in December, the mission to reinforce Wake Island was scrubbed and *Saratoga,* with Task Force 14, delivered her cargo of Marine fighter planes to Midway Island instead. *Enterprise* and Task Force 8, much to Admiral Halsey's disgust, operated on routine escort and submarine patrol duties. All that was about to change.

Officers and Operations

Chester W. Nimitz was 56 years old when, on Christmas Day 1941, he was assigned to succeed Admiral Husband Kimmel as Commander in Chief, Pacific Fleet, CincPAC. Nimitz believed strongly in the aircraft carrier and in taking the offensive and keeping it, essential qualities for the job he would hold until War's end. A 1905 graduate of the Naval Academy at Annapolis, he compiled a distinguished career over the decades as a submariner and aboard destroyers, cruisers and battleships. To Nimitz, Pearl Harbor was not the absolute disaster many took it to be and upon his arrival there, he set about restoring confidence at Pacific Fleet headquarters. He was optimistic about the ultimate outcome of the war and surrounded himself with a first-rate staff of fighting commanders: Halsey, Wilson Brown, Richmond Kelly Turner, Marc Mitscher, Raymond Spruance and top Marine Corps commanders, Holland Smith and Alexander Vandegrift. Nimitz was tactful, patient and tough, with a capacity for detailed thinking and clear-headed planning, an able strategist.

William F. Halsey Jr. graduated from the Naval Academy in 1904, an average student, known on the gridiron as Bull Dog and descended from a long line of seafarers and whaling masters. His early service was aboard destroyers. In 1932, at age 50, he qualified as a pilot and earned his Navy wings. In 1940, Halsey was made Vice Admiral and by December 1941, he was the most senior US carrier Admiral in the Pacific.

Wilson Brown Jr. graduated from the Naval Academy in 1902. During the Great War, he served in London and as a destroyer commander. Between the wars, he skippered battleships, served as Chief of Staff of training for the Atlantic Fleet and was superintendent of the US Naval Academy for three years. Brown completed studies at the Naval War College in 1921 and was naval aide to Presidents Coolidge and Hoover. His promotion to Vice Admiral came in February 1941 as Commander of Atlantic Scouting Force but by December, he was involved in bombardment exercises with the Pacific Fleet.

James Harold Doolittle, born in 1896, served as a flyer in the Army Air Corps in the Great War and between wars worked as a civilian test pilot and a specialist in aeronautics. In 1940, he was given responsibility for converting the US motor car industry to production of military aircraft. The following year, Doolittle rejoined the armed forces as an officer and proved to be a brilliant student of strategic and tactical bombing. His bold Doolittle Raid on Tokyo and other Japanese cities in April 1942 would go down as the first time twin-engine bombers were launched from an American aircraft carrier.

Buildup in the Pacific—December 1941 to June 1942

The Defeat Germany First Policy of Roosevelt and Churchill notwithstanding, the US Navy had no choice after December 7 in its commitment to a two-ocean war. A Pacific victory required more officers, more men and more ships, especially aircraft carriers, but most new surface warships released in early 1942 went to the Atlantic while the Pacific Fleet relied on ships in service.

Yorktown, built at Mare Island near San Francisco in the late 1930s, served in the Atlantic until just after Pearl Harbor when she transited the Panama Canal with destroyers USS *Anderson,* USS *Hughes* and USS *Walke* for San Diego where she was equipped with the new radar system and additional anti-aircraft guns, ready to join *Enterprise, Lexington* and *Saratoga.*

Hornet was next to reach the Pacific. The new 20,000-ton carrier completed her shakedown in the Atlantic in February 1942 and left Norfolk, Virginia, on March 4 with heavy cruiser USS *Vincennes,* light cruiser USS *Nashville,* and USS *Monssen,* a destroyer of the *Benson* class. At San Francisco, *Hornet* took on board 16 North American B-25 twin-engine medium bombers and Army Air Corps personnel under Lt. Colonel James H. Doolittle for a planned raid on Japan.

Wasp, in the Atlantic since joining the fleet in 1940, transferred to the Pacific in June 1942, arriving at San Diego with light anti-aircraft cruiser USS *San Juan* and four Gridley class destroyers: USS *Lang,* USS *Stack,* USS *Sterett* and USS *Wilson.*

Pacific Fleet received one new battleship in June 1942, the 35,000-ton fast battleship *North Carolina.* Heavy cruiser USS *Quincy* arrived at San Diego that month and by then, three new *Atlanta* class light anti-aircraft cruisers were transferred to the Pacific. USS *Atlanta* reached Pearl Harbor in April, *San Diego* reached San Diego in May and *San Juan* escorted *Wasp* to the Pacific in June. Fourteen destroyers built during 1939 and 1940 were transferred to the Pacific Fleet early in the war. Nine were of the 12-ship *Sims* class: *Sims, Russell, Hammann, Anderson, Hughes, Walke, O'Brien, Mustin,* and *Morris,* the first US destroyer to be equipped with fire-control radar. The other five destroyers were those transferred with *Hornet* and with *Wasp.*

Halsey Takes Leave of the Triangle

Enterprise and Task Force 8 under Admiral Halsey spent the first month of war on escort duty and returned to Pearl Harbor December 31 after shepherding *Saratoga* and her cargo of F2A Buffalo fighters to Midway Island. Almost immediately, Halsey's ships were ordered out again to escort a convoy bound for Pearl Harbor from the west coast. By the time Halsey returned from that mission on January 7, Admiral Nimitz was in charge at CincPAC Headquarters and early plans for offensive action against the Japanese were beginning to take shape. That same day, Nimitz dispatched Task Force 17 under command of Rear Admiral Frank Jack Fletcher from San Diego to the South Pacific with 4,800 men of the 2nd Marine Brigade to reinforce Samoa, a US mandate island that strategists believed to be the next Japanese offensive. Task Force 17 included *Yorktown,* heavy cruiser *Louisville,* light cruiser *St. Louis,* and destroyers *Morris, Mustin, O'Brien* and *Walke,* along with transports. Task Force 8 sortied Pearl Harbor for Samoa the morning of January 11 with Halsey in command. The force included *Enterprise* commanded by Captain George D. Murray, heavy cruisers *Chester, Northampton* and *Salt Lake City,* destroyers *Balch, Blue, Dunlap, Fanning, Gridley, Maury, McCall* and *Ralph Talbot.*

Almost immediately upon deployment, Halsey received bad news. In the area of Johnston Island, *Saratoga,* while slowing to recover scout aircraft, was struck by a single torpedo from a Japanese submarine. The blast killed six of her crew. Damage control corrected a slight list by counterflooding, and *Saratoga,* at 33,000 tons one of two of the largest carriers built by the US to date, returned to Pearl Harbor under her own power and on to Bremerton Navy Yard on Puget Sound in the state of Washington. On January 22, Halsey's force suffered its own loss as it neared Samoa. Destroyers *Fanning* and *Gridley* collided during a heavy storm and had to be released back to Hawaii for repairs.

On January 24, Task Force 17 and Task Force 8 rendezvoused near Samoa after Fletcher put the Marines ashore. The two forces sailed northwest over 1,500 miles along the International Date Line toward the equator for carrier raids on the Marshall Islands and on the Gilbert Islands, the US Navy's first offensive mission of the war.

The Gilberts and the Marshalls

Both island groups consist of coral atolls atop volcanic uprisings. The Gilbert Islands lie north and south of the equator just west of the International Date Line and include over 30 coral islands and atolls covering 300,000 square miles of ocean. The Gilberts were for the most part a British protectorate when seized by the Japanese in December 1941. Makin Atoll there was a New Zealand mandate.

North of the Gilberts lie the Marshall Islands that form a double chain of 2,000 islands and islets and cover 600,000 square miles of ocean. Kwajalein in the south is the world's largest coral atoll. Roi and Namur Islands lie to the north. The Japanese occupied the Marshalls beginning in 1914, received a League of Nations mandate to them in 1920 and proclaimed sovereignty there in 1935, at which time the population included 10,000 native Micronesians and about 500 Japanese. A major anchorage on Kwajalein included a seaplane base, and in early 1942, an airfield was being completed on Roi Island. Bases on Roi and on Taroa Island in the Maloelap Atoll were home to units of the Chitose Naval Air Group of the 24th Air Flotilla that flew Claude fighters and Nell medium bombers.

The US offensive began on February 1 when planes of Task Force 17 struck Makin Atoll in the Gilberts and Jaluit and Mille Atolls in the Marshalls. Task Force 8 was assigned Wotje and Maloelap Atolls in the Marshalls. Halsey's mission was extended to include air strikes on Kwajalein after US reconnaissance aircraft reported the entire Marshall group was lightly defended. Halsey split Task Force 8 into three Task Groups. Task Group 8.1 commanded by Rear Admiral Raymond Spruance included heavy cruisers *Northampton* and *Salt Lake City* escorted by destroyer *Dunlap* and was assigned bombardment of Wotje. Task Group 8.3 led by Captain Thomas M. Stock aboard heavy cruiser *Chester* included destroyers *Balch* and *Maury,* its target, Taroa Island. Task Group 8.5, *Enterprise* screened by destroyers *Blue, McCall* and *Ralph Talbot,* would launch simultaneous air strikes against targets on Wotje, Maloelap and Kwajalein. Bombardment by Spruance's and Stock's ships would follow. US planes included TBD Devastator torpedo bombers, SBD Dauntless dive bombers and a squadron of 18 F4F Wildcat fighters.

The early morning hours of February 1 brought calm seas, clear skies and a full moon to Task Group 8.5 east of Wotje. Captain Murray on *Enterprise* began launching at 0443 hours: 36 Dauntless bombers each armed with one 500-pound and two 100-pound bombs toward Roi. Next, eight Devastator torpedo bombers, each with three 500-pound bombs (no torpedoes) headed for Kwajalein. Eleven F4F Wildcats, each carrying a pair of 100-pound bombs, took off at 0700 for Wotje and Taroa; a twelfth veered into the sea on takeoff with the loss of pilot and plane. Six Wildcats served as Combat Air Patrol to protect the carrier. Arriving over Roi before first light, the Dauntlesses circled long enough to alert Japanese anti-aircraft gunners and to allow Japanese pilots to warm up their Claude fighters. Just after 0700, Lt. Commander Halstead Hopping released his 500-pound bomb over the airfield at Roi, the first American bomb of the war to drop on Japanese territory. Hopping was taken down almost immediately by either a Claude just airborne and on his tail or by anti-aircraft fire or both. The Americans lost four planes in the assault on Roi. They claimed four Claudes in the air, some to accurate rear gunners and their twin .30-caliber machine guns, and six on the ground along with considerable damage to the airfield, although it remained operational.

Fifty miles south of Roi at Kwajalein Island, Devastator pilots of Torpedo Six encountered no Japanese planes airborne but heavy anti-aircraft fire. Aircrews reported shipping targets in good number, a light cruiser, two merchant Marus, five submarines, three tankers and a dozen smaller craft, more targets than they had bombs. Dauntlesses of Bombing Six that had not yet released their bombs at Roi were ordered to Kwajalein. A few pilots of Scouting Six also heard the call and headed south, every pilot hoping to find a Japanese carrier. By 0730 hours, the remaining nine Devastators of Torpedo Six left *Enterprise* for Kwajalein, each carrying a 2,000-pound torpedo. Results of US activity over Kwajalein included hits on four Japanese transports, on tankers, cargo ships and submarines. While putting up heavy anti-aircraft fire, light cruiser *Katori* was reported to suffer a direct torpedo hit and left with her bow low in the water. Two Mavis four-engine flying boats and a large launch were hit. Most US aircrews claimed hits on targets, many at point blank range, along with damage to a submarine and the minelayer *Tokiwa*. Though damage reports appeared exaggerated and seemed in conflict, aircrews insisted they would have scored even better if their bombs were armed with delay rather than instant fuses.

At Wotje Atoll, six Grumman F4F Wildcat pilots found a partially completed airstrip. Task Group 8.1 under Spruance met light and inaccurate fire from shore batteries there. It was a different story at Taroa Island. There the Americans found a fully functioning Japanese air base with Claude fighters and several twin-engine bombers parked along the runway. The Wildcats dove to strafe the field with their 100-pound bombs. On a second pass, they mixed with Claudes on Combat Air Patrol, shot down two and saw a third crash on landing. A fourth Claude was also claimed. The Japanese fighters had good maneuverability and climbed rapidly but the Grummans were faster and had armor plates behind the pilots' seats. All six American fighters returned safely to *Enterprise,* now 40 miles east of Wotje.

The work of the Wildcats at Wotje notwithstanding, the mission of Task Group 8.3 to bombard Taroa ran into trouble. A flight of eight Japanese Nell bombers spotted at high altitude repeatedly attacked heavy cruiser *Chester* and destroyers *Balch* and *Maury. Chester* was hit; one bomb exploded aft and tore a six-foot hole in her deck. Eight men were killed and 11 injured. Halsey ordered the refueled and rearmed Dauntlesses of Bombing Six to Taroa to knock out the airfield. Nine launched at 1030 hours and nine an hour later. The first planes caught three Claudes on the ground refueling and successfully dropped their 100-pound and 500-pound bombs in one run. Two Nells on the ground were blown apart; two more caught fire. An hour later when the second flight of Bombing Six arrived, the Japanese were ready with all surviving Claudes airborne. One Dauntless and pilot were lost, another limped back to the carrier. After landing the bombers from the Taroa raid, Admiral Halsey retired *Enterprise* and her Task Groups to the east at maximum speed. It was 1300 hours on February 1, 1942.

As Halsey's force struck atolls in the north of the Marshall Islands that morning, Admiral Fletcher's Task Force 17 hit in the south at Jaluit and at Mille, and at Makin Island in the Gilberts. The missions began in darkness and that, coupled with poor weather, limited their success. Just before 0500 hours, *Yorktown* began launching 28 planes, 11 Devastators and 17 Dauntlesses from about 70 miles east of Mille. The lieutenant in lead of Scouting

Five eventually found and led 20 aircraft toward Jaluit but many of the planes failed to form up and flew separately in twos and threes. Ceiling dropped to 3,000 feet over the anchorage, preventing most Devastators from dropping their bombs and the Dauntlesses from diving on their targets. One Japanese freighter was hit solidly. No airfield was found on Jaluit and anti-aircraft fire was light. New radio homing equipment on *Yorktown* brought several pilots in safely but weather seemed to be the pilots' worst enemy. Two Devastators ditched off Jaluit, one ran out of fuel 20 miles from *Yorktown* and three planes vanished completely.

At Mille, Dauntless crews found no targets. One pilot attacked a pair of storage tanks but when no fire ensued, he assumed he hit water tanks that supplied local residents. Weather over Makin was clear when nine Dauntlesses arrived over its lagoon. Pilots destroyed two Mavis flying boats with machine gun fire and scored one hit on another seaplane there.

Their operations complete, Task Force 17 and Task Force 8 retired east separately toward Hawaii. Wildcats off *Yorktown* encountered one Mavis and shot it down. Radar on *Enterprise* picked up stiffer opposition, six twin-engine Nell bombers at 3,000 feet. Anti-aircraft fire destroyed one plane and fragments flew off others, but five Japanese bombers managed to drop three bombs each near the evading carrier. Some bomb fragments caused a fuel hose fire that killed one man on deck. The Japanese flight leader, knowing he couldn't save his damaged bomber, went into a shallow dive and aimed for the island on *Enterprise*. Hit again on his approach, he veered his plane into the flight deck, clipped the tail of a Dauntless and plunged into the sea. Two hours later, two Nells appeared over Task Force 8 and dropped four bombs from 14,000 feet. Their targets missed, one Nell was downed by Wildcats of the carrier's Combat Air Patrol, the other retreated. By evening, *Enterprise* landed the last of her planes and turned for Hawaii under a protective cloud layer. On February 6, with Admiral Halsey on the bridge, she arrived in Pearl Harbor to an exuberant welcome. *Yorktown* returned a day later.

More Carrier Raids—Wake Island and Marcus Island
Admiral Halsey's next mission was a raid on the Japanese-held island of Wake. The new command was Task Force 16, and like Task Force 8, it was built around *Enterprise* and also included two of the heavy cruisers and the

seven destroyers. Destroyer USS *Craven* replaced the slightly damaged heavy cruiser *Chester*. Again, the ships were formed into task groups. Task Group 16.7, the bombardment group, included heavy cruisers *Northampton* and *Salt Lake City* and destroyers *Balch* and *Maury*. Task Group 16.8 included *Enterprise* and destroyers *Blue, Craven, Dunlap* and *Ralph Talbot*. Tanker USS *Sabine,* escorted by destroyer *McCall,* was on hand to refuel the ships for their 2,500-mile return from Wake to Pearl Harbor.

Task Force 16 reached a launch point 100 miles north of Wake the morning of February 24 (February 23 in Hawaii) with Air Group Six aboard *Enterprise*. It was two months since Wake fell to the Japanese. The bombers were to hit first followed by the naval bombardment, but strong winds and heavy rain postponed the first scheduled takeoff from 0630 to 0645. Launch time was again postponed when a Dauntless crashed into the sea and postponed yet another hour due to heavy fog. By that time, Task Group 16.7 was within 15 miles of Wake and naval bombardment began just as aircraft from *Enterprise* arrived overhead. The Japanese had a seaplane in the air by then; it attacked the ships of the bombardment group without success. The Americans lost three aircraft, one to anti-aircraft fire and two to the weather. Crews estimated Japanese losses at three floatplanes and three small craft, along with hangars, shore batteries, fuel storage and ammunition dumps. After recovering aircraft, the *Enterprise* Task Group and the bombardment Task Group rendezvoused and retired to the northeast for refueling.

The next evening, February 25, Nimitz radioed Halsey, "Desirable to strike Marcus if you think it feasible." Indeed, he did think it feasible. Halsey ordered *Enterprise* and the heavy cruisers to change heading to the northwest, leaving the destroyers back so that he could run at high speed in high seas. Marcus Island, not an atoll but an isolated mountaintop surrounded by the sea, lay halfway between Wake and Iwo Jima. It had an important airfield and a weather reporting station critical to Japanese fleet movements. Early on the morning of March 4, 32 Dauntlesses and six Wildcats were launched toward Marcus. No Devastators—they'd be too slow for the hard, quick strike Halsey envisioned. Arriving over Marcus at 15,000 feet, the bombers and fighters became separated and unable at first to make a coordinated attack. By 0630 hours, 30 SBDs regrouped over Marcus through a break in the clouds. Anti-aircraft fire was intense, worse than in the Marshalls or at Wake, pilots reported. The Americans dropped all their bombs, hitting the airfield and its petroleum tanks and hangars, but no Japanese planes were seen on the ground or in the air. The main purpose of the mission was accomplished, though. When word of the attack on Marcus Island reached Tokyo, Japan's Imperial City went under a blackout order. Halsey and Nimitz had caused the enemy to take notice. One Dauntless crashed at sea and the pilot and his gunner were eventually taken prisoner.

Clashes and Landings South of the Equator

Eleven days after Admiral Halsey's operations in the Gilberts and the Marshalls, but before he raided Wake and Marcus, a task force commanded by Vice Admiral Wilson Brown sortied Pearl Harbor for the New Hebrides Islands on convoy escort duty with Brown's flag on *Lexington*. The New Hebrides, southeast of the Solomon Islands, would remain in Allied hands throughout the war and like New Caledonia to their south and Fiji to the east, would serve as staging and supply areas. By February 16, however, Brown and *Lexington* were assigned a new mission. Radio intercepts and a break into the Japanese code led US strategists to believe a Japanese attack and invasion at the Allied base at Port Moresby on New Guinea's south coast was imminent. Admiral Nimitz and US Chief of Naval Operations Admiral Ernest King agreed a preemptive carrier strike on the Japanese naval base at Rabaul on New Britain Island to the north of New Guinea might stave off such an attack. Rabaul had served as capital of the Australian mandated territory of New Guinea but was taken by the Japanese on January 23 without incident. Australian reconnaissance patrols reported new transports and supply ships arriving there daily.

On February 17, *Lexington* and Task Force 11 left New Hebrides for New Britain 1,300 miles to the northwest. Captain Frederick C. Sherman was *Lexington*'s skipper. The force included heavy cruisers *Indianapolis, Minneapolis, Pensacola* and *San Francisco* and destroyers *Aylwin, Bagley, Clark, Dale, Dewey, Hull, Macdonough, Patterson* and *Phelps*. Aboard the carrier were the Wildcats of Fighting Three who joined *Lexington* after *Saratoga* was torpedoed. Lt. Commander John S. "Jimmy" Thach led Fighting Three. On the morning of February 20, about 400 miles northeast of Rabaul, scout planes spotted a four-engine Mavis shadowing the American ships. A second Mavis appeared and though both were shot down by Combat Air Patrol fighters, Task Force 11 had been discovered. Scout planes went out and flights of Wildcats patrolled within 20 miles of the Task Force. Just before 1700 hours, radar picked up nine Mitsubishi Betty bombers approaching at 11,000 feet. Wildcats led by Thach shot down four of them almost immediately but the five surviving Japanese aircraft maintained course to release their bombs over *Lexington*. Captain Sherman waited until their bomb bay doors opened and the bombs released, then threw the carrier into a turn. The bombs exploded far from the ship. Anti-aircraft fire finished off one crippled Betty and the Wildcat fighters pursued the four escaping bombers.

While Thach's fighters dealt with the early arrivals, a second formation of Bettys was reported at 60 miles out. Six more Wildcats were launched to fan out and intercept the new wave. Two of those made contact but the machine guns on one Wildcat jammed, leaving a lone American fighter pilot against nine Japanese bombers. The pilot was Lieutenant Edward "Butch" O'Hare. Making overhead passes on the formation, O'Hare shot down five of the nine planes. Returning Wildcats led by Thach successfully pursued the remaining four bombers, none of which made it back to base. *Lexington*'s Fighting Three pilots claimed 19 kills of the 20 Japanese aircraft that found Task Force 11 that day. The Americans lost two planes with one pilot recovered. Vice Admiral Brown, believing he was pressing his luck, retired the force. The presence of Task Force 11, however, had for the time being deterred the Japanese in their operation against Port Moresby.

On March 6, Admiral Brown and Task Force 11 with *Lexington* and Admiral Fletcher of Task Force 17 with *Yorktown* rendezvoused near Noumea on New Caledonia with new orders to hit Rabaul. Brown was in overall command of a force that now included eight heavy cruisers and 13 destroyers in addition to the carriers. By March 8 though, as Brown's ships sailed west through the Coral Sea, Allied intelligence reported Japanese forces landing on the northeast coast of New Guinea. These were Special Naval Landing Force assault troops of the 1st Yokosuka Regiment going ashore at Lae and elements of the Imperial Japanese Army's South Seas Detachment landing at Salamaua. Their transports had left Rabaul two days earlier screened by light cruiser *Yubari* and destroyers *Asanagi, Mochizuki, Mutsuki, Oite, Yayoi* and *Yunagi*. Light cruisers *Tatsuta* and *Tenryu* and heavy cruisers *Aoba, Furutaka, Kako* and *Kinugasa* were also in the area to provide additional support.

Again, Admiral Brown called off a raid on Rabaul and planned instead to surprise the Japanese at Lae and at Salamaua from his location 150 miles south of New Guinea in the Gulf of Papua. His combined force included the two carriers, heavy cruisers *Astoria, Chicago, Indianapolis, Louisville, Minneapolis, New Orleans, Pensacola* and *San Francisco* and destroyers *Anderson, Aylwin, Bagley, Clark, Dale, Dewey, Hammann, Hughes, Hull, Macdonough, Patterson, Phelps* and *Sims*. The logistics of getting planes from *Lexington* and *Yorktown* over the 15,000-foot spine of New Guinea's Owen Stanley Mountains was solved on March 9 when Brown learned of a mountain pass at 7,500 feet just 45 miles south of Salamaua.

The US raid began early on March 10. *Lexington* Air Group Commander William B. Ault was first off *Lexington*, followed by eight Wildcats, 31 Dauntlesses and 12 Devastators. From *Yorktown* came 10 Wildcats, 30 Dauntlesses and 12 Devastators. Ault located the mountain pass and flew figure eights within it, guiding the other pilots as they poured through in waves and dove on their targets. The Americans found no Zeros at either base. One floatplane rose but was quickly destroyed. Some Japanese ships were seen fleeing out to sea. Wildcats shot up anti-aircraft guns and dropped small fragmentation bombs on the airfields. Heavy bomb- and torpedo-laden Dauntlesses and Devastators attacked buildings and caught Japanese ships and auxiliary vessels in the harbors and at sea. Aggressive and accurate, the Americans inflicted the worst defeat the Japanese Navy had seen so far in the war. Postwar Japanese sources recorded medium damage to light cruiser *Yubari*, to destroyers *Asanagi* and *Yunagi*, to minelayer *Tsugaru*, to seaplane tender *Kokai*, to 6,800-ton transport *Kiyokawa Maru* and to two converted minesweepers. Army transport *Yokohama Maru* was sunk and Navy transport *Tenyo Maru* ran aground and burned. The Japanese lost 126 sailors, with another 240 wounded. One Dauntless was lost to anti-aircraft fire over Salamaua; all other planes from *Lexington* and *Yorktown* returned to their carriers.

Fletcher's and Brown's forces parted on March 16. Task Force 11 and *Lexington* sailed for Pearl Harbor where on March 26, Lady Lex, as she was now affectionately known, tied up at Ford Island to a resounding welcome. Task Force 17 and *Yorktown* resumed patrols in the Coral Sea, putting in a month later on April 20 in the Tonga Islands east of Fiji for upkeep. The Japanese, meanwhile, made amphibious landings at two islands in the Bismarck Archipelago supported by Rear Admiral Goto's heavy cruisers *Aoba, Furutaka, Kako* and *Kinugasa*. On March 30 (March 29 in Hawaii), Yokosuka Special Naval Landing Force troops from Rabaul went ashore on the small, undefended island of Buka in the western Solomons, and the next day, a small force landed at an Australian settlement on Bougainville, a larger island 90 miles to the south. Then, in early April, as destroyers *Mochizuki, Mutsuki, Uzuki* and *Yayio* patrolled in the Bismarck Sea, Special Naval Landing Force troops of the 2nd Maizuru Battalion from Kavieng on New Ireland Island made amphibious landings on Hermit Island in the Australian mandated Admiralty chain. The next day, Yokosuka Special Naval Landing Force troops from Rabaul landed at the town of Lorengau on Manus Island, also in the Admiralties. The Japanese planned to build airfields on both islands and to improve a deepwater anchorage on Manus.

USS *Hornet,* Jimmy Doolittle and Sixteen Billy Mitchell Bombers

The US Navy's new fleet carrier USS *Hornet* arrived at San Francisco in late March 1942 to play her role in Special Bombing Project One, a joint Army/Navy effort to send a deck load of Army B-25 bombers over Japan for raids on Tokyo and other Japanese cities. The project was the brainchild of US Chief of Naval Operations, Admiral Ernest J. King, and Commander of US Army Air Forces, General Henry H. Arnold. On paper, the plan required *Hornet* to steam within 500 miles of the Japanese coast to launch the B-25s on a low-altitude, overnight run that would bring the planes over their targets in early morning darkness and allow them to fly another 1,000 miles in daylight to Chuchow (on today's maps, Lishui, south of Shanghai) airfield in eastern China. The risky mission was expected to cause only incidental physical damage in Japan but a significant loss of face to the Japanese Army and Navy, while boosting American morale, both military and civilian.

Hornet sortied San Francisco Bay on April 2 with Captain Marc Mitscher in command. Her escort included heavy cruiser *Vincennes*, light cruiser

Nashville and destroyers *Grayson, Gwin, Meredith* and *Monssen*. It was the 20,000-ton carrier's maiden voyage and her deck cargo of 16 B-25 Billy Mitchell bombers perplexed onlookers. The planes were arranged to give the impression they were being ferried to a base in the Pacific, but flight tests that February on shortened runways proved that the fast, new, long-range twin-engine bombers could successfully take off on the length of a carrier deck. Joining officers and men of the US Navy on board were the nearly 100 Army Air Corp personnel who would service the aircraft and the 80 crews who would make the attacks along with the man who would lead them off the *Hornet*, Lt. Colonel James H. "Jimmy" Doolittle.

On April 13, north of Midway Island, *Hornet* rendezvoused with Admiral Halsey's Force that included carrier *Enterprise,* heavy cruisers *Northampton* and *Salt Lake City* and destroyers *Balch, Benham, Ellet* and *Fanning.* Oiler *Cimarron* served the *Hornet* force and oiler *Sabine*, the *Enterprise* group. With the B-25s up top, *Hornet* carried her own search and combat air patrol aircraft below on the hangar deck so *Enterprise* provided those capabilities for both task forces. The huge, combined naval force, Task Force 16, headed due west toward Japan's main island, Honshu. Launch point was planned for 1800 hours on April 18 from 500 miles east of Tokyo. Each B-25 carried four 500-pound bombs, some actually incendiary clusters.

At about 1,000 miles out on April 17, the American ships refueled and began their run toward launch point. At 0300 hours on April 18, *Enterprise* radar picked up two ships ahead and altered course to avoid them. Three-and-a-half hours later, a Dauntless on patrol reported seeing and being seen by a Japanese patrol boat. It was *Nitto Maru No. 23*, part of Japanese Fifth Fleet's defensive picket line set up at 650 miles out. Gunners aboard *Nashville* sank *Nitto Maru* in choppy seas and heavy squalls, but Halsey knew Tokyo was alerted. He had no choice but to launch early. At 0820 hours, Lieutenant Colonel Jimmy Doolittle's plane cleared the bobbing deck of *Hornet* in 50-knot winds. Within an hour, all 15 pilots followed into an overcast sky, keeping their aircraft at just 100 feet above the sea to avoid detection. Halsey and Mitscher retired their forces to the east at 25 knots. Two inbound American planes were sighted by Japanese pilots who mistakenly concluded the aircraft were their own flying boats. Doolittle and the others arrived over their targets between noon and 1300 hours. Ironically, a civil defense exercise in Tokyo had just ended, causing the populace to consider the Americans part of the drill until live bombs began to fall. Anti-aircraft fire was light and although later reports credited Japanese Army units with shooting down some of the attackers, none of the B-25s was lost over Japan.

Doolittle's raiders hit military and industrial targets in Kobe, Kawasaki, Nagoya, Tokyo, Yokohama and Yokosuka. These included aircraft factories, navy yards, power plants, oil tank complexes and steel mills. At Yokosuka Navy Yard, a vessel under conversion to light carrier *Ryuho* was hit along with buildings and repair facilities. The Mitsubishi Company's aircraft factory at Nagoya was bombed, as was Factory No. 1 of the Japan Steel Company. Ninety civilian and military buildings were destroyed, and six schools and an Army hospital were damaged. Fifty civilians died in the raids and 252 were wounded.

The necessary change in the timing of the Doolittle Raid now became a distinct problem for the pilots and crews involved. Instead of flying in daylight toward their destination in China, they faced hours of flight time in darkness and in foul weather. None landed at Chuchow. The only B-25 to make a safe landing arrived on a runway in Vladivostok, Russia, where the aircraft was impounded and the crew interned. Low on fuel, some crews crash-landed on the coast of China while others flew further inland and parachuted into the darkness. One raider died parachuting from his plane, three died of sickness or injuries and four were captured by the Japanese. Of the four, three were executed as war criminals and one died in prison. The pilots and crews that survived owed their lives to local Chinese and to guerilla fighters. To punish them for aiding the Americans, Japanese Army units pillaged and burned whole towns and villages, killing over 250,000 people. The day after the attack on Tokyo, Doolittle was promoted to Brigadier General.

Aftermath

For nearly two months, American outposts in the Pacific had been attacked and overrun as US naval forces suffered continual losses and retreated from the Philippines and the Netherlands East Indies. "Where's our Navy?" had become a recurring question in the early weeks of war. And yet, in February when US carriers finally sailed beyond the Hawaiian Triangle to raid enemy bases in the Marshall Islands, the Gilbert Islands and Wake and Marcus Islands, some observers in Washington thought the long-awaited American offensive operations to be foolhardy. Though Halsey's carrier raids had resulted in only slight damage to Japanese installations and few enemy losses, Japanese bases were no longer immune from attacks. American bombs had finally been dropped on Japanese territory and the raids hit a nerve in Tokyo.

A month following Halsey's raids, a force led by Admiral Brown struck Japanese shipping and bases at Lae and Salamaua in Northeast New Guinea and were the most successful US carrier raids of the war to date. Though raids by aircraft from the Navy's *Enterprise, Lexington* and *Yorktown* had finally struck back at the enemy, it was the Doolittle Raid from the *Hornet* on the morning of April 18, 1942, that stunned the Japanese. It was immediately obvious that although the planes that attacked Japan appeared to be land-based bombers, they were most certainly launched at sea from a carrier. The Japanese Navy blamed the Army for failing to protect the skies over the homeland while the Japanese Army blamed the Navy for allowing the enemy to penetrate home waters. Vice Admiral Nobutake Kondo's Second Fleet, just returned to Yokosuka the previous day, was ordered to sea immediately with Kondo in command of all surface warships in the area, his flag on *Atago*. To support Kondo, Vice Admiral Shiro Takasu's First Fleet and battleships *Fuso, Hyuga, Ise* and *Yamashiro* sortied Hiroshima Bay. Both forces steamed east to attempt to locate and destroy the enemy ships responsible for the raid. Vice Admiral Nagumo learned of the attacks as First Air Fleet passed north of Luzon on its return from the Indian Ocean. He, too, took his force east at top speed to pursue the Americans.

For weeks there had been intense disagreement between and among the admirals of Combined Fleet and of the Naval General Staff about when and where the Japanese Navy might draw the carriers of the US Pacific Fleet into a great and decisive sea battle. Admiral Yamamoto and his Combined Fleet staff favored a plan to send Japan's Fifth Fleet to the western Aleutian Islands in a feint that would lure the US carriers toward the Alaskan chain. In the process, Admiral Nagumo's First Air Fleet would attack and destroy the American carriers, thereby allowing the Japanese to occupy Midway Island and quite possibly force the US Pacific Fleet to give up Pearl Harbor and retreat to the US mainland.

Some senior Japanese admirals thought the Midway plan too much of a gamble, geographically too far east and outside the Japanese Defense Perimeter. They favored a plan to attack Port Moresby, New Guinea, and catch the American carriers between two Japanese carrier forces in the Coral Sea. Actually, it was only days after the Doolittle Raid when the Japanese began moving vessels in preparation for the Port Moresby offensive and within weeks, Japanese warships began gathering in the Inland Sea for the Midway operation. The Doolittle Raid brought the dissenting admirals around; there was now no question that the US carriers had to be destroyed.

When Imperial General Headquarters learned the name of the officer who led the attack on the Japanese cities, they announced to the Japanese public that it was not only a "Do-little" raid but a "Do-nothing" raid. They added that most American planes were shot down or damaged. Commander Mitsuo Fuchida later wrote, however, that it was a "Do-much" raid in that it changed the course of the war at sea in the Pacific.

Some in the United States thought Admiral Halsey's move to the offense foolhardy, that the attacks in February and March caused few Japanese losses and put American carriers and personnel at unnecessary risk. It was true the US carrier raids resulted in relatively light losses for the Japanese, approximately 50 aircraft and a half dozen vessels, none larger than a small transport. The US victories were psychological in nature but there were strategic wins as well.

Halsey's attack on Marcus Island hit a nerve in Tokyo and caused the Japanese to keep Army and Navy air units at home that were previously scheduled for deployment in China and in the Pacific. The success of the attacks by US carrier-based planes at Lae and at Salamaua under Admiral Brown did succeed, as the Americans hoped, in preventing Japanese troops from taking Port Moresby on the south shore of New Guinea.

Halsey and the admirals of Pacific Fleet continued to push the Navy for more warships and more men, and they continued to complain that the Atlantic Fleet was receiving too much in the way of ships, men and materiel. Fortunately, American losses in Halsey's and Brown's raids were light, with 50 US casualties, 21 planes destroyed and no ships lost.

Chapter XII

TO SAVE PORT MORESBY, THE BATTLE OF THE CORAL SEA

Introduction

In an agreement reached in March 1942 between President Roosevelt and Prime Minister Churchill, the United States assumed responsibility for the defense of the entire Pacific Ocean including New Zealand and Australia, while the British undertook defense of the Indian Ocean and the Middle East. Further, the US Military divided its own responsibility in the Pacific Theater at either 159 or 165 degrees east longitude, depending on latitude. East of the line was US territory under Admiral Chester Nimitz, Commander in Chief of the Pacific Ocean Areas, with Vice Admiral Robert L. Ghormley headquartered at New Caledonia commanding an area south of the equator dubbed SOPAC. By this time, MacArthur with SOWESPAC was operating from Melbourne, Australia, and since MacArthur had no ships, the Navy covered the waters of his longitude. This north/south line intersected a generally placid body of water, the Coral Sea, that extends from Australia's Great Barrier Reef in the west to the New Hebrides Islands in the east, from Papua, New Guinea, and the Solomon Islands in the north to New Caledonia in the south.

By early April 1942, Japan's Greater East Asia Co-Prosperity Sphere encompassed much of the Pacific from the International Date Line west. If the Japanese were to monitor Allied movements in the Coral Sea and cut Australia off from US support, it was essential they carry out an operation conceived of as early as 1938 and first set for January 1942, to take over the large Australian military installation on Port Moresby on New Guinea's southeast shore. A base there would give them all Papua and all New Guinea with airfields and deepwater harbors to serve as stepping stones to Australia, the Solomon Islands and later, the New Hebrides, New Caledonia, Samoa, Fiji and New Zealand. Dubbed Operation MO and finally set for early May 1942, the Japanese planned to take Port Moresby and at the same time, satisfy their obsession to draw out American carriers in a final and decisive battle.

The Japanese had used the same naval code since December 1940. An effort to replace it in April 1942 was delayed until May and then again until June. US cryptologists at Pearl Harbor and in Washington began working on the Imperial Navy's JN-25 code in 1940 and by spring 1942, were able to monitor roughly 50 percent of their radio traffic and decipher about 15 percent of that. By mid-April, the Americans deduced that the Japanese were planning an attack for the first week in May and that their target was most probably Port Moresby. Reconnaissance aircraft and Australian coast watchers reporting Japanese ship movements confirmed much of the information gleaned by the code breakers.

Officers and Operations

Admiral Yamamoto, along with Combined Fleet and the Naval General Staff, realized immediately the significance of the Doolittle Raid on Japanese strategy. Now that US carrier-based planes had reached the mainland, an offensive against American carriers was essential. The plan was threefold. In early May, the Japanese Navy would put Army units ashore in the Solomon Islands on the small island of Tulagi and establish a seaplane base there as well as one in the Louisiade Islands off eastern New Guinea. The Japanese fully expected that the US Navy would respond to the Tulagi invasion with a carrier force. Second, the Japanese planned an invasion of Midway Island for June, coupled with a feint in Alaska's Aleutian Islands that together would surely force out the American carriers in the event Operation MO did not. In a third operation, the Japanese planned an invasion of British Fiji and French New Caledonia and thereby circle the Coral Sea with bases and complete the extension of their hegemony in the South Pacific.

Overall command of Operation MO went to Vice Admiral Shigeyoshi Inouye of Fourth Fleet based at Truk in the Caroline Islands. Under Inouye, Rear Admiral Sadamichi Kajioka commanded the Port Moresby Invasion Group whose mission was to escort and protect a group transport force under Rear Admiral Koso Abe. Rear Admiral Aritomo Goto was charged with three distinct missions. His Covering Group was to provide air cover and support for Rear Admiral Kiyohide Shima's Tulagi Invasion Group. Next Goto's force would form one of the pincers intended to destroy any US carriers responding to the Tulagi operation and third, Goto would provide air support to the Port Moresby invasion.

Vice Admiral Takeo Takagi, successful at the Battle of the Java Sea during the Netherlands East Indies Campaign, commanded Carrier Striking Force that included the 5th Carrier Division under Rear Admiral Chuichi Hara. The Carrier Striking Force would cover the Tulagi Invasion and form the main arm of the pincer movement against the Americans and later raid Allied bases across northern Australia. Rear Admiral Kuninori Marumo would lead a small Support Group at Tulagi and then establish a seaplane base in the Louisiade Archipelago southeast of New Guinea.

At Pearl Harbor, Admiral Chester Nimitz responded to the suspected Japanese buildup by dispatching two US carrier forces to the Coral Sea, one led by Rear Admiral Frank Jack Fletcher, the other by Rear Admiral Aubrey Wray Fitch. Nimitz also called on a small naval force under Australian Admiral John Gregory Crace. Fletcher, a 1906 graduate of Annapolis, was also a graduate of both the Naval and Army War Colleges. He received the Congressional Medal of Honor during the Battle of Vera Cruz in 1914 and saw action during World War I. Between wars, his experience was on battleships and cruisers. In late December 1941, he led the aborted mission to reinforce Wake Island and in February 1942, planes from Fletcher's task force raided the Gilbert Islands. In March, he was second in command when US carrier planes hit Japanese bases on New Guinea at Lae and Salamaua, and in April, he was designated Commander Cruisers, Pacific Fleet.

Fitch, also a 1906 graduate of Annapolis, was a gunnery officer aboard the battleship *Wyoming* in World War I and later executive officer on the *Nevada*. By 1930, Fitch had earned his aviator's wings at Pensacola Naval Air Station and served on a seaplane tender and on carrier *Langley*. In 1936, he skippered *Lexington* and then spent two years at the Naval War College. By early April 1942, he was considered the most experienced carrier flag officer in the Navy and was back on *Lexington* as Rear Admiral, replacing Rear Admiral Wilson Brown.

Crace was 15 years old when he joined the British Navy in 1902. He served during World War I and in early 1942, after 40 years of service, he went as a Rear Admiral to Australia in command of the Australian Squadron and the Allied South Pacific Joint Command, ANZAC, or what came to be called MacArthur's Navy. Crace enjoyed a reputation as a fine seaman and an excellent tactician.

Commander Joseph J. Rochefort Jr. set up the Navy's Combat Intelligence Unit in a cellar-type establishment at Pearl Harbor in spring 1941. He enlisted in the Navy during World War I, earned a university degree and studied for three years in Japan. He alternated sea duty with intelligence work and helped set up the Navy's first code breaking center in the 1920s. In the 1930s, he amused himself by breaking the US State Department code. Rochefort, fluent in Japanese, helped crack Japan's JN-25 code but none of this helped alert the Americans to the Pearl Harbor attack. The Japanese had silenced their radio traffic and changed the key to their code. Along with Intelligence Headquarters in Washington, Rochefort's unit quickly regrouped to gather, analyze and puzzle together information on Japanese troop and ship movements, information that would alter the course of the war in the Pacific.

Isolating Port Moresby

By the end of April 1942, Japanese military units were well entrenched in the islands north and east of New Guinea. Kure Special Naval Landing Force troops from Rabaul landed on and secured Buka Island and the town of Kieta on Bougainville in the western Solomons in the last days of March. SNLF troops from Ambon invaded Dutch areas in western New Guinea, taking the fine harbor at Hollandia on April 20. Maizuru SNLF units from

Kavieng on New Ireland hit Hermit Island in the Admiralties on April 7 and the following day, the Japanese extended their control of New Britain Island by taking Talasea west of Rabaul. Australian and Dutch forces at these settlements offered little or no resistance. By late April, Japanese construction units were building airfields and improving harbors in these areas.

While the Japanese secured land and naval bases, Vice Admiral Inouye, his flag on light cruiser *Kashima,* transferred Fourth Fleet HQ at Truk Lagoon south to Rabaul to be close to the upcoming Operation MO. Japanese naval forces gathered at Truk and at Rabaul for their advance on Tulagi and on Port Moresby. The 5th Carrier Division under Rear Admiral Hara arrived at Truk on April 29 with fleet carriers *Shokaku* and *Zuikaku* to provide the nucleus for Vice Admiral Takagi's Carrier Striking Force. Takagi's ships also included heavy cruiser *Haguro* and his flagship heavy cruiser *Myoko,* destroyers *Akebono, Ariake, Shigure, Shiratsuyu* and *Ushio* and oiler *Toho Maru.* The entire force sortied Truk on May 1 for Rabaul.

On April 30, the Covering Group under Rear Admiral Goto left Truk. It included light carrier *Shoho,* her escort destroyer *Sazanami* and four heavy cruisers: *Kako, Kinugasa, Furutaka* and Goto's flagship *Aoba.* Under Goto, Rear Admiral Shima led the Tulagi Invasion Group that sortied Rabaul's Simpson Harbor on April 29. It included two destroyers, *Kikuzuki* and *Yuzuki;* two minelayers, *Koei Maru* and Shima's flagship *Okinoshima,* two subchasers, transport *Azumasan Maru* and five minesweepers, some of them converted for use as troop transports.

Also reporting to Goto, Rear Admiral Kajioka led the Port Moresby Invasion Group that sortied Rabaul on May 3. It included destroyers *Asanagi, Mochizuki, Mutsuki, Oite, Uzuki* and *Yayoi,* and Kajioka's flagship, light cruiser *Yubari.* Under Kajioka, Rear Admiral Koso Abe, his flag on minelayer *Tsugaru,* commanded the transport unit made up of five Navy transports carrying Special Naval Landing Force troops and six Army transports carrying men of the South Seas Detachment. The armada also included five minesweepers, two oilers and a repair ship. A Support Group commanded by Rear Admiral Marumo also left Rabaul in late April and was made up of light cruisers *Tatsuta* and flagship *Tenryu,* seaplane carrier *Kamikawa Maru* and three gunboats.

The Japanese brought a total force of 27 surface warships to Operation

MO. Their heavy cruisers were armed with 8-inch guns, their light cruisers with 5.5-inch guns and destroyers with 5-inch guns. All were equipped with reliable Long Lance torpedoes. Two of their three carriers, *Shokaku* and *Zuikaku,* were the newest in the Japanese Navy, completed in 1941, and together carried 146 aircraft, 125 of them fighters and bombers. Light carrier *Shoho* had 12 fighters and nine bombers aboard. Japan could call on an additional 90 fighters and bombers of the 25th Air Flotilla land based on Truk. Also available were 56 fighters, bombers and scouting aircraft at Rabaul, six fighters at Lae on New Guinea and nine floatplanes based in the Shortland Islands, six of which would be assigned to the new base at Tulagi.

Into the Coral Sea

To meet the Japanese and prevent their taking Port Moresby, Admiral Nimitz ordered *Lexington* from Pearl Harbor and *Yorktown* from south of Samoa to the Coral Sea. The carriers would serve as the centerpiece of Task Force 17, 23 surface warships under Rear Admiral Fletcher. Fletcher was not the Navy's first choice for the job. On April 25, Nimitz met in San Francisco with Admiral Ernest King, Commander in Chief of the US Fleet. King questioned Fletcher's ability to lead the operation and Nimitz, too, was unsure but the man he wanted for the job, Vice Admiral William F. Halsey, was unavailable. Halsey was on his way back to Pearl Harbor with *Enterprise* and *Hornet* from the Doolittle Raid and could not refuel, resupply and take his ships from Hawaii to the Coral Sea by May 1. So, Fletcher it was.

Task Force 17 was divided into task groups. Task Group 17.5 included *Lexington* with escort destroyers *Anderson* and *Morris* along with *Yorktown* and destroyers *Hammann* and *Russell.* Task Group 17.2, led by Rear Admiral Thomas Kinkaid, included heavy cruisers *Astoria, Chester, Minneapolis, New Orleans, Portland* and destroyers *Aylwin, Dewey, Farragut, Monaghan* and *Phelps.* The heavy cruisers in Kinkaid's Task Group would augment Fletcher's firepower. Task Group 17.3, led by Rear Admiral Crace, RAN, included heavy cruisers USS *Chicago* and flagship HMAS *Australia* and light cruiser HMAS *Hobart.* The Australian and US cruisers were supported by destroyers USS *Perkins* and USS *Walke.* Task Group 17.6 was the fleet supply train commanded by Captain John Phillips and included destroyers *Sims* and

Worden and fleet oilers *Neosho* and *Tippecanoe*. Task Group 17.9 under Commander George DeBaun contained a single seaplane tender, USS *Tangier*, with 10 PBY Catalinas to provide reconnaissance east of the Allied line of demarcation in SOPAC territory.

Together, *Lexington* and *Yorktown* carried 141 fighter and bomber aircraft. At five airfields in northern Queensland, General MacArthur's US Army air units and Royal Amsterdam Air Force units had nearly 500 planes, about 300 short-range fighters, 150 older bombers and 48 long-range B-17 heavy bombers. Most US planes were equipped with homing devices that allowed them to find their carriers or their airfields regardless of weather or visibility within a range of 200 miles. The Allies had radar that alerted ships to incoming planes but did not identify their nationality. Weather, good or bad, would favor either the Japanese or the Allies at various times in the upcoming engagement. The greatest advantage to either side was the gathering of intelligence data and here, despite their difficulty in getting information dispersed in a timely manner, the Americans held superiority.

The Japanese Hit Tulagi—the Allies Respond

By 1942, the island of Tulagi had served as the capital of the Solomon Islands for 45 years, since shortly after they were proclaimed a Protectorate by the British in the late 19th century. It was not Tulagi's size, at three miles by one mile, that brought the honor but her central location in the Solomons and her deepwater harbor. When Admiral Shima's Tulagi Invasion Group put Special Naval Landing Force troops and a construction battalion ashore there on May 3, there was no opposition. Within a day, the Japanese began building a seaplane base and installing machine gun emplacements around the harbor. Australian defenders and civilian personnel had evacuated two days earlier. The Covering Group under Rear Admiral Goto remained west of Tulagi near New Georgia Island only until the assault troops were safely debarked, then sortied further west. Rear Admiral Marumo's Support Group turned for the Louisiade Archipelago to establish a seaplane base there at Deboyne Island. On the evening of May 3, Vice Admiral Takagi's Carrier Striking Force remained north of the Bismarck Archipelago with plans to deliver nine Zero fighters to Rabaul, while Rear Admiral Kajioka's Port

Moresby Invasion Group was beginning its sortie south from Rabaul. The Imperial Navy's Operation MO was well underway on all fronts with only the Carrier Striking Force somewhat behind schedule.

Meanwhile, Allied naval forces under Fletcher aboard *Yorktown* and Fitch aboard *Lexington* made their rendezvous in the Coral Sea south of Guadalcanal on May 1 at a point about 250 miles south of Tulagi. Fletcher had intelligence reports of Japanese ship movements to the north and immediately ordered refueling in preparation for the carrier battle thought to be imminent. *Yorktown* and her destroyers fueled from oiler *Neosho*. *Lexington* was to fuel from *Tippecanoe*; however, *Chicago* and *Perkins* had arrived from Australia and were fueling in advance of the *Lexington* group. Fitch estimated his ships would not be ready until noon on May 4.

On the evening of May 2, Fletcher sortied the 100-square-mile area where the Allied forces rendezvoused and headed north and west to look for Japanese carriers. He left orders for Fitch to rejoin him on May 5 at 15 degrees south latitude and 157 degrees east longitude. Admiral Crace was to do the same. Fletcher aboard *Yorktown* moved deeper into the Coral Sea with heavy cruisers *Astoria*, *Chester* and *Portland*, destroyers *Aylwin*, *Farragut*, *Hammann*, *Russell* and *Sims* and fleet oiler *Neosho*. If by chance Fletcher's planes found the Japanese ships, he would be unable to alert Fitch and Crace since the Task Force was under orders to maintain radio silence between groups. But on the night of May 3, Fletcher learned of the Japanese landing on Tulagi from Allied intelligence. He released *Neosho* and *Russell* and sped his ships to a point 100 miles south of Guadalcanal for an air strike on Tulagi the next morning. Dark, overcast skies with rain and high winds reaching north of Guadalcanal gave Fletcher's ships good cover from Japanese search planes.

At dawn on May 4, *Yorktown* began launching aircraft: a squadron of Devastator torpedo bombers, Torpedo Five led by Lt. Commander Joe Taylor; two squadrons of Dauntless dive bombers, Scouting Five, led by Lt. Commander William Burch Jr.; and Bombing Five led by Lt. Wallace Short. Captain Elliott Buckmaster had 20 Wildcats on board that on Fletcher's orders were to be used for Combat Air Patrol only. Six were launched over *Yorktown*. Burch's Scouting Five arrived over the western tip of Guadalcanal at 0800 hours and continued 20 miles further north toward Florida Island. The overcast and rain squalls gave way to clear skies and within minutes, the

Navy pilots saw little Tulagi ahead. Ships of Rear Admiral Shima's Tulagi Invasion Group were in the harbor or patrolling nearby: destroyers *Kikuzuki* and *Yuzuki,* and minelayers *Okinoshima* and *Koei Maru.* Smaller craft and floatplanes were at their moorings. Burch's planes dove from 19,000 feet to 2,500 feet, each pulling up to release a 1,000-pound bomb. Taylor's Devastators followed within minutes and peeled off into shallow dives, some as low as 50 feet above the sea, to release their torpedoes from as close as 500 yards. Japanese anti-aircraft fire was heavy but ineffective. As Burch and Taylor reformed their planes for return to *Yorktown,* Lt. Short led his Dauntless bombers over the harbor in three groups of five each, all armed with 1,000-pound bombs.

All US crews in this first strike on Tulagi returned safely to *Yorktown* and aircraft were quickly inspected for damage, refueled and rearmed. The Americans sank three minesweepers, along with destroyer *Kikuzuki* that beached on a nearby island and sank with the next tide. *Okinoshima* sustained light damage. Within an hour, 14 planes of Bombing Five, 13 of Scouting Five and 11 of Torpedo Five were back in the air and armed with either bombs, torpedoes or belts of .30-caliber machine gun ammunition. Targets of opportunity on this run included a few gunboats and a transport fleeing west. Two float plans rose to meet the Americans. One was shot down. One bomber pilot from Torpedo Five separated from his squadron and failed to return to the carrier. An attempt to rescue him was unsuccessful. Returning pilots blamed missed targets on bomb sights and windscreens that fogged as they descended from cool to warmer air and several reported the need for fighter escorts.

In the early afternoon of May 4, Fletcher agreed to launch four Wildcats with orders to destroy any remaining Japanese floatplanes in Tulagi harbor. In a brief air battle, the fighters took down three of them. Near Savo Island north of Guadalcanal and west of Tulagi, the Wildcats strafed destroyer *Yuzuki,* killing her Captain and nine sailors and wounding 20. Two Wildcats returned to *Yorktown,* two pilots ditched over the south coast of Guadalcanal and were picked up by destroyer *Hammann* that night in high seas. Fletcher ordered a third raid, this one on Japanese vessels heading west. He sent 21 Dauntlesses that attacked several small craft and some landing barges near Florida Island. Anti-aircraft fire was minimal, and all planes returned.

Admiral Nimitz referred to the American strikes on Tulagi as target practice, a major expenditure of ammunition that resulted in minimal losses to the Japanese and that failed to prevent the establishment of a seaplane base in a critical location. The attacks did, however, alert the Japanese to US carriers in the Coral Sea. Now it remained for Fletcher and Takagi to find each other. Both spent the days and nights of May 5 and 6 doing just that.

In Search of the Enemy

After refueling the ships of his Carrier Striking Force near the island of Bougainville, Takagi rounded San Cristobal Island and sailed into the Coral Sea, too late to prevent the attack on Tulagi. Fletcher, meanwhile, moved south for his rendezvous with Fitch and Crace and more refueling. Kajioka's Port Moresby Invasion Group and Marumo's Support Group made for the Louisiade Archipelago. Goto's Covering Group was refueling south of Bougainville. Each side knew the enemy was closing in but suffered the same liability, delay in communication.

Takagi, like the Allies, received intelligence information through channels. Aircraft of the 25th Air Flotilla that were part of the Eleventh Air Fleet performed reconnaissance missions from Rabaul. Their sightings were passed to Eleventh Air Fleet Headquarters and forwarded to Inouye's Fourth Fleet Headquarters, also on Rabaul. From Fourth Fleet, information was forwarded to Tulagi and Hara aboard ship, often several hours later. Communication among the Allies was also convoluted. General MacArthur's US Army Air Corps planes and other aircraft flying from Australia and from Port Moresby performed reconnaissance over the Coral Sea west of 159 degrees east longitude in SOWESPAC territory. Their intelligence together with that provided by coast watchers was sent to Brisbane, Australia, from there to Pearl Harbor for interpretation and finally from Pearl Harbor to US Navy ships at sea.

On the morning of May 5, after the forces of Fletcher, Fitch and Crace made their planned rendezvous and Task Force 17 began refueling, a Wildcat flying Combat Air Patrol over *Yorktown* shot down a Kawanishi Mavis four-engine flying boat from the 25th Air Flotilla. Fletcher knew he had been sighted and his position reported. But it was the evening of May 6 before Takagi learned of the missing plane and assumed it was lost to an

American carrier plane. Throughout May 5 and 6, Japanese land-based bombers from Rabaul softened up Port Moresby, while carrier planes from *Shokaku* and *Zuikaku* continued their search missions. Twenty-four hours after the first Mavis incident, *Yorktown* and *Lexington* crews spotted a second flying boat. Fletcher had no doubt the composition of his Task Force and its position 400 miles south of Tulagi were reported. He finished refueling, released oiler *Neosho* and destroyer *Sims* to the south and ordered a heading correction for his ships to the northwest, certain the Japanese would pass through the Louisiades and make Port Moresby in a day or two.

About the time Fletcher's force was sighted on the morning of May 6, four US Army B-17 Flying Fortress heavy bombers from Port Moresby sighted Goto's Covering Group south of Bougainville and attempted to bomb light carrier *Shoho* without success. At midday, Goto was spotted again by Allied planes that also found the Port Moresby Invasion Group 500 miles northwest of Fletcher's position. It was the morning of May 7, however, before Fletcher received this information. His primary mission was to stop the Japanese transports on their approach to Port Moresby while having no idea of the Japanese plan to envelop his carriers.

Scratch One Flat Top—the *Shoho*

Scout planes began to be launched by both the Japanese and the Americans at first light on May 7. Nakajima Kates from *Shokaku* and from *Zuikaku* searched for Fletcher's Task Force while Douglas Dauntlesses from *Yorktown* looked for the Port Moresby Invasion Force and for Takagi's Carrier Striking Force. Fletcher was 115 miles due south of Rossel Island, easternmost of the Louisiades. He had just released Crace's ships toward Port Moresby to intercept the Japanese transports and transferred destroyer *Farragut* to Crace at this point. Takagi, after sailing his force north during the night of May 6 and early morning hours of May 7, was again heading south and was less than 200 miles northeast of Fletcher. The front of bad weather that rolled across the northern reaches of the Coral Sea days earlier, and that gave the Americans an edge as they hit Tulagi Harbor, continued to play a part in each Navy's ability to find and attack the other's forces.

At about 0730 hours on May 7, a Japanese scout plane crew erroneously identified a lone aircraft carrier and a cruiser at 16 degrees south latitude and

158 degrees east longitude. Actually, these ships were oiler *Neosho* and her escort destroyer *Sims* on station at their coordinates for a future refueling rendezvous with Task Force 17. They were 200 miles south of Takagi's Carrier Striking Force under clear skies. Acting on the scouting report without question, Takagi waited to close the distance, after which Rear Admiral Hara began launching 25 Kate level bombers and 36 Val dive bombers from *Shokaku* and *Zuikaku*. Each plane carried a 500-pound bomb. At 0900, one Japanese plane arrived over *Neosho* and *Sims* and dropped a single bomb that fell far from either ship. Within half an hour, 15 Kates found the same targets and dropped bombs from high altitude, scoring no hits. Within an hour, the remaining Kates arrived and concentrated their bombs on *Sims* that maneuvered to avoid them. Just before noon, the Vals showed up and turned over into their dives to attack in three waves. *Sims* came alongside *Neosho's* port side, firing 20-millimeter anti-aircraft guns in an attempt to protect the oiler but her sailors managed to put only one of Hara's planes into the sea. Three 500-pound bombs struck destroyer *Sims* in rapid succession, breaking her in two to sink within minutes with all but 15 of her 200-man crew. *Neosho* saw eight near misses and took seven direct hits. Although her captain ordered preparations to abandon ship and stand by, many sailors began launching rafts and whaleboats prematurely. Some were taken back aboard and discipline restored while others drifted away from the burning oiler.

Meanwhile, from *Yorktown*, 10 dive bombers fanned out to search for the Japanese. Crew of one of those planes made its own misidentification of vessels that morning, due to a coding error. It reported sighting two carriers and four heavy cruisers in the northern Louisiades. These ships were those of Marumo's Support Group, light cruisers *Tatsuta* and *Tenryu,* seaplane carrier *Kamikawa Maru* and some gunboats.

Another American flying a different search sector reported sighting two Japanese cruisers. Still another off *Yorktown* went out and turned back due to bad weather and missed finding Takagi's Carrier Striking Force. Based on the first report and believing the bomber crew had found the Japanese carriers, Fletcher ordered the launch of 93 planes, Dauntlesses, Devastators and Wildcats, and kept more than 50 planes back.

Lexington began launching at 0930 hours and *Yorktown* half an hour later. Not until all planes were launched did Fitch and Captain Sherman learn of the coding error. Believing there had to be some targets out there, Fitch opted to continue the mission.

Three Dauntlesses off *Lexington* led by Air Group Commander William Ault arrived over the Louisiades at 15,000 feet shortly after 1100 followed by 10 more of Bombing Two led by Lt. Commander Weldon Hamilton, who sighted a force of Japanese ships 25 miles out. These were the 11,000-ton light carrier *Shoho,* her destroyer escort *Sazanami* and four heavy cruisers, not Takagi's Carrier Striking Force but Goto's Covering Group. Ault and his wing men were first to dive on *Shoho,* as a few Zeros rose to break up the attack without success. A near miss by one of the American 500-pound bombs hit close enough to blow five planes off *Shoho's* deck. Hamilton's Dauntlesses showed up, nosed over and headed for the light carrier, followed by a squadron of Devastators that dropped their Mark 13 torpedoes off *Shoho's* starboard.

Shoho's skipper, Captain Ishinosuke Izawa, ran her into the wind to launch three more Zeros and then turned her sharply starboard to elude the torpedoes. Other Japanese ships put distance between themselves to increase maneuverability. At 1120 hours, two 1,000-pound bombs struck *Shoho's* flight deck, penetrated and exploded below in the aft hangar deck. Seconds later, one or more torpedoes struck her astern and starboard. Fires burned out of control and she lost steering, then power. Planes from *Yorktown* continued the attack, scoring 13 more bomb hits and five more torpedo hits.

Izawa gave the abandon ship order shortly after 1130 and within minutes, *Shoho* went down in the first attack by US carrier-based planes on a Japanese carrier underway. This was also the first time in the Pacific War that Dauntless dive bombers and Devastator torpedo bombers executed a coordinated attack. In *Lexington's* radio room, the voice of Scouting Two's skipper, Lt. Commander Robert Dixon, broke through heavy static to announce the victory, "Scratch one flat top! Dixon to carrier. Scratch one flat top!" Of *Shoho's* complement of 736 officers and men, 204 were rescued by the crew of *Sazanami.* All 21 aircraft aboard *Shoho* were lost. The Americans lost three bombers, with one crew never found.

All the morning of May 7, Australian Rear Admiral Crace led Task Group 17.3 toward Jomard Pass in the Louisiade Archipelago, his mission to hold back Kajioka's seven warships and 11 transports headed for Port

Moresby. Crace's ships were zigzagging along in enemy territory with no air cover, in weather that was generally clear with some high clouds. Just after 0800 hours, lookouts aboard heavy cruiser *Chicago* spotted a Japanese flying boat following just out of range of their anti-aircraft guns. Later that morning, Crace's ships were twice flown over by US Army bombers from Australia. Later, at 1400 hours, Crace was 150 miles south of the Jomard when a squadron of single-engine Japanese land-based aircraft flew over and continued away in formation. Soon Crace picked up a group of planes on radar at about 70 miles out and maneuvered into defensive formation. These were twin-engine Betty bombers, 12 of them, armed with torpedoes. The Japanese dropped into shallow dives over the Allies and concentrated their hits on the cruisers, four of them on *Chicago,* three on *Australia* and one on *Hobart.* All missed their mark. Machine gun strafing by the Bettys killed two Allied sailors and wounded 12. Five attackers were brought down by heavy anti-aircraft fire. Within minutes, a squadron of high-level bombers approached at 16,000 feet but again, skillful maneuvering and accurate anti-aircraft fire kept Crace's ships from damage.

Still, the day was not over for Task Group 17.3. Three four-engine bombers appeared overhead at high altitude to drop bombs that narrowly missed destroyer *Farragut.* Men aboard the destroyer identified the planes as B-17s and they were later confirmed to be US Army planes operating from Townsville, Australia. General MacArthur's air commander denied the bombing but later photographs proved otherwise. About midnight on May 7, Crace learned that the Port Moresby Invasion Force had turned back north that morning, so he turned his force south for Australia.

Finally Stopped Short

When Vice Admiral Inouye recalled the Port Moresby Invasion Force from its advance through the Louisiades on May 7, it signaled success for the Allies in that the base remained in Australian hands. For the first time since Pearl Harbor, a Japanese invasion force was ordered by high command to turn away from an objective. But Inouye did not intend this recall to be permanent, just a delay of a day or two until Takagi could deal with the American carriers. Late on the afternoon of May 7 with daylight fading, Takagi had a good idea of Fletcher's location and made the decision to strike. Actually, both the Americans and the Japanese were in a swath of foul weather with Fletcher at 14 degrees south latitude, 156 degrees east longitude, and Takagi 120 miles to the north northeast. At 1650 hours, *Shokaku* and *Zuikaku* began launching planes, 15 Kate torpedo bombers and 12 Val dive bombers, that were to attack the American carriers at sundown. Meanwhile, Fletcher, knowing only the location of *Sazanami* and believing a destroyer wasn't worth the risk of a night launch, decided to wait until morning to once again search for the enemy carriers.

At 1800 hours, the Japanese bombers passed directly over Task Force 17 but failed to find it in poor weather and diminishing light. Only their interception by a squadron of Wildcats flying combat air patrol alerted them to the US carriers below and in the air battle that ensued, the Japanese lost nine bombers and the Americans two fighters. An hour later, the remaining Japanese planes still had not found their own carriers and some of the bombers attempted mistakenly to land on *Yorktown*. Most turned away but one was shot down. Only six of the 27 Japanese bombers launched were able to locate and land safely on their carriers that night.

Task Force 17 radar was able to track the enemy planes and give Fletcher some idea of where to look for Takagi the next morning. At Rabaul, Inouye ordered the warships protecting the Port Moresby Invasion Force to engage the Americans in a night action but rescinded the command in short order and transferred two of Goto's heavy cruisers, *Furutaka* and *Kinugasa,* to Takagi's force. By midnight on May 7, both sides fully expected the following day would bring the decisive carrier battle and both were ready. Fletcher had *Lexington* and *Yorktown* screened by heavy cruisers *Astoria, Chester, Minneapolis, New Orleans* and *Portland,* and seven destroyers, *Aylwin, Anderson, Dewey, Hammann, Monaghan, Morris* and *Russell.* Takagi had *Shokaku* and *Zuikaku* screened by heavy cruisers *Furutaka, Haguro, Kinugasa* and *Myoko,* and six destroyers, *Akebono, Ariake, Shigure, Shiratsuyu, Ushio* and *Yugure.*

The Carrier Battle of the Coral Sea

Early morning May 8, 1942, began with searches for the enemy by both Fletcher and Takagi. Japanese floatplanes and Kate torpedo bombers went out before sunrise to look to the south for the Americans. At 0625 hours, *Lexington* launched 18 Dauntlesses with orders to cover an arc of 360 degrees to 200 miles out. At 0830, *Shokaku* and *Zuikaku* turned into the wind to launch 33 Val dive bombers, 18 Kate torpedo bombers and 18 Zero fighters that would be ready to attack once the American carriers were discovered. Lt. Commander Kuichi Takahashi was in command of the 5th Air Squadron. Within an hour, Kate pilots spotted *Lexington*'s scouts and followed them back to the carrier. By then, Fletcher received a spotting report that gave the size, direction and speed of the Japanese carrier force and its position 175 miles to the northeast. Fletcher's ships were now in clear weather, Takagi's for the most part under cloud cover.

With *Lexington*'s scout planes still out, *Yorktown,* by 0915 launched nine torpedo bombers, 24 dive bombers and eight fighters and Fletcher passed tactical command of the force for the battle to Rear Admiral Fitch. After recovering and servicing her scout planes, *Lexington* turned into the wind to launch a dozen torpedo bombers, 22 dive bombers and nine fighters so that by 1000 hours, 84 US Navy bombers and fighters neared Takagi's carriers while 69 Japanese Navy bombers and fighters followed the Kate scouts toward Task Force 17. Fletcher radioed MacArthur's Headquarters for land-based planes to bomb Takagi's warships but the bombers that did come found only the Port Moresby Invasion Force in retreat and scored no hits. Admiral Inouye did not order Japanese land-based planes of the 25th Air Flotilla at Rabaul and at Lae and Salamaua into the Coral Sea since they were hitting the Australian air base at Port Moresby.

The Dauntlesses of *Yorktown*'s Scouting Five led by Lt. Commander William O. Burch Jr. and Bombing Five under Lt. Wallace C. Short arrived at 17,000 feet over Takagi's force at 1100 hours but to execute a coordinated attack, they waited for the nine slower Devastators of Torpedo Five led by Lt. Commander Joe Taylor. Only *Shokaku* and her escort were visible through a break in the clouds. *Zuikaku* was eight miles to the west under cloud cover. Taylor's planes arrived and dropped into their final approach, while Wildcats flew protective cover above, screening the torpedo bombers from a squadron of Zeros circling the carrier. Anti-aircraft fire was heavy, and the Devastators came in too high and released their torpedoes from too far a distance. None found its target. The Dauntlesses dropped to 2,500 feet to release their 500-pound bombs. One struck *Shokaku*'s starboard bow while another hit her far aft, destroying an engine repair shop and causing heavy casualties. *Shokaku* could land planes but, with her bow engulfed in flames, could not launch. *Yorktown's* Air Group lost four Dauntlesses and two Wildcats while Wildcat pilots claimed they downed a Kate bomber and three Zeros.

Yorktown's planes turned back to their carrier just as *Lexington's* approached; however, only 21 of the 43 *Lexington* planes that launched initially found Takagi's warships. At 1140 hours, four Dauntless dive bombers led by Commander William Ault, 11 Devastator torpedo bombers led by Commander James Brett Jr. and six Wildcats closed on *Shokaku*. One Dauntless scored a single hit on the smoking, damaged carrier and many of *Shokaku's* planes were forced to land on *Zuikaku*. Although fires on *Shokaku* were brought under control, the carrier lost 108 of her crew with 40 wounded. Still, it was not a good showing by the Americans. All their torpedoes had missed their mark and there were only three bomb hits and eight near misses on *Shokaku* by the 28 Dauntlesses that found her that day. Once again, pilots blamed fogging windscreens along with heavy cloud cover.

Shortly before 1100 hours, *Lexington's* radar picked up approaching enemy aircraft 70 miles out. Eight Wildcats on combat air patrol over the carriers were running low on fuel. Nine more were launched. Twenty-three Dauntless dive bombers went up as well to compensate for lack of fighter planes. At about 1120, with the sun behind them, 10 Kate torpedo bombers approached the American carriers now at flank speed and sailing two miles apart. Four Kates singled out *Lexington,* went into shallow dives and dropped to under 200 feet. Two came in from starboard, two from port. Captain Frederick Sherman ordered the 33,000-ton ship to starboard in response to a torpedo off his port bow, but two Kates approached from starboard and dropped torpedoes that hit *Lexington* forward port side and amidship starboard. Still, she maintained her speed. Her escort vessels put up heavy anti-aircraft fire. Gunners on *Minneapolis* took down four Japanese planes while their ship dodged at least two torpedoes. Destroyers *Anderson, Dewey* and *Morris* did their best to keep up with Sherman's maneuvers and protect the carrier. The Dauntlesses shot down four Kates but lost four of their own. A squadron of Vals continued the attack, nosing over from 17,000 to 2,500 feet. A bomb off one of the Vals struck the carrier's main deck port side forward while another hit her large smokestack. Damage control contained the fires, but *Lexington* was listing eight degrees to port, three of her 16 boilers were out and her aircraft deck elevators were damaged. She maintained 25 knots and by noon, her list was corrected and her elevators repaired so that she could launch and recover aircraft.

Two miles southwest of *Lexington,* Kate bombers found *Yorktown* and at 1120 hours released their torpedoes off the carrier's port quarter. Captain Buckmaster increased speed and maneuvered violently to take the carrier out of danger. Cruisers *Astoria, Chester* and *Portland* and destroyers *Aylwin, Hammann* and *Russell* kept the Japanese planes under continuous fire with their 5.5-inch guns and smaller weapons. Within minutes, a squadron of Vals nosed over and screamed down to drop 500- and 800-pound bombs. *Yorktown,* agile and elusive even at 20,000 tons, dodged each of them until at 1127 hours, a single 800-pound bomb smashed through her deck less than 20 feet from her island and penetrated four decks before detonating and killing 40 men and injuring 26. By 1140, the Japanese broke off their attack and *Yorktown* like *Lexington* continued to maintain 25 knots.

Their bombs and torpedoes spent, both Japanese and American planes turned for their carriers after history's first sea battle in which opposing admirals never saw the other's ships. Of 69 planes launched by the Japanese that morning, 40 returned, most landing on the undamaged *Zuikaku.* Those lost included 15 Vals, eight Kates and six Zeros. The Japanese lost an additional 14 aircraft, some Combat Air Patrol Zeros and others damaged aboard *Shokaku.* Based on reports by returning Japanese pilots that both American carriers were sinking and certain to be lost, Takagi ordered Rear Admiral Hara to release *Shokaku* back to Japan for repairs.

Yorktown recovered 35 of 41 aircraft that took part in the attack that day, losing four Dauntlesses and two Wildcats. Of 43 aircraft from *Lexington,* 36 returned, 19 of them to *Yorktown. Lexington* lost two Devastator torpedo bombers and three Wildcat fighters. Together, the two carriers lost an additional 20 aircraft on May 8, predominantly Dauntlesses and Wildcats performing Combat Air Patrol. A significant loss to the crew of *Lexington* was the fall of their Air Group Commander Bill Ault. It was Ault who shepherded *Lexington*'s planes through New Guinea's Owen Stanley Mountains in February in the successful attack on the Japanese at Lae and Salamaua. On May 8, in the dogfight that followed the attack on *Shokaku,* Ault's plane and another Dauntless were hit and Ault's gunner wounded. Both planes remained airworthy but with not enough fuel to return to their carriers or to find land. Both were presumed lost at sea.

End of a Fighting Lady—the *Lexington*

At 1247 hours, a huge internal explosion, thought to be the result of a generator igniting gasoline vapors, rocked *Lexington*. That blast was followed by several others that tore apart the carrier's interior, claiming casualties from the officers and men of the damage control unit. Even so, it appeared at first that both US carriers would survive what came to be called the Battle of the Coral Sea. Soon after landing her planes, however, *Lexington* suffered yet another explosion that all but destroyed her engine rooms, boilers and ventilation system. Fires raged out of control and at 1456 hours, Captain Sherman gave the semaphore signal for help, life rafts were loosened, and flight operations transferred to *Yorktown*. Destroyer *Morris* was first to come alongside to fight fires and over the course of the afternoon, men from *Morris, Anderson* and *Hammann* carried *Lexington*'s wounded to safety in whaleboats and life rafts. Destroyer *Dewey* searched for airmen without success.

By 1630 hours, *Lexington* was dead in the water. More explosions followed and by 1707, Captain Sherman gave the abandon ship order. By 1800 hours, most sailors and Marines had left the carrier without panic for cruisers *Minneapolis, New Orleans* and *Portland* standing by. Sherman was last off after confirming no living man remained aboard and transferred to *Minneapolis* where Fitch's flag now flew. Just before 2000 hours, it fell to destroyer *Phelps* to torpedo the smoldering, listing carrier and send the beloved Lady Lex to the bottom. Of her crew, 2,735 were rescued, and 216 men went down with her along with 36 aircraft on board.

Aftermath

The Japanese did not meet their goals in the Coral Sea and never returned to take Port Moresby. Even their occupation of Tulagi was short lived, their seaplane base there and another on Deboyne Island abandoned before long. They didn't satisfy their desire to draw out and destroy the entire US carrier fleet. Nevertheless, the Battle of the Coral Sea appeared a victory for them, a tactical victory because of the sinking of *Lexington* and damage to *Yorktown*.

It proved a strategic victory for the United States because for the first time in the war, the Japanese Navy was denied a planned target.

Both Japanese and US admirals made major mistakes that first week in May. Based on faulty reconnaissance, both sides committed all their carrier-based planes to targets that were not the other's carrier force. Japanese errors, in retrospect, were more critical. Returning pilots claimed that both American carriers were sinking. If that information was passed on to Vice Admiral Inouye at Rabaul, why didn't he order the Invasion Force back toward Port Moresby? If Takagi was not sure the American carriers were sunk, why did he release *Zuikaku* back to Japan with *Shokaku* and not send her planes against them? These mistakes would haunt the Japanese a month later. Japanese ship losses included light carrier *Shoho* sunk, carrier *Shokaku* heavily damaged and out of service until July, destroyer *Kikuzuki* sunk, several smaller craft destroyed and over 85 war planes and veteran pilots lost. Carrier *Zuikaku* did not return to service until mid-June due to plane and pilot losses. The Japanese downplayed their human losses, bringing wounded sailors home under cover of darkness and forbidding them communication with their families. On May 10, minelayer *Okinoshima* was lost to a US submarine south of Rabaul and the Port Moresby Invasion Group was ordered back to Truk.

In the United States, news of the Battle of the Coral Sea was received amid claims of victory, welcome news after the surrender of Corregidor and the fall of the Philippines that same week. The American public did not learn of the loss of *Lexington* until after the Battle of Midway a month later. Admirals King and Nimitz refused to talk to the press and when the Imperial Japanese News Agency published exaggerated reports of US losses, the American press curtailed its enthusiasm. When the loss of *Lexington* was made known, the news was disheartening to civilians and military personnel alike. She was the Navy's largest and oldest fleet carrier and it was on Lady Lex that most senior carrier pilots of the day had trained. There were 543 US Navy officers and men who died at Coral Sea. The Navy lost or had damaged beyond repair nearly 80 carrier planes and in addition to *Lexington*, destroyer *Sims* and fleet oiler *Neosho* were sunk.

The story of *Neosho* is particularly tragic. After she and *Sims* were attacked the morning of May 7, *Neosho*, listing over 20 degrees, drifted steadily westward as her Captain and crew worked to keep her afloat. Catalinas flying from Noumea looked for survivors and destroyer *Henley* was dispatched but a plotting error by the oiler's navigator early on caused incorrect coordinates to be sent. She was finally spotted on May 11 and *Henley* came alongside to take off the remaining crew for transfer to Brisbane. On May 17 destroyer *Helm* found a raft with four survivors of the 68 who prematurely abandoned *Neosho* when she was attacked 10 days earlier.

Rear Admiral Fletcher took Task Force 17 south after the battle and then east until May 11 when he divided the force in two. *Yorktown* with heavy cruisers *Chester* and *Portland* and destroyers *Aylwin, Dewey, Farragut, Monaghan* and *Phelps* made for port south of Samoa and then home to Pearl Harbor for repairs. Rear Admiral Kinkaid on *Minneapolis* went to Noumea with heavy cruisers *Astoria* and *New Orleans* and destroyers *Anderson, Hammann, Morris* and *Russell.* Lack of a decisive US victory in the Coral Sea affirmed Admiral King's dissatisfaction with Fletcher but Admiral Nimitz, though disappointed, did not move to change Fletcher's command. With the loss of *Lexington,* Rear Admiral Fitch was made director of land-based planes in the South Pacific after recommending to Nimitz the need for such planes to work with naval units.

Admiral Isoroku Yamamoto, too, was less than pleased with the outcome of the Battle of the Coral Sea. It was he who understood the industrial capacity of the United States and it was he who warned that the Imperial Japanese Navy must run wild in the Pacific for six months, forcing the US to sue for peace and allowing Japan to keep much of her gains. Five of those months had passed.

Chapter XIII

MIDWAY: TURNING POINT IN THE PACIFIC

Introduction

With the fall of US stations on Guam and Wake Island, the small atoll of Midway became the most important piece of American real estate in the Pacific after Pearl Harbor. Located at the western edge of the Hawaiian Ridge and just east of the International Date Line, Midway is closer to Tokyo than to San Francisco. It lies 2,000 miles south of Alaska's Aleutian chain and about equidistant from Wake to the southwest and Oahu to the southeast. Early in May 1942, the atoll's importance was further enhanced when the Philippines surrendered and Midway became the most western US Pacific outpost.

A month before, a Japanese plan centered on the invasion of Midway was being hotly debated between admirals of Combined Fleet and the Imperial Navy's General Staff. The Doolittle Raid on April 18 ended some dissention while the invasion of Port Moresby scheduled for early May could have lengthened the timeline for taking Midway by drawing out the US carriers for the one decisive naval battle the Japanese so desired. When that crucial battle never developed in the Coral Sea, however, Japanese planning for Midway continued in earnest.

Even so, some Japanese admirals remained cautious. They were concerned that the plan was designed around a carrier battle when two of Japan's newest fleet carriers, *Shokaku* and *Zuikaku,* were heavily damaged, their aircraft and crews reduced by 50 percent. Light carrier *Shoho* had been lost in the Coral Sea. Unlike preparation for the Pearl Harbor attack that used one-fifth the warplanes and warships planned for Midway, too little time was given to the practice of attack techniques among air and naval crews.

Most worrisome was the continued overconfidence exhibited by certain senior naval officers, by then including Admiral Yamamoto. Some termed it victory fever. After all, Japan's six fleet carriers and their supporting warships had been deployed almost continually since war began and had compiled a nearly flawless combat record. The optimism was based in some way, however, on erroneous reports from returning Japanese carrier pilots after the Battle of the Coral Sea that two US carriers, *Yorktown* and *Saratoga,* had been sunk. If true, this left only two American carriers, *Enterprise* and *Lexington,* in the Pacific. Amidst optimism on one hand and doubt on the other, the plan to take Midway moved forward. Named Operation MI, its thrust was based on bombing and invading the atoll, coupled with attacks in the Aleutian Islands and minor feints at Sydney Harbor and on Madagascar. On April 23, carriers *Akagi, Hiryu* and *Soryu*, after an absence of almost four months, entered the anchorage at Hashirajima in Japan's Inland Sea. There they joined *Kaga,* the fleet carrier left back for maintenance at the time of the Indian Ocean campaign, along with a good portion of the impressive body of warships assigned to the Midway operation. It included more vessels than most Japanese sailors had ever seen or imagined existed.

Officers and Operations

Imperial Headquarters' official order for Operation MI came down on May 5, 1942, and read, "Commander in Chief Combined Fleet will, in cooperation with the Army, invade and occupy strategic points in the western Aleutians and Midway Island." For the first time in the war, Commander in Chief Admiral Yamamoto would go to sea in battle and for the first time, as many as six of the Imperial Japanese Navy's nine Fleet Admirals would serve under him in a single operation.

Vice Admiral Chuichi Nagumo had served as Commander in Chief of First Air Fleet since April 1941. He was not Yamamoto's choice but Yamamoto was overruled by the Navy's General Staff. Nagumo led what the Imperial Japanese Navy called the Kido Butai, its main carrier group, in the attack on Pearl Harbor, the bombing of Darwin and Operation C in the Indian Ocean, and now he would lead at Midway. Nagumo was criticized for failing to launch a third attack on Pearl Harbor, a move that might have left the US Pacific base useless and changed the course of the war.

Vice Admiral Shiro Takasu was Commander in Chief, First Fleet, and for him too, it was to be the first time in the war that he sailed into battle, his flag on the 30,000-ton battleship *Hyuga*.

A transport group reporting to Vice Admiral Nobutake Kondo's Midway Invasion Force was let by Rear Admiral Raizo Tanaka, his flag on light cruiser *Jintsu*. At Midway, he would command a Close Cover destroyer flotilla of transports and later run what came to be known as the Tokyo Express in the battle for Guadalcanal. Another Close Cover Support Group under Kondo was led by Vice Admiral Takeo Kurita aboard heavy cruiser *Kumano*.

Vice Admiral Boshiro Hosogaya, who in 1939 was charged with all vessels in Chinese waters, now would lead Northern Force from flagship *Nachi* toward sites in the Aleutian Islands.

An Elaborate Plan

Vice Admiral Nagumo's First Carrier Striking Force reached Hashirajima Harbor in Hiroshima Bay on April 23 and joined two groups of warships moored there. Nagumo's force dropped anchor north of super-battleship *Yamato*, the new 63,000-ton flagship of Combined Fleet's Admiral Yamamoto. The 18 vessels under Yamamoto's direct command were dubbed Main Force and would sortie Hashirajima for Midway at the same time the ships of the Aleutian Guard Force sailed north. Also in harbor was First Fleet, 20 vessels under Vice Admiral Shiro Takasu that would serve as Aleutian Guard Force.

South of Yamamoto's and Takasu's forces were some ships of Vice Admiral Nobutake Kondo's Midway Invasion Force, the largest number of vessels under a single command in the operation. From heavy cruiser *Atago,* Kondo would personally lead the 21 vessels making up the Main Body of the force. Other ships of the Midway Invasion Force were anchored off Saipan in the Mariana Islands, 1,500 miles to the south. Designated Transport Group, Rear Admiral Raizo Tanaka aboard light cruiser *Jintsu* led 36 ships, including a dozen transports carrying assault troops.

South of Tanaka's force off the former American outpost of Guam were ships of the Midway Invasion Force Support Group led by Vice Admiral Takeo Kurita aboard heavy cruiser *Kumano.* Kurita's force would escort Tanaka's Transport Group on a parallel course to Midway.

Off the northern tip of Japan's Honshu Island, Vice Admiral Boshiro Hosogaya, now Commander in Chief of Fifth Fleet, was in overall command of Northern or Aleutian Force. Staging in Ominato Harbor, it included four naval groups totaling 34 vessels, its mission to assault and secure objectives in the Aleutian Islands and draw American forces to the north. Hosogaya's own Main Force included eight vessels, his flag on heavy cruiser *Nachi.*

Air protection for Northern Force included eight ships of the Second Carrier Striking Force under Rear Admiral Kakuji Kakuta. At its center was the newly revamped 4th Carrier Division that included Kakuta's flagship, light carrier *Ryujo,* and Combined Fleet's newest fleet carrier, the 19,000-ton *Junyo.* Remaining units of Northern Force were built around two amphibious forces, Attu Invasion Force led by Rear Admiral Sentaro Omori aboard light cruiser *Abukuma* and Kiska Invasion Force commanded by Captain Takeji Ono, his flag on light cruiser *Kiso.*

Late in May 1942, all surface vessels assigned to Operation MI were anchored at either Hashirajima or in the Mariana Islands or at Ominato Harbor. By May 23, a Japanese submarine force had sortied Kwajalein Atoll in the Marshall Islands. Vice Admiral Teruhisa Komatsu, the Commander in Chief of Sixth Fleet and Combined Fleet's submarine force, had released 20 fleet submarines for Operation MI reconnaissance and special missions. From light cruiser *Katori,* Komatsu led 10 subs and their tender.

US Navy Regroups

For the Americans, Vice Admiral William F. Halsey, with carriers *Enterprise* and *Hornet,* was ordered back to Pearl Harbor from the Marshall Islands after a long and uneventful search in the Coral Sea for enemy carriers *Shokaku* and *Zuikaku*. He was back at Pearl on May 26 where he received a quick debriefing and, within days, was admitted to the hospital with a severe case of shingles. Now, Admiral Chester Nimitz, with his top carrier commander out of action, asked Halsey to choose his own replacement. Without hesitation, Halsey named Vice Admiral Raymond Ames Spruance. Spruance commanded a cruiser division under Halsey in the first months of the war, part of the task force built around USS *Enterprise* that carried out raids on the Gilberts, the Marshalls and on Wake Island. Spruance was known to be rational and calm, a steadied leader who demanded commands aboard his ship be given clearly and concisely.

A day back in port, carriers *Enterprise* and *Hornet* with the other ships of Task Force 16 were being refueled and resupplied. The damaged *Yorktown* had just limped into Pearl from Tongatabu, her internal strength weakened by an explosion from a single bomb and her watertight integrity reduced by numerous near misses. Estimated time for repairs on *Yorktown* varied, but within 50 hours, with over 1,400 men working long shifts, the carrier the Japanese thought they had sunk at Coral Sea was being fueled and readied for action with her own air group and replacement aircraft. At 0900 hours on May 30, *Yorktown* with Task Force 17 under Rear Admiral Frank Jack Fletcher headed for open water and her planned rendezvous with Task Force 16 on June 2 at Point Luck, 200 miles northeast of Midway. Thanks to clever manipulations by the US code breakers at Pearl Harbor, US Intelligence confirmed Japanese plans to extend their defense perimeter in the Pacific and Nimitz had some idea of Yamamoto's plan for Operation MI. The US Pacific Fleet would not be drawn into the trap envisioned by the Japanese.

With only 26 warships including the carriers to defend Midway, Nimitz called on Rear Admiral Robert A. Theobald to command the Alaskan Sector. On May 27, Theobald, aboard his flagship light cruiser *Nashville,* arrived at Kodiak Island to take command of all US Forces in the Aleutians and head the newly formed Task Force 8. At Pearl Harbor and in Washington, it was assumed the Japanese Navy's Northern Force would attack Dutch Harbor on Unalaska Island and land troops there. They theorized there would be raids and amphibious assaults at Cold Bay on the Alaskan Peninsula and at Umnak Island.

Deception at Sydney

Coupled with operations of Northern Force in the Aleutian Islands, the Japanese planned a second, smaller action to draw US ships away from Midway, this at Australia's Sydney Harbor. It would mimic the midget submarine operation that preceded the carrier-based attack on Pearl Harbor. Although unsuccessful at Pearl Harbor, with all five midget subs beached or sunk, a similar operation at Sydney might just confuse the Americans. Five Japanese I-class fleet submarines arrived off Sydney's Outer Heads on May 31 (May 30 in Hawaii). Four carried two-man midget subs, and a fifth carried a floatplane. Sydney Harbor had no protective submarine nets, but the subs did have to navigate a winding, six-mile channel. Woolloomooloo Pier was lit with floodlights the night of the 31st as civilians and sailors strolled the waterfront. Ferries and water taxis shared the waters with military ships. Heavy cruiser USS *Chicago* and destroyer USS *Perkins*, after maintenance at the Garden Island Naval Station, were ready to rejoin MacArthur's Navy. An American destroyer tender, two Australian corvettes and a Dutch submarine were at anchor.

By 2230 hours and a few miles to the east, fishermen on a trawler spotted one of the midget subs following them up the channel and signaled authorities. Warships were put on alert but the harbor's ferries continued to run and the bright lights illuminating the harbor and boardwalk never dimmed. Just before 2300 hours, lookouts on *Chicago* spotted a sub's conning tower 300 yards starboard and opened fire with 5-inch guns and raked the target with machine gun fire. Most shells overshot the target, ricocheted off the water and some landed in a residential district.

The midget sub dove as *Perkins* got underway but the effectiveness of the destroyer's sonar was hampered by the movement of ferries and pleasure craft. After midnight, lookouts on *Chicago* spotted the wake of a torpedo that struck a dock and caused an explosion that tore out the bottom of an anchored barracks boat, killing Australian sailors bunked aboard. A second torpedo ran up on the beach but did not explode. The next day, two midget submarines and the bodies of their crews were discovered in Sydney Harbor and the USS *Chicago* and USS *Perkins* were ordered out to sea. That week, the Japanese staged a similar deceptive action on the island of Madagascar and a week later, a Japanese I-class fleet submarine was seen operating off Sydney Harbor. In both cases, the US Navy did not take the bait.

More Than a Diversion

Japan's Combined Fleet leaders had little knowledge of the Aleutian Island chain. Their charts and maps were more than 30 years old, their knowledge of harsh weather conditions and low temperatures overlooked. They believed their attacks on the islands of Attu, Kiska, Adak and Unalaska that lay across 1,500 miles at the south end of the Bering Sea would be completed before the onset of winter. But attacks on the Aleutian chain were to serve as more than a diversion from their move on Midway Atoll. A military presence in the Aleutians would provide a site for air bases and prevent long-range bombing raids from the north on the Japanese homeland. Control of the Aleutians would obstruct communication between the United States and the USSR.

On May 26, 1942 (May 25 in Hawaii), the Japanese Navy's Second Carrier Striking Force sortied east from Ominato Harbor on its 3,500-mile journey across the North Pacific. Planes from carriers *Junyo* and *Ryujo,* would strike American installations at Dutch Harbor on Unalaska Island and provide air cover for amphibious landings on the islands of Adak, Attu and Kiska. *Junyo* carried 21 Val dive bombers and 24 Zero fighters, while *Ryujo,* Rear Admiral Kakuta's flagship, could launch 21 Kate bombers and 16 Zeros. Supporting the 4th Carrier Division were heavy cruisers *Maya* and *Takao,* screened by destroyers *Akebono, Sazanami* and *Ushio* and served by oiler *Teiyo Maru.*

Vice Admiral Boshiro Hosogaya followed Kakuta's force from Ominato aboard heavy cruiser *Nachi* and led Northern Force's Main Body for Paramushiro in the Kurile Islands. Escorted by destroyers *Ikazuchi* and *Inazuma,* three cargo vessels and two fleet tankers, the ships would refuel there and head east for the Aleutians on June 2.

On the morning of May 27, the Kiska Invasion Force weighed anchor from Ominato. Captain Takeji Ono on light cruiser *Kiso* led light cruiser *Tama,* auxiliary cruiser *Asaka Maru,* destroyers *Akatsuki, Hibiki,* and *Hokaze,* three minesweepers and two troop transports. Ono was to land assault troops on Kiska, secure the island and put a construction force and supplies ashore.

Transport *Hakusan Maru* carried 550 amphibious assault troops of the Maizuru Special Naval Landing Force. Transport *Kumagawa Maru* carried 700 labor troops with construction supplies and equipment.

Vessels of the Attu Invasion Force took up a parallel course 800 miles south of the Kiska Force. From the bridge of light cruiser *Abukuma*, Rear Admiral Sentaro Omori led destroyers *Hatsuharu*, *Hatsushimo*, *Nenohi*, and *Wakaba*, a minelayer and a single troopship, *Kinugasa Maru*, that carried 1,200 assault troops of the Army's North Sea Detachment. It was to put some troops ashore at Adak and the remainder on Attu at the westernmost tip of the Aleutians. All landings were to begin on the morning of June 5 covered by aircraft from *Junyo* and *Ryujo* with bombardment and additional support from the guns of Hosogaya's Main Body.

From off Kodiak Island south of Alaska's mainland, US Navy Captain Ralph C. Parker was responsible for the patrol of shorelines and defense of installations under construction in the Aleutian chain. Parker's forces included his flagship, gunboat USS *Charleston*, two old four-stack destroyers, *Gilmer* and *Humphreys*, three Coast Guard cutters and several converted fishing trawlers. He had 20 PBY Catalinas based off three tenders for reconnaissance and a single B-17 heavy bomber for search missions.

On May 27, Rear Admiral Robert Theobald, the US Navy's new commander of the Alaska Sector and recently activated Task Force 8, arrived at Kodiak. His flag on light cruiser *Nashville*, his small force included light cruiser *St. Louis* and destroyers *Gridley* and *McCall*. Theobald expected Task Force 8 would be reinforced by heavy cruisers *Indianapolis* and *Louisville*, light cruisers *Honolulu*, destroyers *Brooks*, *Case*, *Dent*, *Kane*, *King*, *Reid*, *Sands*, *Talbot*, and *Waters*, six submarines, three seaplane tenders, two fleet tankers and a few smaller vessels. Most of the cruisers and destroyers on the way to Theobald, however, would not reach the Aleutians in time for the Japanese attacks. US patrol vessels in the Aleutians were used to establish a 500-mile-long defense line south of the Aleutians and west of the Alaskan Peninsula. A second picket line of vessels was on station to northwest. The US Navy had 20 PBY Catalina flying boats and their seaplane tenders stationed at Cold Bay near the western tip of the Alaskan Peninsula, at Sand Point on an island just off the peninsula and at Dutch Harbor on Unalaska Island.

American aircraft based in the Aleutians or on the Alaskan mainland belonged to the US Army. A single airstrip had just been completed at Otter Point on Umnak Island. There were a dozen Curtiss P-40 Warhawk fighters based there and another 21 Warhawks and a squadron of medium bombers stationed at Cold Bay. On Kodiak Island, there was a squadron of Bell P-39 Airacobra fighters, a squadron of P-40 Warhawks and five Boeing B-17 Flying Fortress heavy bombers. At Anchorage on the mainland, the US Army had a squadron of Airacobras, two squadrons of the new Lockheed P-39 twin-fuselage, twin-engine Lightning fighters and two dozen other medium and heavy bombers. All 150 plus US Army aircraft assigned to the Alaskan Sector fell under the command of the Navy's Theobald.

Strikes in the Aleutians

Just after midnight on June 3, Kakuta's Second Carrier Striking Force reached its launch point less than 200 miles south of Unalaska Island. Expecting first light before 0300 hours, officers on carrier *Ryujo* at the head of their column prepared to launch six fighters and 11 level bombers for the first strike at Dutch Harbor. One thousand yards astern, *Junyo* would launch six fighters and a dozen dive bombers. As launch time neared, under overcast skies and heavy fog, there was little hint of daylight. From *Ryujo's* bridge, Rear Admiral Kakuta, with the carrier's skipper, Captain Tadao Kato and the Aviation Officer, Lieutenant Commander Masatake Okumiya, looked east, waiting for some sign of light. By 0235 hours, the fog lifted somewhat. The carriers became visible to each other, turned into the wind and began launching aircraft from a point 180 miles southeast of Dutch Harbor. With cloud cover under 1,000 feet and intermittent layers of overcast and fog, flying in formation was difficult and many Japanese aircraft failed to find their targets.

Through thick clouds and under overcast skies, nine Kates and three Zeros off *Ryujo* approached the north coast of Unalaska Island and the new Ft. Mears military base at Dutch Harbor. It held an Army Air Corps landing field, four oil storage tanks, barracks, a hospital and a radio station. A seaplane tender and several moored PBY Catalinas were in the harbor, no US planes in the air. It was 0400 hours. Kates bombed and destroyed or heavily damaged the radio station, a wing of the hospital, Army barracks and all four storage tanks while Zeros strafed a couple of the Catalinas. A few US Army P-40 Warhawk fighters took to the air and anti-aircraft fire from the ground was heavy but by 0830 hours, the attack was over and the Japanese had lost just a single Zero. *Junyo*'s planes never found their target.

On his return to *Ryujo,* a Kate pilot spotted what appeared to be five US destroyers at Makushin Bay off Unalaska's north coast and reported the sighting. Kakuta ordered all available aircraft launched but since *Ryujo*'s aircraft were not yet recovered and *Junyo*'s were still in the air, the two carriers could launch only 20 more fighters and bombers. Kakuta ordered four Pete open cockpit Mitsubishi float-biplanes launched from his heavy cruisers. Of his 24 planes, only the Petes found Makushin Bay where they were jumped by a pair of Warhawks with two shot down and two damaged. The same weather front that kept *Junyo*'s planes from finding Dutch Harbor now obscured the American destroyers. Running low on fuel, the second wave of Kates and Zeros headed back to their carriers. Second Carrier Striking Force reversed course to the southwest and refueled its escorting destroyers. It was 100 miles from Unalaska.

US Navy picket boats had failed to spot Kakuta's carriers but one Catalina on patrol did make contact. Shortly after learning Kakuta's position, a flight of B-17 heavy bombers and B-26 medium bombers located the Japanese force. No bombs found their targets, but one B-17 Flying Fortress and one B-26 Marauder were lost in the attack.

The next morning, June 4, Kakuta's carrier aircraft were to hit the island of Adak, 400 miles west of Dutch Harbor, in advance of an amphibious assault scheduled the following day. With a prediction of poor weather on Adak and clear skies expected over Unalaska Island, Kakuta decided to hit Dutch Harbor again. *Ryujo* and *Junyo* launched 11 Val dive bombers, six Kate level bombers and 15 Zero fighters in better weather conditions. By 0830 hours, they again hit targets at Dutch Harbor including an aircraft hangar under construction and a moored barracks ship. No Japanese planes were lost in the second raid. The US Navy's Northern Force lost six aircraft while on the ground, and the Army saw more than 40 American casualties.

As Japanese pilots reformed over Unalaska's western cape for their return flight, they spotted the airfield at Otter Point on the small island of Umnak to the west. They were jumped by eight P-40 Warhawks, and in the dogfight,

US aircraft downed two Val bombers and a Zero. Two more Vals were lost as they tried to return to their carriers. Kakuta's Second Carrier Striking Force remained south of Unalaska long enough to land planes and retired to the southwest.

Advance Toward Midway

May 27, 1942, was Japan's Navy Day and the 37th Anniversary of the Battle of Tsushima, Admiral Togo's brilliant one-sided victory against the Russian Fleet. First Air Fleet's primary striking force, now dubbed First Mobile Force, sailed from Hashirajima Bay on Vice Admiral Nagumo's order to sortie as scheduled. *Akagi, Kaga, Hiryu* and *Soryu* moved out slowly past the anchored warships that would follow within days. The carriers were accompanied by battleships *Haruna* and *Kirishima,* heavy cruisers *Chikuma* and *Tone,* light cruiser *Nagara,* and destroyers *Arashi, Hagikaze, Hamakaze, Isokaze, Kazagumo, Maikaze, Makigumo, Nowaki, Tanikaze, Urakaze* and *Yugumo.* Cheering crewmen aboard the ships of Yamamoto's Main Force and the Main Body of Kondo's Midway Invasion Force gathered at deck rails, waving as each ship passed single file toward Bungo Strait and the open Pacific. Aircraft of the Kure Naval Air Corps and Sacki Defense Force patrolled above and ahead of the long column.

After clearing the strait and on a southeasterly heading into the Pacific, the ships took up their positions in formation. Light cruiser *Nagara* continued to lead as carriers *Akagi* and *Kaga* formed a starboard column and *Hiryu* and *Soryu* formed to port. Heavy cruisers *Tone* and *Chikuma* moved ahead of *Akagi* and *Hiryu*, respectively, as battleships *Haruna* and *Kirishima* took up similar positions to the rear of the columns. Destroyers accompanied the columns of moving warships.

Next day, May 28, and 1,500 miles south of Japan's Inland Sea, vessels making up units of the Midway Invasion Force began moving east from the Mariana Islands. Off the island of Saipan, Rear Admiral Raizo Tanaka on light cruiser *Jintsu* led the Invasion Force's Transport Group. A dozen transports carried 5,000 assault troops of the Midway Landing Force. Destroyers *Amatsukaze, Arare, Hatsukaze, Kagero, Kasumi, Kuroshio, Oyashio, Shiranuhi, Tokitsukaze* and *Yukikaze* protected the transports while air support for Tanaka's vessels was provided by ships of the Seaplane Tender Group. Cruiser

Chitose carried 20 floatplanes, 16 float Zero fighters and four Pete reconnaissance aircraft. Tender *Kamikawa Maru* had a dozen aircraft aboard, eight fighters and four reconnaissance type. Destroyer *Hayashio* and a small patrol boat escorted the tenders.

A second group moored off Saipan sortied with Tanaka's ships. Under the command of Captain Sadatomo Miyamoto, four minesweepers, three sub-chasers and a supply vessel took a more southerly approach to Midway, stopping first at Wake Island. Their mission would be canceled before the battle took place.

A third unit of the Midway Invasion Force was anchored 100 miles south of Saipan off the former US possession of Guam. From heavy cruiser *Kumano*, Vice Admiral Takeo Kurita led the Midway Invasion Force's Close Support Group, heavy cruisers *Mikuma, Mogami,* and *Suzuya,* destroyers *Arashio* and *Asashio* and a fleet tanker. Departing the Marianas with Tanaka's Transport Group, Kurita remained 40 miles to the southwest off Tanaka's starboard flank, providing protection and support for the Midway bound transports.

The Main Body of the Midway Invasion Force led by Vice Admiral Nobutake Kondo left Japan's Inland Sea on May 29 and followed the route taken by Nagumo's First Mobile Force from Hashirajima, Kondo's 21 ships continued further south before heading east, taking a more direct approach toward Midway. His flag on heavy cruiser *Atago,* Kondo led battleships *Hiei* and *Kongo,* heavy cruisers *Haguro* and *Myoko,* light cruiser *Yura,* and destroyers *Asagumo, Harusame, Minegumo, Murasame, Natsugumo, Samidare* and *Yudachi.* Light carrier *Zuiho* carried a dozen Zero fighters and a dozen Kate bombers, air cover for the Main Body, and was escorted by destroyer *Mikazuki.* Kondo's ships would be kept fueled and supplied by four tankers and a repair vessel of the Supply Group.

The last Japanese ships to sortie in Operation MI were Combined Fleet's Main Force under Admiral Isoroku Yamamoto aboard battleship *Yamato.* It included battleships *Mutsu* and *Nagato;* a Special Force of seaplane carriers, *Chiyoda* and *Nisshin;* light cruiser *Sendai;* and destroyers *Ayanami, Fubuki, Hatsuyuki, Isonami, Murakumo, Shikinami, Shirayuki* and *Uranami.* In addition, light carrier *Hosho* carried eight bombers to provide air cover in addition to floatplanes carried on the battleships and cruisers. Seaplane carriers *Chiyoda* and *Nisshin* had been converted to submarine tenders for Operation

MI and carried midget submarines. Destroyer *Yukaze* escorted *Hosho* and two fleet tankers of the 1st Supply Unit that would refuel Yamamoto's Main Force as it moved east.

Weighing anchor with Yamamoto's Main Force at Hashirajima were the ships of Vice Admiral Shiro Takasu's Aleutian Guard Force. His flag on battleship *Hyuga*, Takasu led battleships *Fuso, Ise* and *Yamashiro*, light cruisers *Kitakami* and *Oi* and destroyers *Amagiri, Ariake, Asagiri, Kawakaze, Shigure, Shirakumo, Shiratsuyu, Suzukaze, Umikaze, Yamakaze, Yugiri* and *Yugure*. The 2nd Supply Unit, which included two tankers, would keep Takasu's warships fueled. Yamamoto's and Takasu's forces followed a heading set by Nagumo's Carrier Force. After reaching a point more than 2,000 miles to the east of Japan's Inland Sea, Yamamoto's Main Force would continue northeast as Takasu's ships split away to the north to support landing operations in the Aleutians.

Nagumo's ships reached a planned position southeast of the Japanese homeland on May 29 and rendezvoused on schedule with vessels of the Midway Supply Group. They would remain together until June 2 when refueling was complete and destroyer *Akigumo* detached itself from the supply train and joined the carrier force sailing to the northeast. Late afternoon on June 2 (June 1 at Midway), Nagumo's First Mobile Force ran into dense fog that slowed progress and impaired movement for nearly two days. Not only did the foul weather require a reduction in speed that would upset Yamamoto's time schedule, but a course change was planned for the following day. If conditions continued and the force maintained radio silence, there was a good chance ships would be lost when changing course in heavy fog.

Heavy weather persisted as Nagumo neared the International Date Line early the following morning. Searchlights could not be used for signaling the impending course change. Unwilling to break radio silence, Nagumo used medium-frequency radio to signal the heading change. From *Akagi*, the order was given and the 21 ships made the necessary corrections without incident. Later that day, the fog lifted and that night, Nagumo's force reached map coordinates less than 300 miles northwest of Midway.

Elusive American Carriers

Information regarding the location of US naval forces was critical to the success of Operation MI and to drawing out the American carriers. A month had passed since the main carrier battle in the Coral Sea and almost three weeks since the last US carriers were reported there. Japanese planners were confident the American ships were back at Pearl Harbor but Nagumo had no confirmation. The Japanese estimated that if the US carriers were at Pearl Harbor, it would take them two days to respond to initial attacks in the Aleutians and at Midway. With those raids scheduled to commence at Dutch Harbor on June 3 and at Midway on June 4, a response by American naval units from Hawaii would not come until June 5 or more likely June 6. All these dates were east of the International Date Line. Still, Nagumo worried. A new plan, Operation K, was devised to confirm that the American carriers were indeed back in their home port.

Operation K involved an aerial reconnaissance mission over Pearl Harbor employing the Japanese Navy's longest-range aircraft, the 31-ton, four-engine Kawanishi Mavis flying boat. Maximum range of a Mavis was 4,000 miles and Pearl Harbor was 2,100 miles from their base at Wotje in the Marshall Islands. The solution called for two submarines carrying aviation fuel to put in at French Frigate Shoals, a point between Midway and Pearl Harbor. The Mavis flying boats would refuel there, fly on to Pearl Harbor and return to the Marshalls. The subs were to arrive off French Frigate Shoals on May 30 and service the reconnaissance aircraft the morning of May 31.

As the Mavis flying boats readied for takeoff from Wotje in the Marshalls, however, headquarters on Kwajalein received a disturbing report. One sub upon arrival at the rendezvous point radioed that two American ships were anchored in the harbor along with two flying boats. The US was using French Frigate Shoals as a seaplane base. Operation K was postponed for 24 hours. When the US ships did not sortie, Operation K was canceled, a fact unknown to Nagumo who was keeping radio silence.

Meanwhile, submarines that sortied Kwajalein with the light cruiser *Katori* on May 23 had been assigned various missions within the Hawaiian Triangle, the area of the Pacific Ocean east of the International Date Line between Hawaii, Midway and Johnston Island. Submarine *I-168* would patrol Midway Atoll. Submarines *I-169, I-171, I-174* and *I-175* would form a cordon line west of the Hawaiian Islands. Submarines *I-156, I-157, I-158, I-159, I-162, I-165* and *I-166* were to form a second cordon to the northwest between Hawaii and Midway. Unfortunately for the Japanese, the submarines assigned to both cordon lines did not arrive on station until the early morning of June 4. Fortunately for the Americans, Spruance's Task Force sortied Pearl Harbor on May 28 and Fletcher's Task Force 17 followed two days later. They rendezvoused on June 3 at Point Luck, ahead of and well north of the Japanese submarines.

Early that day, US Navy PBY Catalinas on patrol 600 miles west of Midway spotted Rear Admiral Tanaka's Transport Group still two days out. Tanaka's flagship *Jintsu* alerted Yamamoto's *Yamato* they had been discovered. In the first attack in the battle, a flight of B-17 bombers hit Tanaka's ships without success. A group of four PBY Catalinas, each armed with an aerial torpedo, found Tanaka and scored one hit on tanker *Akebono Maru*, causing 24 casualties. The vessel kept its speed and remained in column.

Nagumo was concerned about beginning Operation MI without two of his best commanders, Mitsuo Fuchida and Minoru Genda. Fuchida was *Akagi*'s Air Unit Commander. Six months earlier, he led the first wave on Pearl Harbor. In January, he led air operations in the Bismarck Archipelago and the following month, against British ships in the Indian Ocean. Scheduled to lead the attack on Midway, Commander Fuchida, two days after leaving Hashirajima, was in sick bay on *Akagi* recovering from an emergency appendectomy. He would be replaced by Lt. Joichi Tomonaga. Genda, First Air Fleet's Operation Officer, was in sick bay with a severe case of influenza. An outstanding air tactician, Genda had a major role in planning the attack on Pearl Harbor under Yamamoto and was a continuing source of support to Vice Admiral Nagumo. Early on June 4, he made his way to the bridge, weak and apologetic, to confer with Nagumo. It was then, not knowing the location of the US carriers and unaware his own force had been discovered, Nagumo made the decision to attack.

Air Raid Midway

First Air Fleet carriers *Akagi, Kaga, Hiryu* and *Soryu* adjusted their headings into the wind in calm seas and a slight breeze just after 0400 hours on Thursday, June 4, 1942. They launched 108 carrier aircraft in the first wave against Midway Atoll to begin the most crucial battle of the Pacific War. First in the air were nine Zero fighters from *Akagi* followed by 18 Val dive bombers, each armed with a 500-pound bomb. *Kaga* launched nine Zeros and 18 Vals. Well to *Akagi's* portside, *Hiryu* put nine fighters and 18 Kate level bombers into the air. Her sister ship, *Soryu,* launched the same number and types of aircraft. By 0445 hours, all 108 aircraft were airborne. To protect the Japanese ships from enemy aircraft and submarines, and in the event a second Midway strike was needed, 153 planes were held back: 48 Zeros, 48 Vals and 57 Kates. Lt. Tomonaga in a Kate level bomber led the 108 into a brightening southeastern sky toward the Midway Atoll, 190 miles distant.

Although Tanaka's transports had been spotted the previous day and although the US Navy and the US Army had B-17s, Marauders and Catalinas flying search patterns, the actual position of Nagumo's force was still unknown to the Americans. At Pearl Harbor, Commander Rochefort's cryptologists had deciphered enough of Japan's Naval Code JN-25 to alert Fletcher and Spruance that Nagumo's carriers would approach Midway from the northwest. Then, just after 0530 hours, as the first wave of Japanese aircraft headed toward Midway, a message from a Catalina was received aboard both *Enterprise* and *Hornet* saying: "Enemy Carriers." Ten minutes later, the same flying boat sent a second message: "Many enemy planes heading Midway bearing 320 distance 150." Then just after 0600 hours, a third message from the same plane: "Two carriers and battleships bearing 320 distance 180 course 135 speed 25." The sighting placed Nagumo's carriers 200 miles west of Spruance's Task Force 16.

Fletcher ordered *Enterprise* and *Hornet* to continue their current headings and begin attacks on the enemy carriers. *Yorktown* would launch after her Dauntless search planes were recovered. If the American carriers stayed on their southwesterly course and the Japanese carriers maintained their current southeasterly heading, the two forces would meet about 40 miles north of Midway.

All serviceable aircraft at Midway were ordered into the air. Six of the Navy's new Grumman TBF Avenger torpedo bombers led by Lt. L.K. Fieberling headed out with the Army's B-17 and B-26 bombers toward the map coordinates of the sighting. US Marine Corps Major Lofton R. Henderson led 27 aircraft, 16 SBD Dauntlesses and 11 SB2U Vindicator bombers. Remaining over Midway to defend the atoll were 27 Marine Corps fighters assigned to VMF-221 commanded by Major Floyd B. Parks: seven Grumman F4F Wildcats and 20 Brewster F2A Buffaloes. Parks's fighters, most of them obsolete, would go up against more than 100 Japanese aircraft, including 36 Zeros.

Just before 0645 hours, as Japanese aircraft approached in V-formations at 12,000 feet and the Marine fighters gained altitude and prepared to engage the enemy, warnings were sounded on Eastern and Sand Islands. High over Midway, the Wildcats and Buffaloes tore into the Japanese formation. Zero fighters, commanded by Lt. Masaharu Suganami, did not allow a single US fighter to attack a Japanese bomber. Though anti-aircraft fire was heavy, Vals accurately bombed installations on Sand and Eastern Islands. Tomonaga, leading the Kates, bombed hangars and hit the airstrip on Eastern Island. Early in the attack, Tomonaga was not satisfied with the raid's results and seeing no enemy aircraft on the ground, signaled Nagumo to prepare for a second wave.

Japanese planes destroyed aircraft hangars and fuel tanks on Eastern Island, seaplane hangars and storage tanks on Sand Island and caused more than 20 casualties on the ground. Eastern Island's runway remained operational. Anti-aircraft fire from land troops on Midway was heavy and accurate and Tomonaga led only 68 of 108 aircraft back to the carriers. In the air, Marine fighters had been less effective, losing 13 of 20 Buffaloes and two of seven Wildcats and with them, Major Parks.

Nagumo's Dilemma: Bombs or Torpedoes

As Tomonaga's planes attacked Midway, US Navy Task Force 16, moving at 21 knots, was 250 miles to the northeast of the atoll, its location still unknown to the Japanese. Aboard *Enterprise*, Rear Admiral Spruance led a task group that included heavy cruisers *Northampton*, *Pensacola* and *Vincennes* and destroyers *Aylwin*, *Balch*, *Benham*, *Monaghan* and *Phelps*. A second task group, centered around carrier *Hornet*, included heavy cruisers *Minneapolis* and *New Orleans*, the new anti-aircraft light cruiser *Atlanta* and destroyers *Conyngham*, *Ellet* and *Worden*. Trailing well astern of Task Force 16 was the newly repaired *Yorktown* and the ships of Task Force 17. Aboard the *Yorktown*, Rear Admiral Frank Jack Fletcher led the heavy cruisers *Astoria* and *Portland* and destroyers *Anderson*, *Hammann*, *Hughes*, *Morris* and *Russell*.

West of Task Force 16, Nagumo awaited the return of planes from Midway, concerned with developments that occurred that morning. In a period of three hours, attitudes aboard *Akagi* had gone from resolute determination and total confidence to questioning, skepticism and doubt. A Catalina had discovered Tanaka's First Mobile Force and shadowed it until driven off. As planes for the Midway strike were airborne, a Japanese floatplane reported a squadron of American bombers heading toward First Air Fleet. Minutes after 0700 hours, with the Midway strike over, Nagumo received the message from Tomonaga that a second attack was needed. Six of the US Navy's newest torpedo bombers, Fieberling's TBF Grumman Avengers, were approaching in single file formation in the distance.

Knowing the assault troops aboard Tanaka's transports could not invade the atoll until enemy air strength on Midway was destroyed, Nagumo agreed to a second strike. This meant planes already on deck, armed with armor-piercing bombs and torpedoes, would be lowered to hangar decks for rearming with general-purpose bombs for use on land targets. But just before 0730 hours, *Akagi* received a message from heavy cruiser *Tone*. One of its floatplanes messaged, "Ten ships, apparently enemy, sighted. Bearing 010 distance 240 miles from Midway, course 150, speed more than 20 knots." American ships 240 miles away? Their composition? In all Japanese war games and improvised scenarios, the Americans were not to appear this soon. US ships were expected to remain at Pearl Harbor until Midway was attacked. Instead, it appeared they were waiting for the Japanese. The importance of a second strike on Midway began to fade. Warning sirens sounded on *Akagi* as the *Tone*'s sighting report was debated. By now, Zeros had taken out all but one of Fieberling's Avengers. Patrolling Zeros took down three of four Martin B-26 Marauder medium bombers approaching Nagumo's ships. It was apparent the Marauders, like the Avengers, had launched from Midway.

Rearming of the Kates from torpedoes to bombs was halfway complete when Nagumo ordered the activity halted and notified his entire force to prepare for battle against enemy ships. Then another report was received from *Tone*'s floatplane indicating the enemy force had executed a heading change. Frustrated by a sighting report that failed to describe the ships spotted, Nagumo ordered the aircraft to ascertain and transmit the composition of the enemy force immediately.

At 0755 hours, while Nagumo and his staff awaited a reply from *Tone*'s search plane, a second wave of US planes approached. This was a squadron of 16 Dauntlesses of Marine Scout-Bomber Squadron VMSB-241 led by Major Lofton R. Henderson. They were followed by 11 SB2U-3 old Vindicators led by Major Benjamin W. Norris. A twelfth returned to Midway with mechanical problems. For months, Henderson and Norris had been training their squads of raw, inexperienced pilots and aircrews off Midway and were well respected by their crews. Once over *Hiryu,* Henderson attempted a skip-bombing attack on the Japanese fleet rather than a dive bombing. A dozen Zeros sent half the Dauntlesses into the sea. The remaining bombers went after carriers *Hiryu* and *Soryu* but were again jumped by Zeros and no hits were scored. Last to approach *Hiryu,* Henderson's plane was singled out by *Hiryu*'s combat air patrol and crashed into the sea, his left wing aflame. Although a parachute was seen, Henderson and his young gunner, Lee Walter Reininger, were not found. The Vindicators dove on battleship *Haruna* and on *Akagi.* The Marine pilots were jumped by Zeros, scored no hits and only nine of their squad returned to Midway.

At 0809 hours, those on *Akagi*'s bridge were relieved to learn the American ships were described from *Tone* as five cruisers and five destroyers. Minutes later, a squadron of Boeing B-17 Flying Fortresses flying at 20,000 feet, out of anti-aircraft range and threats from Zeros, released their bomb loads over carriers *Hiryu* and *Soryu*. Without success, the 14 heavy bombers headed back to Midway.

Nagumo decided that rearming the Kates from torpedoes to bombs could continue because a second strike on Midway would knock out further threats to the First Mobile Force. Returning planes would then be refueled and rearmed with armor-piercing bombs and torpedoes so that a large strike force could be sent against the American warships. Again, however, a new message from *Tone*'s floatplane reported an aircraft carrier accompanied the advancing American ships and soon, two cruisers were spotted 250 miles from Midway.

The mood on *Akagi*'s bridge changed with every disturbing confirmation from *Tone* and now, aircraft returning from the Midway strike were spotted in the distance. It was apparent an American naval force of at least a dozen warships had been waiting for Nagumo's force. It was within striking range and included at least one aircraft carrier. A second strike on Midway was suspended until the threat from the enemy ships was eliminated. Rearming the Kate bombers aboard *Akagi* and *Kaga* was ordered stopped. Those armed with torpedoes would be sent topside while Kates rearmed with bombs would have their armament changed—again. Before a strike on the US ships could be launched, however, aircraft returning from the first attack on Midway were ready to land, low on fuel and some damaged. Nagumo ordered all four Japanese carriers to clear their decks to recover planes. By 0900 hours, all recovery operations were handled expeditiously and within an hour, Nagumo ordered a heading change to the northeast and *Akagi, Kaga, Hiryu* and *Soryu* were ready to launch.

The Americans Launch

Rear Admiral Spruance also faced a dilemma. He received the first report of Nagumo's position northwest of Midway at 0530 hours on June 4, 1942. Task Force 16 was 225 miles from the Japanese, too distant for his torpedo bombers and fighters to find the enemy in poor visibility, attack and return safely to *Enterprise* and *Hornet*. The Douglas Devastator torpedo bombers and Grumman Wildcat fighters had an effective combat range of under 200 miles. If they had to hunt for the Japanese ships, the planes would certainly run out of fuel. But Spruance was also aware of the attack on Midway. By launching now, instead of waiting to close the distance, his planes might catch Nagumo's carriers in the process of recovering and refueling aircraft. Most important perhaps, an enemy search plane had just been sighted following Task Force 16 and Spruance was sure he had lost the advantage of surprise. He decided to launch an all-out strike before his own carriers came under attack.

Shortly after 0700 hours, *Enterprise* and *Hornet* turned into the wind to launch the first of 67 Dauntless dive bombers, followed by 20 Wildcat fighters and then 29 TBD Devastator torpedo bombers. Eight Dauntlesses were committed to submarine patrol duty and 36 Wildcats were retained to protect the ships. *Enterprise* launched 33 dive bombers, 15 torpedo bombers and 10 escorting fighters. *Hornet* would send out 34 dive bombers, 14 torpedo bombers and 10 fighters.

Over the horizon, the *Yorktown* and Task Force 17 trailed *Enterprise* and *Hornet* to the southwest. Rear Admiral Frank Jack Fletcher waited to launch

Yorktown's aircraft until all his scout planes had been recovered and when he was certain that sighting reports received earlier that morning were accurate. Although the Japanese were expected to have four or five carriers heading toward Midway, only two had been sighted. A month earlier at Coral Sea, Fletcher launched an all-out strike of 93 aircraft based on inaccurate information. The target turned out to be a single light carrier. At Midway, Fletcher would be more cautious.

As Fletcher waited and *Yorktown* continued recovering aircraft, *Enterprise* and *Hornet* began launching in two waves each, Dauntless dive bombers first with armament changed from 1,000-pound to 500-pound bombs. Wildcats and Devastators were to follow. Launch went as scheduled aboard *Hornet* but on *Enterprise,* the second wave was delayed. Waiting Dauntlesses circled overhead while many Devastators and Wildcats on *Enterprise* remained below in the hangar deck, making the possibility of dive bombers, torpedo bombers and fighters arriving over the target in a coordinated attack unlikely.

Lt. Commander Clarence Wade McClusky, Air Group Leader on *Enterprise,* waited for the Dauntlesses to reach altitude and form up, assuming all units would launch within 30 minutes. When they did not, the Dauntlesses were released and ordered to proceed independently to conserve fuel. Fighters and torpedo bombers would follow. In the delay and confusion, the 10 escorting Wildcat fighters from *Enterprise,* led by Lt. James S. Gray, mistook *Hornet*'s squadron of torpedo bombers for those of *Enterprise.* As the Wildcats followed the wrong group of Devastators to the southwest, *Hornet*'s fighters, unable to locate their torpedo bombers, headed toward the map coordinates with *Hornet*'s dive bombers. *Enterprise*'s dive bombers and torpedo bombers, unable to locate their fighter escort, took different headings, flying separately to the southwest.

On *Yorktown,* Rear Admiral Fletcher, though still skeptical of the sighting reports, ordered a partial strike, sending up 17 Dauntless dive bombers, 12 Devastator torpedo bombers and six Wildcat fighters. The dive bombers, led by Lt. Commander Maxwell F. Leslie, were escorted by six Wildcats of Commander John S. "Jimmy" Thach's Fighting-Three squadron. The slower torpedo bombers, led by Lt. Commander Lance E. Massey, headed west unescorted. Fletcher held back 20 Dauntlesses and 19 Wildcats in the event more Japanese carriers were sighted.

At 0915 hours and about 130 miles to the west of Task Force 16, Nagumo's First Mobile Force, after undergoing various attacks by American land-based bombers, had recovered aircraft from the first Midway strike and prepared to launch a second raid on the atoll. However, reports of enemy ships in the area convinced him that at least one American carrier had been sighted and he ordered a course change to the northeast, to close the distance and launch a major strike against the enemy. Just before 0920 hours, though, a squadron of aircraft was spotted approaching from the east.

Death of the Devastator

The first American planes to find Nagumo's First Air Fleet, now dubbed First Mobile Force, were the 15 TBD Devastators of *Hornet*'s Torpedo-Eight Squadron led by Lt. Commander John C. Waldron. Wildcat fighters off *Enterprise* circled above, ready for a prearranged signal to drop down to protect the torpedo bombers, but Lieutenant Gray in the lead Wildcat waited for a signal that never came. The fighters lost sight of the Devastators in heavy clouds and with no call for assistance, Gray contacted his group leader, Lieutenant Commander McClusky, and reported that the Wildcats were running low on fuel and would have to break off and head back to the *Enterprise*. Other planes launched from *Hornet* that morning, 34 SBD Dauntlesses and 10 F4F Wildcats, set out on a different heading and never found the Japanese. At about 0920 hours, the Devastators off *Hornet* began their descent from 1,500 feet but before leveling off for their final run, Waldron's planes were hit by a swarm of Zero fighters that swooped down on the squadron and shot down each and every one of the TBDs.

One person survived the attack on Torpedo-Eight. Ensign George H. Gay Jr. piloted the trailing Devastator of the formation. As the squadron's navigator, he flew a loose formation, more concerned with bearing than his interval with the other aircraft. His was the last of his squad to be attacked and the last of Torpedo-Eight to plunge into the sea but not before he did his best to drop his torpedo on Japanese carrier *Soryu*. Wounded and with his gunner dying, Gay headed toward the carrier at low altitude, dropped his torpedo and thought for a moment of crashing into *Soryu*'s deck. Instead, his bomber cartwheeled into the sea in a hail of machine-gun fire, his torpedo ineffective. He was able to exit his plane and float under a seat cushion to hide from the Japanese. At dark, he inflated his life raft and spent 30 hours in the water before being rescued by a PBY Catalina. In that time, he was witness to the sinking of three Japanese carriers and would later personally describe that victory to Admiral Nimitz.

Devastators from *Enterprise* reached Nagumo's force minutes after Gay's plane crashed into the sea. Led by Lt. Commander Eugene E. Lindsey, they approached the Japanese ships from the south and fared only slightly better than the *Hornet*'s aircraft. Within 12 minutes, 10 Devastators off *Enterprise* were shot down, no Japanese ships were hit and no defending Zeros were lost. In less than half an hour, 29 American torpedo bombers had attacked Nagumo's Force and just two survived.

At 1000 hours, a third squadron of Devastators approached the Japanese who by now knew they were dealing with at least one American carrier, perhaps more. This was Torpedo-Three off *Yorktown* led by Lt. Commander Lance E. Massey and covered by six Wildcats of Lt. Commander Jimmy Thach's Fighting-Three. Above the Devastators, the Wildcats tangled with more than 20 Zeros as other Japanese fighters, 5,000 feet below, tore into the lumbering Devastators. Before long, the Wildcats were routed by the faster, more maneuverable Zeros. Unescorted, *Yorktown*'s Devastators ran a gauntlet between fighters and anti-aircraft fire. Ten were shot down and no torpedo hits were scored. As the surviving Devastators headed away from Nagumo's force with Zeros still in hot pursuit, men aboard the Japanese ships were astonished by the determination of US pilots in pressing home their attacks. They were amazed, too, at the slow speed of the Devastators and the fact they had attacked mostly without fighter escort.

A total of 35 of 41 Devastators were lost, and 69 men, among them, squadron commanders Waldron, Lindsey and Massey. What seemed a disaster for the US Navy, however, directly contributed to American success in the carrier battle that followed. Nagumo's force had been put on the defensive and was distracted from the Dauntless dive bombers waiting in the wings.

Pacific Turning Point

First Mobile Force had successfully dodged bombs and torpedoes from almost 100 land-based and carrier-based aircraft. Nagumo was now certain he was dealing with more than a single enemy carrier. It was time to deliver

Japan's final, decisive attack against the elusive Americans carriers, put ground troops ashore on Midway Atoll and extend the Japanese defense perimeter in the Pacific. *Akagi, Kaga* and *Soryu* remained northeast of Midway in the center of an eight-mile box formation with battleships, cruisers and destroyers positioned around them. *Soryu* was three miles off *Akagi*'s starboard beam. *Kaga* trailed more than a mile astern of the flagship. *Hiryu* was 10 miles ahead, all ships on a northeast heading. At 1020 hours, Nagumo gave the order for the four carriers to turn into the wind and launch aircraft.

Three hours earlier, Lt. Commander Wade McClusky led two squadrons of SBD Dauntless dive bombers off USS *Enterprise*. These planes of Bombing-Six and Scouting-Six were searching to the southwest and further from the Japanese position. Three of his planes, running low on fuel, had left the formation. At 0955 hours and flying at 19,000 feet, a Dauntless crew spotted a Japanese destroyer moving to the northeast at high speed and McClusky's planes changed course to follow, now with five more having left their formation. Before long, they spotted the Japanese carrier force in the distance. McClusky broke radio silence and reported the Japanese position to *Enterprise.* He signaled Lt. Commander Richard H. Best and Bombing-Six to attack the carrier furthest to the north in the group. McClusky, along with Lt. Wilmer E. Gallaher and Scouting-Six, would attack the closer carrier.

Lt. Commander Maxwell Leslie and the Dauntlesses of Bombing-Three off *Yorktown* had also spotted Nagumo's First Mobile Force and were closing from the southeast. As 17 Dauntlesses of Bombing-Three and 25 bombers off *Enterprise* prepared to dive, neither Leslie nor McClusky was aware of the other group's presence. While *Yorktown*'s Bombing-Three tried to contact the planes of their torpedo squadron five miles to the west, *Enterprise*'s planes were going into their dives. In the excitement and confusion, a combination of SBD Dauntlesses from Scouting-Six and Bombing-Six followed McClusky while five of their aircraft continued to the north and stayed with Best and Bombing-Six.

Nosing over above the nearest Japanese carrier, McClusky with Gallaher led 17 Dauntlesses against carrier *Kaga*. American aircrews were surprised at the absence of Japanese fighters, and as they dove further under 10,000 feet, the light response by Japanese anti-aircraft fire was equally encouraging. Plunging at 300 miles per hour, McClusky released his bomb at 1,800 feet and missed the target. A second Dauntless bomb also missed but a third, Gallaher's, struck forward of *Kaga*'s bridge. Ensuing explosions tore a refueling cart apart and bathed the bridge in high-octane aviation fuel and scorching flames. Every officer and sailor on the bridge, including *Kaga*'s skipper, Captain Jisaku Okada, perished. *Kaga* took three more hits. On her flight deck, abandoned bombs, torpedoes and refueling lines erupted in blazing gasoline fires.

Aircraft were thrown overboard and gaping holes were seen in *Kaga*'s deck.

To the northwest, the remaining SBDs from *Enterprise*, now following Lt. Best, dove on *Akagi,* her deck filled with perhaps 40 aircraft awaiting takeoff. Best saw his bomb miss and explode in the water off the carrier's bridge. The next bomb, dropped by Lt. Edward J. Kroeger, hit the carrier near the amidships elevator and opened a gaping hole in the flight deck. A third bomb, dropped by Ensign F.T. Weber, struck the end of the carrier's flight deck and tore off a huge piece of *Akagi*'s deck while planes stood on their noses, tails in the air, and fires raged topside and below on *Akagi*.

Lt. Commander Leslie had hoped to make a coordinated attack with Devastators of Torpedo-Three but lacking contact, he signaled his squadron to attack the nearest Japanese carrier. This was *Soryu*, sailing to the east of *Kaga* and *Akagi*. Beginning at 1025 hours, three 1,000-pound bombs struck *Soryu* in rapid succession, one hitting in front of the forward elevator, two straddling the amidships elevator. Explosions knocked aircraft over the sides and fires fueled by gasoline and munitions destroyed 18 Kate bombers ready for launch. The last of Leslie's *Yorktown* planes changed targets and attacked a Japanese battleship and a destroyer.

From the first American bomb released at approximately 1021 hours and the last dropped six minutes later, three of Combined Fleet's finest aircraft carriers, *Akagi, Kaga* and *Soryu,* were ablaze. Only Zero fighters flying Combat Air Patrol were spared but low on fuel, and no place to land, they too would be lost. Just before 1030 hours, it was over and the Dauntlesses set their headings to the east and back to *Enterprise* and *Yorktown.*

A small boat from the light cruiser *Nagara* was sent to remove Vice Admiral Nagumo and other senior officers from the *Akagi*'s bridge. At first, Nagumo refused to leave his flagship but by 1046 hours, with all passageways on the *Akagi's* bridge blocked by flames, Nagumo climbed through a forward-facing porthole and shimmied down a rope to be rescued and transfer his flag to light cruiser *Nagara*. *Akagi's* captain, Taijiro Aoki, attempted to go down with his ship but was removed to safety by his crew. Aboard *Soryu*, seriously burned Captain Ryusaku Yanagimoto gave the order to abandon ship, walked back into the flames and disappeared. Destroyers *Hamakaze* and *Isokaze* came alongside to remove *Soryu's* survivors.

Attack and Counterattack

By 1050 hours, June 4, 1942, Vice Admiral Chuichi Nagumo, now safely aboard light cruiser *Nagara*, transferred tactical command of First Mobile Force to Rear Admiral Hiroaki Abe aboard heavy cruiser *Tone*. Abe immediately notified Rear Admiral Tamon Yamaguchi and Captain Tomeo Kaku on *Hiryu* of the burning Japanese carriers and gave the order for *Hiryu's* planes to attack the American carriers. Yamaguchi confirmed *Tone's* message and radioed Battleship *Yamato* the following message: "Fires are raging aboard *Kaga, Soryu* and *Akagi* resulting from attacks carried out by enemy land-based and carrier-based attack planes. In the meantime, we are temporarily retiring to the north." Hundreds of miles to the northwest and unaware of developments centered around the carriers of First Mobile Force, Admiral Yamamoto on *Yamato* was stunned. Any hope of a Japanese carrier victory at Midway now rested with *Hiryu's* 43 remaining planes. Six Zero fighters and 18 Val dive bombers began launching from *Hiryu* at 1058 hours. Lt. Michio Kobayashi leading the Vals followed a scout plane from *Chikuma*. Still below on *Hiryu's* hangar deck, 10 Kates, some just returned from bombing Midway Atoll, were being armed with torpedoes. Six Zeroes remained over the carrier.

The first sighting reports from *Tone's* number four search plane were now hours old but sightings by other Japanese aircraft, including a floatplane from heavy cruiser *Chikuma*, updated the American positions. More recent reports of enemy ship coordinates gave Yamaguchi reason to believe that as many as five enemy carriers were within striking range. This misinformation was corrected when downed American aircrews who were picked up out of the water and interrogated gave the actual number and even the names of the three US carriers.

About the same time Lt. Kobayashi's squadron of dive bombers was being led to the east, Rear Admiral Fletcher awaited the return of *Yorktown*'s planes from the strike on Nagumo's carriers and ordered the launch of 10 Dauntlesses to patrol to the west and south of Task Force 17. He was concerned that a fifth or even a sixth enemy carrier might be in the area and had seven dive bombers fueled and armed with 1,000-pound bombs waiting on the *Yorktown*'s hangar deck. A dozen F4F Wildcats from *Enterprise* and *Hornet* were in the air overhead. There were 15 Grumman fighters being refueled on *Yorktown*'s flight deck. Approaching from the west, Lt. Commander Leslie's Dauntlesses returned from their attack on *Soryu*. Still in the air and dangerously low on fuel were Thach's five Wildcats. At about 1145 hours, *Yorktown* radar picked up a group of enemy aircraft approaching from 40 miles out. Captain Buckmaster gave the order to stop refueling the fighters and ordered Leslie's bombers and Thach's fighters, now ready to land, to stay in the air. Heavy cruisers *Astoria* and *Portland*, screened by destroyers *Anderson*, *Hammann*, *Hughes*, *Morris* and *Russell*, were ordered to general quarters and battle stations.

Just before noon, Kobayashi's Vals escorted by six Zeros neared Task Force 17. More than a squadron of Wildcats jumped the Vals before they reached *Yorktown*. The American fighters shot down 11 enemy bombers, but seven remaining Vals got through and dove on the American carrier. Heavy anti-aircraft fire met the Vals but didn't stop them from diving as low as 500 feet before releasing their bombs. Gunners downed two more attackers, but the Japanese pilots gave everyone watching from below a lesson in dive-bombing accuracy. Three bombs hit *Yorktown* in rapid succession. The first explosion tore a hole in the flight deck. The second bomb hit near the smokestack, shutting down the carrier's ventilation system and snuffing out her boiler fires, which resulted in a loss of the carrier's power. A third bomb penetrated the flight deck, hangar deck and third deck storage locker, finally exploding four decks below. Within twenty minutes, *Yorktown* was dead in the water. The second bomb also knocked out her radar and all bridge communications. At 1315 hours, Rear Admiral Fletcher transferred his flag to the heavy cruiser *Astoria*. Heavy cruiser *Portland* took *Yorktown* in tow. Though two bombs had penetrated deep into the carrier, fire-fighting parties and damage control crews quickly brought the fires under control. By 1340 hours, all fires were out, the flight deck had been patched, power was partially restored and *Yorktown* could obtain a speed of 20 knots and once again launch and recover aircraft. Leslie's Dauntlesses and Thach's Wildcats, critically low on fuel, needed to land and Wildcats protecting the task force did also. Leslie's SBDs landed on *Enterprise,* while the fighters flying Combat Air Patrol headed for *Hornet.* Four of Thach's Wildcats returned to the quickly repaired *Yorktown* while a fifth fighter was recovered by *Hornet.*

By 1400 hours, *Yorktown's* radar picked up the approach of a second formation of enemy aircraft and a dozen Wildcat fighters were in the air, ready and waiting. They downed half the Vals and three of the six Zeros but within half an hour, five Kates dropped down in final runs and released torpedoes. Two struck *Yorktown* port side, and explosions ruptured her fuel tanks, jammed her rudder and caused an immediate loss of power. *Yorktown* took on a list to port. Considering the quick repair work done at Pearl Harbor along with that day's recovery from attack, Captain Buckmaster was concerned with the carrier's ability to withstand more battle damage before her watertight integrity was affected. He gave the order to abandon ship and by 1500 hours, destroyers *Anderson, Hammann, Hughes, Morris* and *Russell* began to transfer crew and to pick up sailors from the water.

On *Hiryu,* Rear Admiral Yamaguchi and Captain Kaku planned to launch a third attack on the damaged *Yorktown* at 1630 hours but their bomber crews and fighter pilots were near exhaustion. Plus, they were left with just four Kates, five Vals and six Zeros. Since returning Kate aircrews reported *Yorktown* burning and listing, Kaku postponed the time of launch to 1800 hours. A 90-minute delay would give the pilots and crews time for rest and a meal. The delay would doom *Hiryu.*

At about 1700 hours, 25 Dauntless dive bombers that launched from *Enterprise* arrived undetected over the Japanese ships. Lt. Gallaher, filling in for Lt. Commander McClusky who had been injured in the morning attack, led 14 of *Yorktown's* SBDs along with aircraft from *Enterprise.* Approaching from out of the sun, Gallaher ordered 10 of *Yorktown's* planes to attack the escorting Japanese battleships and cruisers while the remaining Dauntlesses dove on *Hiryu.* The few Zeros on patrol failed to stop the attackers before the SBDs began their dives. One bomb struck the forward elevator, tearing it apart and throwing its platform against the carrier's portside island in the explosion. A second bomb hit the flight deck amidships and the next two penetrated the flight deck forward of the island. The few planes spotted topside caught fire along with bombs and torpedoes left in the open. Aircraft on the hangar deck below erupted in flames so that moments after the first bombs hit, the 17,000-ton *Hiryu* was engulfed in flames. Still, she continued to move forward at nearly 30 knots. Except for anti-aircraft gunners, the crew formed bucket brigades and escorting destroyers *Kazagumo* and *Makigumo* came alongside to discharge their fire hoses. When flames reached the lower deck, *Hiryu's* engines stopped, she began to flood and took on a 15-degree list to port. Explosions could be heard deep within the ship.

Deaths of Five Carriers

Soryu, on June 4, 1942, was the first of the Japanese carriers to sink. While rescuing survivors, destroyers *Hamakaze* and *Isokaze* attempted to take the burning hulk in tow but finally, at 1915 hours, she sank. There was a gigantic underwater explosion as *Soryu* disappeared into the Pacific.

Kaga was also finished. About 1700 hours, her acting skipper, Flight Officer Amagai, ordered abandon ship but as destroyers *Hagikaze* and *Maikaze* came alongside to take survivors, two huge explosions rocked the burning carrier. At 1930 hours, Combined Fleet's largest carrier sank.

Akagi, flagship of Vice Admiral Nagumo and the pride of First Air Fleet, was burning but still making way late on June 4 and was considered salvageable. Late that night, however, after an enormous explosion rocked the ship, Captain Taijiro Aoki and most of his crew were taken off the burning carrier by *Arashi* and *Nowaki*. Aoki went back aboard and was forcibly removed by a boarding party on June 5 after which Yamamoto ordered *Akagi* scuttled. Destroyers *Arashi, Hagikaze, Maikaze* and *Nowaki* each fired a single Type-93 torpedo into the carrier and before 0500 on June 5, *Akagi* disappeared in an explosion that rocked the four destroyers.

Hiryu, by dawn on June 5, was still afloat. Captain Kaku ordered abandon ship but he and Rear Admiral Yamaguchi stayed aboard. Destroyers *Kazagumo* and *Makigumo* moved in to transfer what remained of the crew. That done, destroyer *Makigumo* was ordered to torpedo and sink *Hiryu*. One of two torpedoes hit the carrier, caused a significant explosion and the destroyers returned south to First Mobile Force. Next morning, a search plane from light carrier *Hosho* reported *Hiryu* still afloat with men on deck, waving. It seems the engine room crew had been freed from their entrapment below by *Makigumo*'s torpedo. The men were found at sea and rescued by an American ship. Nagumo dispatched a seaplane to search for *Hiryu* and destroyer *Tanikaze* to take her down but she was not seen again.

US carrier *Yorktown*, 100 miles east of Midway Atoll, was adrift and listing badly and destroyer *Hughes* was sent to guard her. Later on the night of June 4, Fletcher merged the ships of Task Force 17 with Spruance's Task Force 16 and retired to the east. Pearl Harbor believed *Yorktown* could be saved. Minesweeper *Vireo* was dispatched from French Frigate Shoals and destroyer *Gwin* from Pearl Harbor to assist while *Yorktown* was down in the bow, listing 25 degrees to port and taking on water. Fletcher released destroyers *Balch, Benham* and *Hammann* to bring the carrier in and a salvage team from *Hammann* was put aboard.

At 0700 hours on June 5, a Japanese floatplane spotted the drifting *Yorktown* and reported her position to battleship *Yamato*. Admiral Yamamoto dispatched submarine *I-168* to *Yorktown*'s coordinates where, that afternoon, undetected by ships working around the carrier and destroyers forming a defensive ring, the sub fired four torpedoes. The first missed, the second and third struck *Yorktown*, passing under *Hammann,* and the fourth struck *Hammann* amidships. Within minutes, the destroyer went down along with most of her crew but the carrier continued to drift and burn. Two days later, on the morning of June 7, USS *Yorktown* finally rolled over to port and sank.

Final Actions

While *Akagi, Kaga, Soryu* and *Hiryu* were being attacked by land-based planes from Midway and by American carrier planes on June 4, Kondo's powerful Midway Invasion Force was 300 miles to the northwest, followed by Tanaka's troop transports and by Kurita's escorting cruisers. Yamamoto's Main Force was 500 miles out. Although surprised by the appearance of American forces so early in the operation, Yamamoto remained optimistic about the battle's outcome. He was convinced that only two US carriers were operating in the Pacific, certain that *Hiryu* had disposed of one of them. Believing Midway could still be taken and the battle won, Admiral Yamamoto ordered Rear Admiral Kakuta's Second Mobile Force, with carriers

Ryujo and *Junyo* in the Aleutians, to rendezvous with Kondo's Invasion Force and Yamamoto's three battleships. In this revised plan, planes from the light carriers were to neutralize any land-based enemy aircraft remaining on Midway. The air attack would be followed by a bombardment from Kondo's warships and by Tanaka's transports putting amphibious troops ashore. With Midway secured, Japanese naval forces could seek out and destroy what remained of American naval forces in the area.

At about 1700 hours on June 4, however, Yamamoto received the unsettling information that none of Nagumo's four fleet carriers were operational and the US Navy had not two but three carriers in the area. He ordered *Ryujo* and *Junyo* to reverse course back to the Aleutians. Two hours later, Yamamoto learned the Americans were spotted retiring to the east and he ordered Kondo's Invasion Force to bombard Midway that night. A few hours later still, he learned that Nagumo had transferred his flag to the light cruiser *Nagara*. Just before 0100 hours on June 5, Yamamoto replaced Vice Admiral Chuichi Nagumo with Vice Admiral Nobutake Kondo as head of First Mobile Fleet.

Kondo's Invasion Force merged with Kurita's Close Support Group 200 miles west of Midway, a battle line 30 miles long that included eight heavy cruisers, a light cruiser and 10 destroyers. Nagumo's force, two battleships, two heavy cruisers and 12 destroyers, was 75 miles from the atoll and expected to begin bombardment by 0200 hours, when Yamamoto learned that Kondo's Force would arrive off Midway an hour late. Beginning the bombardment at 0300 hours would be risky. Japanese ships would have to remain off the atoll until they were certain all American air power had been neutralized or they would be subject to attacks from both land-based and carrier-based aircraft. With the loss of Nagumo's carriers and by canceling *Ryujo* and *Junyo* as reinforcements, the only air protection would come from the light carriers *Hosho* and *Zuiho*. The *Hosho*, however, traveling with Yamamoto's Main Force, carried no fighters, while the *Zuiho*, moving with Kondo, carried a dozen Zeros. With the Americans retiring to the east, Yamamoto realized the much sought after surface night battle would not occur, and at 0255 hours on June 5, he ordered a general withdrawal. Operation MI was canceled—permanently.

Before midnight on June 4, the 7th Cruiser Division, led by Vice Admiral

Takeo Kurita aboard heavy cruiser *Kumano,* was 80 miles west of Midway and heading east. It included heavy cruisers *Mikuma, Mogami* and *Suzuya,* escorted by destroyers *Arashio* and *Asashio.* Kurita's ships had been spotted crossing the US submarine picket line on station west of Midway when he received the message that Operation MI was canceled. Kurita reversed course and headed west but an hour after midnight on June 5, his column again approached the US picket line and was detected. A signal to reverse course in a 45-degree port turn was flashed to the Japanese ships. As *Mogami* executed the maneuver, she rammed the port quarter of *Mikuma* in a collision that damaged both cruisers. *Mikuma's* portside oil tanks ruptured and the bow of the *Mogami* was bent sharply to port, back to the number one 8-inch gun turret. Kurita aboard *Kumano* led *Suzuya* to the rendezvous point and left *Arashio* and *Asashio* with the damaged ships, *Mikuma* leaving a trail of oil.

The US task force was northeast of Midway on a westerly heading. Before dawn on June 5, all the Navy's serviceable Catalina flying boats from Sand Island were searching to the west. At the same time, from Eastern Island, 12 of the Army's B-17 Flying Fortress heavy bombers had launched and were also heading west. At 0630 hours, a Catalina reported Japanese cruisers retiring, 125 miles west of Midway. The B-17s never located the enemy cruisers but the last serviceable Marine bombers, six Dauntlesses and six Vindicators that launched from Midway, spotted an oil slick and found the damaged ships. Dauntless pilots kicked over into steep dives as Vindicators descended to lower altitudes before attempting their glide-bombing attacks. *Mogami,* *Mikuma* and the destroyers put up heavy anti-aircraft fire and the Americans achieved only a few near misses. A Vindicator bomber piloted by Captain Richard E. Fleming, after being hit and bursting into flames, dove into the *Mikuma* and crashed into her aft gun turret. The explosion knocked out the cruiser's two rear-facing 8-inch guns, both floatplane catapults and destroyed all anti-aircraft mounts from amidships aft.

Earlier that morning of June 5, Spruance received a report on the position, heading and speed of Kurita's ships from Lt. Commander J.W. Murphy, skipper of the submarine USS *Tambor.* By dawn, Task Force 16 launched all remaining Dauntlesses from *Enterprise* and *Hornet,* because Spruance, like Fletcher, believed at least one more Japanese carrier was out there. The two carriers launched more than 100 reconnaissance sorties but no targets were reported. Just before 1600 hours, 32 SBD Dauntlesses from *Enterprise* and 26 from *Hornet* were launched on search missions 300 miles to the west. There were no sightings on the outward leg but after the bombers turned back for their carriers, a Japanese destroyer was spotted. It was *Tanikaze*, dispatched to check on the location and condition of *Hiryu*. By then, *Tanikaze* had undergone two attacks by B-17 heavy bombers from Midway, and now she would elude more than 50 bombs dropped by the US carrier planes, taking only slight damage. Nevertheless, *Tanikaze's* anti-aircraft guns shot down one of the Dauntlesses and continued to search for the *Hiryu*.

By June 6, the Japanese surface warships that had participated in Operation MI were withdrawing to the northwest: Kondo's Midway Invasion Force; the destroyers of Tanaka's Escort Group; the battleships *Haruna* and *Kirishima,* with heavy cruisers *Chikuma* and *Tone* of Nagumo's First Mobile Force; the battleships, cruisers and destroyers of Takasu's Aleutian Force; the heavy cruisers *Kumano* and *Suzuya* of Kurita's Close Support Group. They were all heading for a rendezvous with Yamamoto without firing a single round at an enemy ship.

More than 300 miles east, Rear Admiral Spruance couldn't reach the merging Japanese forces with his aircraft even if he knew their exact location, but he could find those two Japanese heavy cruisers as they moved west from Midway. He ordered Dauntlesses and Wildcats off *Enterprise* and *Hornet* into the search. Later, a second strike of 31 dive bombers, three torpedo bombers and 12 fighters was launched from *Enterprise.* And later still, with the range between the American carriers and Japanese cruisers reduced to under 90 miles, 24 dive bombers and eight fighters were launched from *Hornet.* In little more than five hours, the two Japanese heavy cruisers and their two escorting destroyers were subjected to 81 dive bombings and three torpedo attacks. In the early attack, heavy cruiser *Mogami* took two bomb hits, one killing all members of a gun crew. Less than three hours later, she took two bomb hits by *Enterprise* dive bombers that started fires throughout the ship and reduced her speed even further. Slightly ahead and west of the *Mogami,* heavy cruiser *Mikuma,* burning and leaking oil, took a single bomb hit during the two morning raids. The explosion started more uncontrollable fires and by noon, Captain Shakao Sakiyama gave the order to abandon ship. Raging fires aboard *Mikuma* prevented destroyers *Arashio* and *Asashio* from moving alongside to transfer the crew. Men on *Mikuma* went over the side and *Arashio* picked up more than 100 survivors from the water. By afternoon, the third wave of dive bombers and the second group launched from the *Hornet* appeared. *Mogami* took a single hit that penetrated the cruiser's deck and exploded in the engine room, killing 90 men. The attack also finished off the *Mikuma*. One bomb killed most of the crew still on deck while a second struck torpedo racks, detonating torpedoes that sealed the ship's fate. The destroyers avoided all bombs until the last attack when *Arashio* was hit with a loss of 37 men and *Asashio* with the loss of 22. Yet neither speed nor the ability to navigate was affected on either vessel. Moving from the drifting and deserted *Mikuma,* the destroyers escorted the heavily damaged *Mogami* westward and left behind *Mikuma*, listing badly, before she rolled over and disappeared. Three months earlier in the Battle of Sunda Strait off Java, it was *Mikuma* and *Mogami* that were credited with sinking Allied cruisers USS *Houston* and HMAS *Perth.*

In the Aleutians on the morning of June 7, Rear Admiral Sentaro Omori aboard light cruiser *Abukuma,* led the Attu Invasion Force toward the westernmost island in the chain. As the minelayer *Magane Maru* swept the invasion approaches, the transport *Kinugasa Maru* protected by destroyers *Hatsuharu, Hatsushimo, Nenohi* and *Wakaba,* debarked an Army detachment of 1,200 assault troops of the Attu Landing Force led by Major Matsutoshi Hozumi. At the same time 200 miles to the east, Captain Takeji Ono aboard the light cruiser *Kiso* led the Kiska Invasion Force to the middle of the island chain. With light cruiser *Tama,* auxiliary cruiser *Asaka Maru* and screened by destroyers *Akatsuki, Hibiki* and *Hokaze,* they protected the transports *Hakusan Maru* and *Kumagawa Maru,* moving toward Kiska. Minesweepers *Hakuho Maru, Kaiho Maru* and *Shunkotsu Maru* swept the landing approaches as the *Hakusan Maru* put ashore 550 amphibious troops commanded by Lieutenant Commander Hifumi Mukai from the 3rd Battalion, Maizuru Special Naval Landing Force. The *Kumagawa Maru* carried 700 labor troops and construction equipment. Both Attu and Kiska were nearly deserted and the landings were unopposed. Operation MI had put troops ashore at two of the three Aleutian objectives, but without Midway and with the loss of four of Combined Fleet's best carriers, operations scheduled for July were suspended. In the South Pacific, there would be no invasions of

New Caledonia, the New Hebrides, Fiji or Samoa. Plans aimed at severing communication and supply lines between the west coast of the United States and New Zealand and Australia were also put on hold. The Empire of Japan and its Combined Fleet would have to look elsewhere in the Pacific to keep up pressure on America and her Allies.

Aftermath

The Imperial Japanese Navy came to Midway with 375 carrier-based aircraft. Vice Admiral Nagumo's ships carried 261 planes. Kurita's Second Mobile Force had 82 aircraft. Light carriers *Hosho* and *Zuiho* carried a total of 32 planes. Aircraft at Wake or in the Marshall Islands 1,500 miles from Midway were too distant to contribute but the Navy's four-engine, long-range Mavis flying boats were within range. Pilots of the 1st and 2nd Carrier Divisions were some of the best in the Japanese Navy. American pilots and aircrews aboard *Enterprise* were experienced; *Hornet*'s pilots were green. Pilots and aircrews on *Yorktown* were made up of air personnel from *Lexington, Saratoga* and *Yorktown* and had varying degrees of combat experience, from untried and green to aces. Until the morning of June 4, many Marine and Navy pilots at Midway had never attempted a bomb or torpedo attack or had ever flown the type of aircraft they would pilot that day. Comparing equipment, the Mitsubishi Zero was faster, more maneuverable and could easily outclimb the Grumman Wildcat. The Nakajima Kate bomber, when loaded with a torpedo, was almost twice as fast as a torpedo-laden Douglas Devastator. The dive-bombing proficiency of the Aichi Val crews was consistently more accurate than those flying the Douglas Dauntless.

Though a strong proponent of carrier operations and carrier-based aircraft, Admiral Yamamoto at Midway led a force built around battleships. Vice Admiral Takasu's Guard Force was also heavy in battleships. Vice Admiral Kondo's Midway Invasion Force was cruiser heavy. The Japanese plan envisioned two or three of these surface forces surprising and neutralizing American aircraft on Midway, after which Nagumo's carriers would bait the enemy and draw out US carriers in a final battle. The Pearl Harbor operation with its single strike force had been beautifully simple. As war progressed and Japanese victories continued, so did the complexity of each operation. For the Midway portion of Operation MI alone, eight Japanese

forces sortied from four staging areas. Assuming the Americans reacted as
the Japanese had planned, Nagumo's carrier-based planes could knock out
Midway's aircraft, soften up the atoll for the upcoming landing, protect the
troop transports as they arrived and still have time to attack and disable the
US carriers when they appeared. But the US carriers were not 1,000 miles
away at Pearl Harbor or in the Coral Sea. They were lying in wait, 200 miles
away. There were not two US carriers, but four. As Japanese scouting reports
evolved hour to hour from destroyers to cruisers to an aircraft carrier in the
area, the mood on *Akagi's* bridge rose and fell with each correction. Nagumo
was hesitant, he waited, he ordered his planes to change armaments from
bombs to torpedoes and then, from torpedoes back to bombs. Planes sat too
long on flight decks and in hangar decks.

How luck or the idea of good or bad fortune ultimately affected the Battle of Midway can always be debated and the number of "what ifs" is long.
What if the floatplane from *Tone* had been launched on time and what if it
had given accurate information more quickly? What if Operation K had proceeded as planned and the Mavis flying boat had arrived over Pearl Harbor
as scheduled? What if McClusky hadn't spotted the destroyer *Arashi*? What
if the four Japanese carrier captains had insisted on proper storage of bombs
and torpedoes? And what if Yamamoto had sent the carriers *Akagi, Kaga,
Hiryu* and *Soryu* with *Junyo, Ryujo, Hosho* and *Zuiho* to attack Midway?

The Imperial Japanese Navy lost four fleet carriers and a heavy cruiser. A
second heavy cruiser was severely damaged, while a Japanese battleship,
three destroyers and an oiler were lightly damaged. Carrier *Akagi* lost 221
men, *Kaga* lost 800, *Hiryu* 416 and *Soryu's* losses totaled 718. The heavy
cruiser *Mikuma* went down with 648 of her crew, while the severely damaged
Mogami lost nearly 100 men. The lightly damaged battleship *Haruna,*
destroyers *Arashio, Asashio,* and *Tanikaze* and oiler *Akebono Maru* lost
approximately 75 men. The 261 operational aircraft aboard the four carriers
were all lost, and with them, most of Combined Fleet's best pilots and aircrews. With losses of approximately 3,400 officers, sailors and airmen, the
Battle of Midway was Japan's greatest naval loss since the 13th century.

The United States Navy lost a fleet carrier and a destroyer. *Yorktown* went
down with 82 of her crew and destroyer *Hammann* lost more than 40 men.
On Midway, the Marines lost 20 men, while in the air, the Army lost 20

airmen, the Navy lost 26 and the Marines lost more than 40 officers and men. Air losses from the three carriers totaled approximately 150 naval airmen and 113 aircraft.

Before the battle, the Japanese Navy had seven operational fleet carriers in the Pacific to four of the United States Navy. Now, fleet carrier strength between the two navies was virtually equal. However, by July 1942, the Japanese Navy had under construction two fleet carriers, a light carrier and two escort carriers. The United States had six 27,000-ton *Essex* class fleet carriers, six 11,000-ton *Independence* class light carriers and 16 escort carriers of the *Bogue* and *Sangamon* classes being built.

History would prove the Battle of Midway the most pivotal engagement in the Pacific War, one of history's major turning points. Fate saw some famous and some not-so-famous players at Midway go on to fight future battles and others who did not live to see war's end. Some were idealized, others denigrated. Joseph Rochefort and his team of cryptologists at Pearl Harbor are remembered for the intelligence data they supplied to the US Navy. The leadership of Rear Admiral Raymond Spruance favorably impressed Admiral Ernest King in Washington and Pacific Fleet Commander Admiral Chester Nimitz while the performance of Rear Admiral Frank Jack Fletcher did not. Admiral Isoroku Yamamoto, who had studied at Havard and served as Japan's naval attaché in Washington, and who predicted the Imperial Japanese Navy would have only six months to overcome the United States in the Pacific, died when his plane was shot down by a US Army Air Force plane on April 18, 1943. US code breakers in Hawaii had successfully determined his flight plans. Vice Admiral Chuichi Nagumo never recovered from the defeat at Midway and took his own life on July 6, 1944, while refusing to be taken prisoner at the Battle of Saipan. Japan would not surrender until September 2, 1945. It would be a long war.

Chapter XIV

AN ISLAND CALLED GADARUKANARU

Introduction

After the Japanese failed to take Port Moresby in the Battle of the Coral Sea and after their loss of four of Combined Fleet's carriers in the Battle of Midway, Admiral Yamamoto canceled some future naval operations and postponed others. The Japanese Army, however, stayed on the offensive and remained committed to taking Port Moresby even though it would have to provide its own land-based air cover. On January 23, 1942, Japanese forces had taken Rabaul on New Britain Island in the Bismarck Archipelago. An Australian base, it was 500 air miles north of Port Moresby. They improved harbor facilities there and would eventually add three airfields to the two already in service. On March 23, Japanese assault troops went ashore on Northeast New Guinea at Lae and at Salamaua and secured both objectives. Within a month, their amphibious forces landed to the north at Dutch settlements in Netherlands New Guinea and overran the deepwater anchorage at Hollandia. By May, only the southern territory of Papua remained in Allied hands, with Port Moresby and its adjacent airfields and with an Australian sea base in far eastern Papua at Milne Bay.

Officers and Operations

Admiral Ernest J. King, Commander in Chief US Fleet, expected a Japanese advance in the Solomon Islands, a British Protectorate, and his concerns were justified in late March 1942 when enemy troops secured the small island of Buka and a settlement on Bougainville in the western Solomons. A March 31 directive from King advised Admiral Nimitz to prepare his forces for a major amphibious operation. Nimitz was in command of all Navy, Marine, Army and Army Air Force units in the Pacific Ocean Area, SOPAC, except for forces temporarily assigned to General MacArthur's Southwest Pacific Area, SOWESPAC. In the first days of May 1942 as Japanese troops landed on Tulagi just north of Guadalcanal, King and Nimitz were planning the first major Allied land offensive of the war. If approved by the Joint Chiefs, King would need an overall commander to head the operation, a carrier commander to protect transports and an officer in charge of land-based aircraft of the US Navy, US Army and Royal Australian Air Force units. Meanwhile, General George Marshall, head of the Joint Chiefs, received a proposal from General MacArthur for an Allied invasion in the Bismarck Archipelago at Rabaul. Under this plan, MacArthur expected to command all naval and marine units south of the equator. The Navy disagreed. It did not want its precious flat tops exposed to Japanese land-based and carrier-based attacks and King was certain he did not want his forces under the command of MacArthur. King went ahead with his plans.

Vice Admiral Robert L. Ghormley was recalled from London where he served as a special naval observer. In Washington, King advised Ghormley he wanted him for overall commander of the Solomons campaign and warned him of the shortage of ships, aircraft, men and supplies he'd inherit. Ghormley accepted and traveled to Pearl Harbor to meet with Nimitz. Next, and still without Joint Chiefs' approval, King and Nimitz met with Rear Admiral Richmond Kelly Turner in San Francisco in late June. Turner was Director of the Navy's War Plans Division and although he told King he had no experience in amphibious operations, King told Turner he'd learn and appointed him Commander, South Pacific Amphibious Force. Because the Solomons were a British protectorate, ships of the Royal Australian Navy would be under Rear Admiral Sir Victor Alexander Charles Crutchley who replaced Rear Admiral Crace. With land-based Allied aircraft too far distant, Admiral King wanted either Bill Halsey or Ray Spruance to serve as tactical commander of carrier-based aircraft in the campaign. Halsey was recuperating from shingles and Spruance was serving as Chief of Staff to Nimitz so the assignment went to Rear Admiral Frank Jack Fletcher. Fletcher would lead Task Force 61, three fleet carriers, one battleship, six cruisers and 16 destroyers, designated Expeditionary Force. The Joint Chiefs approved the Navy's Solomons operation on July 2 and the same day, moved MacArthur's SOW-ESPAC and Nimitz's SOPAC two longitudinal degrees west. Ghormley met with MacArthur in Melbourne on July 18, both men pessimistic about plans for the operation dubbed Watchtower that some sailors and Marines later called Operation Shoestring. Ghormley established his headquarters at Noumea on New Caledonia, 1,000 miles south of the Solomon Islands.

On May 3 and 4, Japanese Army troops of the 3rd Kure Special Naval Landing Force landed on the two-mile-long by one-mile-wide island of Tulagi in the Eastern Solomons, 18 miles north of Guadalcanal. Construction workers there installed a refueling facility and communication center and the Japanese Navy maintained a squadron of floatplanes in the deepwater harbor. A second seaplane base was established less than three miles east between the islands of Tananbogo and Gavutu. In mid-May, Captain Shigetoshi Miyazaki, Commander of the Yokohama Air Group, suggested that an airfield be constructed on the north coast of Guadalcanal, an idea approved by General Harukichi Hyakutake, Commander of the IJA 17th Army at Rabaul. By mid-June, a labor force escorted by combat troops sailed from Tulagi to Guadalcanal to begin construction.

On June 25, a US Army aircrew on reconnaissance over Guadalcanal's north coast reported the clearing of palm trees, underbrush and the burning of a grassy field east of an area called Lunga Point. More flight crews reported tents in a bivouac area near the clearing and a wharf under construction. Within a week, an Australian coast watcher provided more information. The Japanese were awaiting the arrival of units to begin building an airfield that if completed, would give Japanese planes control of the skies over the Coral Sea and put the Japanese in range of Allied bases as far south as New Hebrides and New Caledonia. On July 4, Allied reconnaissance discovered and reported the nearly completed airfield and for the next five months the United States of America and the Empire of Japan would send all available ships, aircraft and ground troops to the eastern Solomons for control of that airstrip.

US Reinforcements

On June 14, elements of Major General Vandegrift's 1st Marine Division arrived in Wellington, New Zealand, expecting its 19,000 men would train in amphibious tactics until early 1943. Vandegrift was amazed to learn on June 26 that he had less than five weeks to prepare his men for an assault on enemy-held islands. Knowledge of the Japanese airfield nearing completion prompted the change in plans and the US Navy's amphibious assault would have to be executed before the facility was up and running. America's first land offensive of the Pacific war was scheduled to begin August 1. Not only was there little time to prepare but there were no current maps available on the topography of the islands nor were there charts of the surrounding waters. The nearest US base was at Espiritu Santo in the New Hebrides, 500 miles to the southeast. Vice Admiral Ghormley postponed the landing invasion to August 7.

Six months after Pearl Harbor, Admiral Yamamoto's prediction of the ability of the Japanese Army and Navy to run wild in the Pacific for half a year, before the US Navy regrouped, became a reality. American shipbuilding programs released the most substantial number of naval reinforcements to date. In June, the 35,000-ton battleship USS *North Carolina* completed her shakedown in the Atlantic and headed for the Pacific, the first US battleship deployed in the Pacific War. She would be joined by sister ships *Washington* and *South Dakota*. No heavy cruisers were received by the Navy but five light cruisers of the 10,000-ton *Cleveland* class were completed: *Cleveland, Columbia, Montpelier, Denver* and *Santa Fe*. Only USS *Columbia* reached the Pacific by year's end. Three new 6,000-ton light anti-aircraft cruisers arrived in the Pacific between April and June: *Atlanta, San Diego* and *San Juan*. *Atlanta* and *San Juan* sailed for Guadalcanal. *San Diego* sailed for Espiritu Santo where she would escort troop and supply convoys to Guadalcanal. By early September, a fourth light anti-aircraft cruiser of the *Atlanta* class, USS *Juneau*, was stationed off Guadalcanal.

Although most of the 78 new 1,700-ton *Bristol* class destroyers were assigned to Atlantic duty, *Aaron Ward, Buchanan* and *Laffey* commissioned in March, *Farenholt* and *Duncan* commissioned in April, and *McCalla* and *Barton* commissioned in May, were sent to the Pacific, all committed in the battles for Guadalcanal. The largest class of US destroyers produced during the war, the 2,100-ton *Fletchers,* were primarily assigned duty in the Pacific including the namesake, *Nicholas, O'Bannon, Chevalier, Redford, Jenkins, Strong, LaVallette, Saufley, Taylor, DeHaven* and *Waller.* Most saw action in the Solomons campaigns. By the end of 1942, three more of the *Fletcher* class were commissioned: *Bache, Guest* and *Beale.*

In addition to new US warships released to the Pacific Fleet, several old veterans were transferred to Nimitz from the Atlantic. The 15,000-ton fleet carrier *Wasp,* in the Atlantic since Pearl Harbor, joined *Enterprise, Hornet* and *Saratoga,* giving the USN four fleet carriers in the Pacific for the first time. Eleven fast carriers of the 27,000-ton *Essex* class were approved for the Navy and by December 1941, three were laid down. *Essex* was launched in July 1942 and commissioned in December. Four of eight light carriers of the 11,000-ton *Independence* class were laid down in 1941, and in 1942, the class was increased to nine vessels. The namesake was launched in August, commissioned in January 1943. USS *Long Island,* the first of more than 100 escort carriers produced during the war, was ordered into the Pacific. Unlike the warships that followed, she, *Archer* and *Charger* were conversions built on the hulls of old merchantmen. Only *Long Island* saw action while *Archer* and *Charger* served as training vessels. Six escort carriers of the 10-ship, 7,800-ton *Bogue* class and all four of the larger 12,000-ton *Sangamon* class were laid down in 1941 but none sailed west of Pearl Harbor in 1942.

Japanese Reinforcements

Before the Battle of Midway, Admiral Yamamoto and Combined Fleet expected to create several new naval units to protect the expanding area of the Greater East Asia Co-Prosperity Sphere. In the first eight months of war, First Air Fleet's carrier aircraft and Eleventh Air Fleet's land-based planes had formed Combined Fleet's air strength. Fourth Fleet under Vice Admiral Shigeyoshi Inouye was based at Truk, 850 miles north of the Solomons. Japan envisioned adding six new fleets from Second to Thirteenth, all needing to be staffed and supplied, an overly optimistic projection and never realized.

The last battleship Japanese shipbuilders would launch during the war and one of the world's largest was the super battleship *Musashi,* sister ship of the 63,000-ton *Yamato. Musashi* would not join Combined Fleet until 1943. Fleet carrier *Hiyo,* second of the two-ship 19,000-ton *Junyo* class, was completed in July 1942, converted from a luxury liner. *Junyo* entered service in May, but *Hiyo* did not receive its full crew or its complement of aircraft nor did it complete its shakedown cruise until the end of the year. Light carrier *Ryuho,* near completion in April at Yokosuka, was damaged in the Doolittle Raid. She finally sortied on December 11 but was torpedoed the next day and returned to Yokosuka. One flush-deck, 19,000-ton escort carrier entered service in 1941, *Taiyo,* converted from a former passenger liner. Work on sister ships *Chuyo* and *Unyo* was begun in 1942—*Unyo* ready in May, *Chuyo* in November—but neither saw duty that year.

The Imperial Japanese Navy went to war with 18 heavy cruisers, the last of which, the 8,500-ton *Chikuma,* was completed in 1939. The Navy received no additional heavy cruisers during the war. Plans for five new light cruisers saw only the 6,600-ton *Agano* completed in November. She would not join the fleet until 1943; *Noshiro, Yahagi, Sakawa* and *Oyodo* would follow. Early in the war, most Japanese flag officers saw the aircraft carrier or the battleship as their ultimate weapon. However, at Guadalcanal in the last half of 1942, it would be destroyers with their maneuverability and speed, their ability to carry cargo and assault troops, and their Long Lance torpedoes that made them the new weapon of choice. They were in short supply.

After the Battle of Midway, the IJN suspended future expansion and by July 1942, only the Eighth Fleet at Rabaul was operational. In command there since June 29 was Vice Admiral Gunichi Mikawa, a veteran of Pearl Harbor and Midway. The Eighth or Outer South Seas Force initially included a combat force of five heavy cruisers, three light cruisers, four destroyers, troop transports and small auxiliary vessels and barges. By July, Rabaul's airstrips were home to 24 twin-engine Mitsubishi Betty bombers and 30 Zeros of the 25th Air Flotilla. An additional 20 reconnaissance and fighter floatplanes were stationed at Tulagi, Tananbogo and Gavutu. Mikawa was unaware of the US naval force approaching the Solomons.

Operation Watchtower Begins

A pre-invasion meeting for the Allies' Operation Watchtower was held on July 27 aboard Fletcher's flagship, USS *Saratoga*, sailing with carriers *Enterprise* and *Wasp* and 23 escorting warships 400 miles southeast of Fiji that rendezvoused with Rear Admiral Turner's South Pacific Amphibious Force. The meeting included Rear Admiral Daniel J. Callaghan representing Ghormley, Marine Major General Alexander Vandegrift and Rear Admiral John S. McCain Sr., the new head of Land-Based Air, South Pacific Force. McCain, his flag on seaplane tender *Curtiss*, was headquartered at Efate Island in the New Hebrides. A shock to some, Fletcher announced he would keep his carriers at Guadalcanal no more than two days and they would provide air support from south of the island. Protecting the carriers were battleship *North Carolina*; heavy cruisers *Minneapolis, New Orleans, Portland, Atlanta, San Francisco* and *Salt Lake City*; and destroyers *Phelps, Farragut, Worden, Macdonough, Dale, Balch, Benham, Maury, Gwin, Grayson, Lang, Sterett, Aaron Ward, Stack, Laffey* and *Farenholt*.

Watchtower began at 0300 hours on August 7 when planes off *Wasp* bombed Tulagi, Tananbogo and Gavutu Islands, softening them up and surprising the Japanese. US bombers destroyed 15 seaplanes at Tulagi, some with crews in them. By 0500 hours on August 7, Marine transports and screening warships rounded the western tip of Guadalcanal and entered the seven-mile-wide channel separating the big island from Savo to the north. Cruiser *Quincy* fired on Guadalcanal, west of the landing beaches. *San Juan* and destroyers *Buchanan* and *Monssen* bombed landing sites on the small islands. Destroyer *Selfridge* sank a schooner. First Marine Raider Battalion under Colonel Meritt Edson and 2nd Battalion under Lt. Colonel Rosecrans went ashore on Tulagi to little early resistance. Captain Miyazaki's radio message at 0625 hours for help at Tulagi was heard from Rabaul throughout Japanese-held territory. A second message was received at Rabaul at 0805 that 20 enemy ships were attacking and that Miyazaki's men were destroying equipment and papers. They would defend to the last man. No further broadcasts were received and none was received from crews on Guadalcanal. At Rabaul, in response to the messages, Admiral Mikawa met with Army Lt. General Hyakutake to discuss reprisal. Both men agreed that the appearance of the Americans was a good sign. The sooner they were defeated, the better.

Marines on Tulagi fought all that day, August 7, and the next, overtaking caves and machine gun pits, often in hand-to-hand combat in which they faced their first Banzai charge. Marine paratroopers jumped on Gavutu Island where one in 10 Americans was killed or wounded. Japanese resistance ended by noon on August 9 with almost 500 Japanese casualties and 70 US Marines and naval personnel lost or injured. Of 20 prisoners taken, most were Korean construction workers. Before long, the US Navy would turn the deep harbor at Tulagi into a refueling facility and another on Gavutu into a base for motor torpedo boats. Across the channel at Guadalcanal on August 7, Marines went ashore west of Lunga Point at "Red Beach" to little resistance, mostly slowed by jungle terrain. They easily took the Japanese airfield the next day as construction crews and native workers retreated into the rain forest. It would be the last easy day, or easy night, that US soldiers, sailors and Marines would live through on the densely forested, humid, insect- and malaria-ridden island. There would be a six-month-long, fierce, bloody land campaign for control of the airfield that the Americans named Henderson Field in honor of US Marine Corps Major Lofton Henderson, the first Marine aviator to perish in the Battle of Midway. More names like Edson's Raiders, Cactus Air Force, Bloody Ridge and others would be written into the history of Guadalcanal. In the waters off its north coast, Allied and Japanese ships would conduct six sea battles over the next four months that would result in an extraordinary loss of ships and men on both sides. The First is remembered as the Battle of Savo Island.

The Battle of Savo Island

In reprisal, the Japanese followed a plan quickly prepared by Captain Shigenori Kami for a night attack on the Allied forces in the Solomons. Following it, Vice Admiral Gunichi Mikawa, aboard heavy cruiser *Chokai*, led a force southeast from Rabaul late day on August 7 with light cruisers *Tenryu* and *Yubari*, heavy cruisers *Aoba*, *Furutaka*, *Kako* and *Kinugasa* and destroyer *Yunagi*. A US submarine and two Allied scout planes reported the enemy on a southeast course but the alerts either did not reach US officers or were missed in the heat of battle and an endless attempt to unload supplies. By evening August 8, the Japanese neared what would soon be called Iron Bottom Sound south of Savo Island. A floatplane off *Aoba* reported the Allies having one battleship, four cruisers, seven destroyers and 15 transports off Guadalcanal and two heavy cruisers, 12 destroyers and three transports off Tulagi. Mikawa surmised there had to be carriers in the area. For an attack in darkness, he ordered each ship to display a 1 × 7-meter white banner on their bridges to be seen by his other ships over the dark, night waters. This worked better than Allied radar, it seems. An Australian coast watcher keyed an alert to Malaita near Guadalcanal that announced 24 Japanese torpedo bombers headed toward the Allies. Radar on *Chicago* picked them up and called in planes from the carriers. The second of two Japanese attacks resulted in a hit on destroyer *Mugford*, killing 22 men. Japanese lost 14 bombers and the Americans, 11 fighters and a dive bomber.

Admiral Crutchley executed a night plan for his ships that included a picket line: destroyer *Blue* in the channel south of Savo, and *Ralph Talbot* to the north, and two cruiser groups, HMAS *Australia,* HMAS *Canberra* and *Chicago* behind *Blue,* and *Vincennes, Quincy* and *Astoria* behind *Ralph Talbot.* To counter an attack, the *Australia* group would also include *Selfridge, Patterson* and *Bagley.* The *Vincennes* group would use *Henley, Helm, Jarvis* and *Mugford.* At the eastern approach with *San Juan* were HMAS *Hobart* and destroyers *Monssen* and *Buchanan.* All went well the night of August 7 and ships broke formation the morning of the eighth. Just before noon, Japanese planes came in from over Florida Island's east end. Gunfire from the cruisers took down 20 of them. Destroyer *Jarvis* was hit and badly damaged. Unloading of supply ships went on during August 8, with and without help from the Marines.

After midnight August 9, Japanese and Allied warships met east and north of Savo Island. The first salvo from *Kako* hit *Vincennes,* after which the cruiser took 85 direct hits but not before sinking the *Kinugasa.* Hit by fire from *Furutaka,* shells from *Tenryu* and *Yubari,* and torpedoes from *Chokai,* Captain Frederick Riefkohl gave the abandon ship order. *Vincennes* sank just east of Savo with the loss of 332 killed or missing and 258 wounded. Earlier, *Aoba* focused her fire on *Quincy* while flagship *Chokai* hit *Astoria.* Fueled planes and cartridge cases of star shells burned on *Quincy's* deck, surrounded by dead and wounded. Men were trapped below jammed hatches. At 0204 hours, two torpedoes from *Tenryu* struck portside, then she followed with shell fire. Captain Samuel Moore steered the burning *Quincy* between *Furu-*

taka and *Chokai* that was firing on *Astoria*. *Quincy* got off several 8-inch shells, her last, that penetrated *Chokai's* bridge. At 0235 hours, *Quincy* sank bow first leaving 167 wounded in the water and 370 dead, including Captain Moore. His body washed up on Savo Island and was buried by natives, one of whom kept Moore's Annapolis class ring.

Japanese star shells lit the cruisers so that Captain Greenman on *Astoria* saw how fiercely *Vincennes* and *Quincy* were burning when his ship took a hit on the starboard side of the bridge. The aft engine room below was abandoned, and boilers could give only eight knots while Japanese shells raked *Astoria* from her foremast aft, just after 0200 hours. She managed some minor damage to *Kinugasa* and 12 shots on *Chokai*, as the enemy turned back. Mikawa had ordered all his ships away. Destroyer *Bagley* came alongside *Astoria*, bow to bow, at 0445 and took off wounded. There was hope *Astoria* could be saved and at 0600, *Bagley* returned with electricians, ship fitters and water tenders while still able officers pitched in. *Bagley* backed away and destroyer *Hopkins* attempted a tow to shallow water. Destroyer *Wilson* pumped water on the fires for an hour but by noon, *Hopkins* and *Wilson* were ordered away. Two more destroyers were brought in but at 1100 hours, a blast was heard below and *Astoria* listed 45 degrees. Captain Greenman called abandon ship, was last to leave, and she quietly sank at 1215 hours.

Early in the battle, HMAS *Canberra* and USS *Chicago* were struck by bombs from Japanese floatplanes as they sailed between the enemy and Allied transports north of Guadalcanal. *Canberra* was also hit by torpedoes and shells from *Chokai* and *Furutaka*. Destroyer *Patterson* came alongside at 0400 hours to fight fires on *Canberra* but by 0630, her 398 Australian seamen along with 18 Japanese prisoners were removed by transport USS *Barnett*. She was scuttled by destroyers *Ellet* and *Selfridge*, an effort that required 300 shells and five torpedoes. *Canberra's* wounded totaled 109 men, with 84 killed or missing. Destroyer USS *Jarvis* with her crew of 247 was not seen again, vanished in the Coral Sea southwest of Guadalcanal.

Aftermath

Fearing an attack by American carrier planes, Admiral Mikasa withdrew his ships to the west against forceful advice from his team to attack the Allied transports, a decision that eventually led to an Allied victory in the Solomons. The Japanese would be back, however, to engage their enemy in five more sea battles and to land thousands of troops in an attempt to retake Henderson Field. The mistakes of US admirals were many and there was plenty of blame to go around. Only British Admiral Crutchley, who was likely most at fault, escaped criticism. *Time* magazine called Savo the "worst blue-water defeat in US history." Lessons learned after Savo were bitter but from the wreckage emerged a United States Navy of men and ships without equal in the world.

Chapter XV

A CHANGING TIDE

Introduction

As Japanese forces sailed west and Allied forces east, Vandegrift's Marines were digging in on Guadalcanal to help bring supplies ashore, fight Japanese in the air and on land, and complete and keep Henderson Field. Failure on any count was not an option. Vandegrift knew Turner would send more stores and weapons, he knew his Marines would hold the enemy, and he knew once the airfield was ready, McCain would fly in planes. Four old destroyer transports, *Colhoun*, *Gregory*, *Little* and *McKean*, brought in fuel, bombs and ammunition on August 15, 1942, along with Marine Major Charles Hayes to run the airport and 120 men to service the planes. Another three transports brought in rations and departed safely. The first flight to land at Henderson was a Catalina followed on August 20 by 19 Wildcats and 12 Dauntlesses off light carrier *Long Island*. One early skirmish at the Matanikau River caused the loss of four Marines and 65 Japanese, after which General Hyakutake at Rabaul assigned Colonel Kiyonao Ichiki and his detachment to retake Guadalcanal. Estimated time to accomplish the operation was three days. Six destroyers from Truk landed Ichiki with less than 1,000 troops east of the airfield in the belief there were only 2,000 Marines on the island when actually there were 17,000. In the first hours of August 21, US Marines met the Japanese at the Ilu/Tenaru River, or Alligator Creek, and obliterated most of Ichiki's detachment, after which he took his life. By this time, Yamamoto was ready to commit his Combined Fleet in Operation KA.

Allied Operations

Nightly attacks on Henderson Field by Japanese raiders, nicknamed Tokyo Express by the Marines, were for the most part a source of aggravation, but an early significant loss was destroyer USS *Blue.* She was hit by a torpedo off destroyer *Kawakaze* on August 21 in Iron Bottom Sound and towed by USS *Henley* toward Tulagi where she was scuttled outside the harbor. By then, Japanese naval forces were on their way from the North in five groups and the American admirals knew they were coming. Alerted by one of Admiral McCain's patrol planes at 0950 hours on August 23, Dauntlesses and fighters from carrier *Saratoga* and land-based Marine planes launched from Henderson Field that afternoon found no transports, no Japanese. Rear Admiral Tanaka aboard light cruiser *Jintsu,* alerted by the patrol, had turned them back. Early on August 23, the American carrier force was north of Malaita Island, 150 miles east of Guadalcanal. Task Force 11 under Admiral Fletcher included *Saratoga* with 36 Wildcats, 36 Dauntlesses and 15 Avengers; cruisers *Minneapolis* and *New Orleans*; and destroyers *Dale, Farragut, Macdonough* and *Worden. Enterprise* carried the same number of planes as *Saratoga* and was covered by USS *North Carolina,* light cruisers *Atlanta* and *Portland;* and destroyers *Balch, Benham, Ellet, Grayson, Maury* and *Monssen.* Carrier *Wasp* had 28 Wildcats, 36 Dauntlesses and 15 Wildcats, and sailed with cruisers *Salt Lake City, San Francisco* and *San Juan* and destroyers *Aaron Ward, Buchanan, Farenholt, Lang, Selfridge, Stack* and *Sterrett. Wasp,* however, had been turned back for refueling at 1800 hours.

Japanese Operations

Yamamoto's ships, meanwhile, refueled at sea, not north of Truk as the American admirals assumed, but heading south nonstop. Vice Admiral Kondo led Advance Force aboard his flagship, heavy cruiser *Atago,* with *Maya* and *Takao;* Vice Admiral Takagi with *Myoko* and *Haguro*; and Rear

Admiral Tomatsu Tokama on light cruiser *Yura* with destroyers *Asagumo, Hayashio, Kuroshio* and *Oyashio*. A Support Group included battleship *Mutsu;* destroyers *Harusame, Murasame, Natsugumo* and *Samidare;* and seaplane carrier *Chitose* with 22 planes. A Striking Force under Vice Admiral Nagumo included carrier *Shokaku* with 26 fighters, 14 bombers and 18 torpedo bombers; and *Zuikaku* carrying 17 fighters, 27 bombers and 18 torpedo planes. The carriers were screened by destroyers *Akigumo, Kazagumo, Makigumo, Shikinami, Uranami* and *Yugumo*. Their vanguard under Rear Admiral Abe included battleships *Hiei* and *Kirishima*, cruisers *Chikuma, Kumano* and *Suzuya*. Their screen was light cruiser *Nagara* with destroyers *Akizuki, Hatsukaze, Maikaze, Nowaki, Tanikaze* and *Yukikaze*. A diversionary group held heavy cruiser *Tone*, light carrier *Ryujo* carrying 16 fighters and 21 torpedo planes, along with destroyers *Amatsukaze* and *Tokitsukaze*. An Advance Expeditionary Force from Truk included light cruiser *Katori* and nine submarines. From Rabaul on New Britain Island, Vice Admiral Mikawa on *Chokai* headed Outer South Seas Force, with Rear Admiral Tanaka leading a reinforcement group on *Jintsu* with five destroyers that were to shell Henderson Field the night of August 24: *Isokaze, Kagero, Kawakaze, Mutsuki* and *Yayoi,* and three others, *Suzukaze, Umikaze* and *Uzuki*. Rear Admiral Goto led heavy cruisers *Aoba, Kinugasa* and *Furutaka*. A transport unit with *Kinryu Maru* carried SNLF troops and more of the Ichiki detachment on four patrol boats. There were 100 land-based aircraft assigned and three submarines.

Battle of the Eastern Solomons

On the morning of August 24, Admiral Kondo sent light carrier *Ryujo* and cruiser *Tone* ahead to lure the American carriers into attacking, and the ruse was successful. From his base at Noumea, Ghormley ordered Fletcher to intercept and attack the big Japanese carriers. Poor communication caused Fletcher to launch most of his torpedo and dive bombers on *Ryujo* instead of on *Shokaku* and *Zuikaku*. *Ryujo* took several bombs and one torpedo and sank that evening with the loss of 100 of her crew. At 1400 hours, Nagumo launched 36 Vals that ran into 53 Wildcats that had fought through a swarm of Zeros. A dozen Vals were destroyed and the remainder hit *Enterprise* with three bombs that ruptured her decks. She was saved by damage control.

North Carolina fought off all attackers and her gunners took down 14 Japanese planes. *Saratoga's* planes found *Chitose* and caused severe damage. Fletcher moved his ships south at 2000 hours and though Kondo tried to find them, he gave up by midnight. On the morning of August 25, land-based Dauntlesses along with dive bombers off *Enterprise* found *Jintsu*, leaving her severely damaged. Transport *Kinryu Maru* was hit with a 1,000-pound bomb and as survivors were being rescued, eight B-17s from New Hebrides showed up and quickly sank destroyer *Mutsuki*. Destroyer *Yayoi* was damaged. A Japanese attempt to land reinforcements on Guadalcanal failed, leaving the Battle of the Eastern Solomons a tactical victory for the Americans.

Defending Cactus at Bloody Ridge

The Allied code for Guadalcanal was Cactus and the Marine and Army planes based at Henderson Field were the Cactus Air Force. The Japanese, in the weeks after their defeat in the Eastern Solomons, made nightly raids on the airfield and its environs. They paid a heavy toll, though, as Marine pilots scored a five-to-one kill ratio on the attackers. On August 30, two squadrons of Marine Air Group 3 arrived at Cactus along with planes of the Army's 67th Fighter Squadron, 14 P-400s, a version of the Airacobra. Their air commander Roy Geiger arrived four days later, and his firm optimism served well as mechanical breakdowns and the muddy airstrip wore down men and equipment.

In late August, Tanaka's ships began delivering Japanese troops from Santa Isabel to the far west of Guadalcanal at Cape Esperance. These were 3,000 men of Major General Kiyotake Kawaguchi's 35th Brigade, to be debarked from destroyers and barges, many that were lost to Dauntlesses. Kawaguchi's plan to recapture Henderson Field took his men on a six-day jungle march to a position two miles south of the airfield where Col. Meritt Edson's Raiders were dug in and waiting. Kawaguchi had support from the air and from destroyers and a cruiser that bombarded the ridgeline. At 2100 hours on September 13, Kawaguchi launched the first of two attacks on Edson's men that left his own detachment with 500 dead. A second Japanese line east of the airfield was also repulsed, leaving 400 wounded to be carried back behind Japanese lines, an eight-day slog through jungle terrain. The bloody ridge the Marines held would become known to US history as Edson's Ridge.

With this defeat, the Japanese made control of Guadalcanal their main military objective and planned a major attack on the Allies for mid-October. Lt. General Hyakutake would take personal command of the land operation. Meanwhile, the Tokyo Express continued its nightly passage through the Slot and began delivering additional troops to Kawaguchi almost immediately after Bloody Ridge. Even with their victory in mid-September, Vandegrift's Marines were low on supplies, had no tanks and were down to 30 operational aircraft. The US Army canceled a delivery of its planes. The General in command of US Army forces in the Pacific thought Guadalcanal a lost cause and MacArthur and the chief of Army Air Force agreed. Ghormley in Noumea thought otherwise and sent the 7th Marines from Espiritu Santo as reinforcements, five transports and two supply ships. He ordered a carrier group centered on *Hornet* and *Wasp* for long-range cover, 100 miles distant. On September 15, *Wasp* was hit by three torpedoes from Japanese submarine *I-19*. She sank with the loss of 150 men and three days later, Admiral Turner delivered the Marines to Guadalcanal. USS *North Carolina* and destroyer *O'Brien* also were torpedoed but survived. The last day of September, Admiral Nimitz visited the island and subsequently ordered the Americal Division's 164th Regiment to be assigned there. Attacks and counterattacks would continue for months while losses on both sides tallied up from fighting and from illness.

Battle of Cape Esperance

On October 11, while screening a landing of US Army troops near Henderson Field, Admiral Norman Scott on heavy cruiser *San Francisco* learned of a Japanese force under Admiral Goto covering Japanese troop landings at the far northwest of Guadalcanal at Cape Esperance. Scott's group sailing west of Savo Island included heavy cruiser *Salt Lake City*, light cruisers *Boise* and *Helena* with destroyers *Buchanan*, *Duncan*, *Farenholt*, *Laffey* and *McCalla*. Goto, heading southeast down the Slot, had heavy cruisers *Aoba*, *Furutaka* and *Kinugasa* with destroyers *Fubuki* and *Hatsuyuki*. The reinforcement group under Rear Admiral Takaji Joshima had seaplane carriers *Chitose* and

Nisshin carrying 728 Army personnel, field guns, howitzers, supplies and landing craft. Joshima had six destroyers: *Akizuki, Asagumo, Murakumo, Natsugumo, Shirayuki* and *Yamagumo*. The American ships had radar, some with an early version and some more modern, while the Japanese had sailors with good night vision.

Kingfishers catapulted off *San Francisco* tracked the unsuspecting Goto; however, a plane off *Salt Lake City* accidentally ignited flares that gave him warning. At 2330 hours, a scout plane confirmed Joshima's landing group off Esperance and Scott strategized he'd remain between the two forces and hit Japanese either approaching or retiring. Scott's ships sailed in a snake-like line from northeast to southwest, with destroyers to port. Radar from *Helena* at 2342 reported a surface or air target six miles distant on a direct heading. Communication between ships was poor and caused confusion when Scott ordered his line of ships to turn southwest. When *Duncan*'s skipper saw *Farenholt* turn west, he stayed the course to attack the enemy, but *Farenholt* went southwest. *Laffey* followed *Farenholt*.

By 2345 hours, most ships followed *San Francisco* southwest. *Duncan* and *Helena,* relying on her modern radar, attacked an unsuspecting Goto. *Salt Lake City* fired her guns and star shells and was hit by fire off a Japanese ship, killing several of her crew. *Boise* fired on *Hatsuyuki, San Francisco* fired as did *Farenholt,* and *Laffey* raked *Aoba. Duncan* hit *Furutaka* and a destroyer, perhaps *Hatsuyuki*. At 2347, Scott ordered a cease fire because he was worried his ships were firing on each other. This halt would have been a disaster for the Americans had not Admiral Goto made the same decision after which exploding shells near *Aoba*'s bridge left him mortally wounded. Gunners on some US ships failed to follow the Rear Admiral's order and once he was reassured there was no friendly fire, he quickly reversed his order. *Duncan* took a serious hit in her fireroom and several more followed but not before releasing a torpedo on *Furutaka* that sunk her hours after the battle ended.

Despite Scott's confidence, *Farenholt* was hit in what might have been friendly fire. When an unidentified ship was seen sailing west, the Americans attacked as a group and saw *Fubuki* explode and sink. *Aoba* and *Furutaka* were burning. *Furutaka* sank 20 miles northwest of Savo Island. At midnight, just as Scott again called a cease fire, *Kinugasa* opened up. In the milieu, ships continued firing and *Boise* took enormous damage, yet with fires quelched by flooding, she remained at 20 knots. *Boise* lost 107 officers and men, 35 wounded. Heroic attempts to save *Duncan*, notwithstanding, she was abandoned and sank six miles north of Savo. *McCalla* rescued 197 of *Duncan*'s crew and took three Japanese prisoners. While Admiral Goto fought and died, Joshima landed troops and supplies east of Cape Esperance. *Murakumo* and *Shirayuki* returned to rescue 400 survivors, but *Murakumo* had to be scuttled after an attack by bombers and fighters from Henderson Field. The same planes took out *Natsugumo*, also on a rescue mission. During the sea battle, fresh Japanese troops were successfully landed at Tassafaronga east of Esperance, along with heavy artillery that would mean trouble for the Marines. The battle was a morale booster for the American public. The US Navy was left with some lessons to learn.

Henderson Field Takes a Pounding

As Admiral Nimitz promised, the 164th Infantry Regiment of the Americal Division arrived on Guadalcanal early on October 13 courtesy of Admiral Turner's transports. Things were looking up for the Marines there until afternoon when high level Japanese bombers in two attacks turned Henderson Field into Swiss cheese. Crews, mostly Seabees, repaired the cratered runways with Marston mats, the perforated steel strips of planking that allowed for rapid reconstruction. However, field artillery the Americans called Pistol Pete that was delivered days before to enemy troops continued to tear up the runway until destroyers *Gwin, Nicholas* and *Sterett* put it out of business for a time, along with its Japanese operators.

After midnight, however, Henderson was in for more abuse. Vice Admiral Kurita with battleships *Haruna* and *Kongo*, screened by light cruiser *Isuzu* and several destroyers unleased a bombardment of armor-piercing shells that set the runway aflame. Of 90 US planes, only 35 Wildcats and seven dive bombers were left to use a supplementary grass landing strip. Four motor torpedo boats from Tulagi came across Sealark Channel to torpedo Kurita's ships and by 0230 hours, he ceased firing and backed off to north of Savo. The Americans lost 60 Marines, others wounded, and most of their aviation fuel. On the night of August 14–15, Mikawa on *Chokai* along with *Kinugasa* continued their shelling and early morning saw six Japanese transports loaded with Hyakutake's troops lying off Tassafaronga. Three of the six were beached and the other three withdrawn, thanks to pilots from Henderson along with B-17s from Espiritu Santo, torpedoes off Geiger's own PBY, and Wildcats and ground troops that took down a dozen Japanese bombers and five Zeroes. Planes off carrier *Hornet* took out a dozen enemy seaplanes on Santa Isabel and added to the beaching of the transports at Tassafaronga.

Even so, the next few weeks left hope of an American victory at Guadalcanal in doubt. Destroyers *Meredith* and *Vireo* were sunk on October 15 while towing barges of fuel to Henderson. Days later, Destroyers *Grayson* and *Gwin* rescued 88 men while 236 were lost, many to sharks. On October 16, destroyer *McFarland* was hit delivering oil at Lunga Point. The barge she towed exploded but her survival story is legendary. On October 17, destroyers *Aaron Ward* and *Lardner* shelled Kokumbona between Tassafaronga and Lunga, relieving the enemy of an ammunition dump. And on and on it went.

Battle of Santa Cruz Islands

By the last week of October 1942, despite attention to the war in Europe and in North Africa, Navy Secretary Knox, and President Roosevelt himself, shared their strong opinions with the Chiefs of Staff that Vandegrift must be given all he needed to hold Guadalcanal. The 25th Infantry Division would be sent from Hawaii, the 8th Marines from Samoa, the 37th Division rerouted, the 2nd Raider Battalion and the 43rd Division sent. Cactus Air Force, down to 29 planes, would be resupplied. On October 18, when Admiral Halsey arrived on Noumea in French New Caledonia, supposedly for a tour of the situation, he was handed a message from Nimitz that he, Halsey, was to replace Gormley. In another personnel move, Admiral Fletcher was replaced by Rear Admiral Thomas Kinkaid to lead the main naval strike force. Halsey called a conference at Noumea for October 23 to include Vandegrift, Turner, Commander Patch of the Americal Division, Marine Commandant Holcomb and others. The decision was made to give Vandegrift everything he needed. Nothing would be held back.

Yamamoto on battleship *Yamato* at Truk continued to believe the Imperial Japanese Navy could draw out and destroy the American fleet in their next encounter and he had been promised by the Army that it would have Henderson Field sewed up by the night of October 24. Japanese naval forces were to rendezvous north of the Santa Cruz Islands, east of the southern

Solomons and 850 miles north of Noumea. Nagumo was in command of main force with *Shokaku* and *Zuikaku,* light carrier *Zuiho,* battleships *Hiei* and *Kumano,* four heavy cruisers and 12 destroyers. Admiral Hiroaki Abe had battleships *Hiei* and *Kirishima.* Kondo commanded Advance Force with carrier *Junyo,* battleships *Haruna* and *Kongo* now equipped with radar, seven cruisers and 12 destroyers. Their planes would have to find the Americans before their fuel supplies ran low.

To meet the Japanese, Admiral Kincaid and Task Force 61 had *Enterprise,* battleship *South Dakota,* two cruisers and eight destroyers. Rear Admiral George Murray and Task Force 17 brought *Hornet,* four cruisers and six destroyers. A PBY located the Japanese just after midnight on October 25 and before dawn on the 26th two Dauntlesses off *Enterprise* successfully attacked *Zuiho.* By 0930 hours, Nagumo's dive and torpedo bombers left *Hornet* dead in the water but not before her planes hit *Shokaku* with six bombs that put it out of commission. *Hornet* was under tow when hit by planes from *Junyo,* hit again that afternoon, abandoned and sunk by Japanese torpedoes after midnight. Cruiser *Chikuma* was hit and forced to return to Truk.

Enterprise fought off attacks until hit by a 500-pound bomb that exploded through her flight deck. *South Dakota* was hit and cruiser *San Juan* and destroyer *Smith* damaged. Kondo sent a fast vanguard to find *Enterprise,* but Kincaid took her away from the action. After Kondo's ships were hit by torpedoes from PBYs, he retired to Truk. The Japanese lost 69 of their 212 planes at Santa Cruz, 500 total in Guadalcanal battles. and many of their best pilots. By then, Yamamoto learned that ground forces had not taken Henderson Field.

The Battle of Santa Cruz was fought in waves of aircraft attacks, ship movements north and south, and although sinking *Hornet* gave the Japanese a tactical win, two of their carriers and one cruiser would be out of action for months. Most telling on Yamamoto's side, however, was his reassignment of Admiral Nagumo to shore duty. The Americans not only held Henderson Field, Vandegrift's Marines pushed the Japanese westward with the help of heavy guns off cruisers *San Francisco* and *Helena.* B-17s, bombers and Airacobras hammered enemy troops, killing hundreds, until Vandegrift learned of an enemy landing east of Henderson. A Japanese attempt to build another airfield there failed after US cruisers, destroyers and land-based howitzers killed 400 of the enemy troops and drove the remainder into the jungle and toward the hills near Mount Austen.

Naval Battles of Guadalcanal

The last days of October saw cruiser USS *Atlanta* and four destroyers deliver transports and artillery to the Marines along with a bombardment that pushed Japanese land troops farther west yet again, beyond Point Cruz. Japanese destroyers delivered more troops and supplies to western Guadalcanal, more than the Americans imagined. Five battalions of Vandegrift's newly arrived Marines and an Army battalion began a new offensive west on November 10 but Hyakutake's new force of 5,000 men held the Americans back from their leader's command post at Kokumbona and the road to Mount Austen. The Marines pulled back east of the Matanikau River, destroying bridges they had built. The big action turned to the waters off Guadalcanal the next day when the Japanese Navy and Army began an enormous, combined effort to smash the Americans on land and at sea. Rear Admiral Hiroaki Abe's battleships *Hiei* and *Kirishima* bombarded the Henderson Field defenders day and night to allow Admiral Tanaka's transports to land troops at Tassafaronga on November 13. Kondo with carriers *Hiyo* and *Junyo* and battleships *Haruna* and *Kongo* would provide cover from 150 miles north. Admiral Turner on attack transport *McCawley,* with an escort of three heavy cruisers, two light cruisers and eight destroyers, delivered an infantry regiment on the 12th. Rear Admiral Norman Scott on *Atlanta* arrived with four destroyers that day and Turner ordered in Callaghan on *San Francisco* with destroyers *Helena, Juneau, Pensacola* and *Portland* to intercept Abe. Halsey sent Task Force 16 with battleships, cruisers, destroyers and, if she were finished with repairs at Noumea, *Enterprise.* If not, Rear Admiral W. A. Lee on *Washington* would command. The Americans had 14 submarines in the Solomons, Rear Admiral Fitch's planes at Espiritu Santo and Geiger's air wing at Henderson.

Action began at 0145 on Friday, November 13, just off Lunga Point when Callaghan's destroyers ran into Abe's vanguard. A Japanese torpedo put *Atlanta* out of commission early and a salvo that hit its bridge killed Rear Admiral Scott and most of his staff there. *Atlanta* sank that evening. Callaghan on *San Francisco* formed his ships into a line as he had done at Cape Esperance a month earlier. This time he lost *Laffey* and *Cushing* that were in the lead. Confusion reigned among both the Americans and the Japanese, including a puzzling cease fire order from Callaghan, most likely to avoid friendly fire. *O'Bannon's* skipper, however, continued launching torpedoes on battleship *Hiei,* covering her in flames, after an earlier set of salvos from *San Francisco* hit her. But *San Francisco* suffered next when hit by *Kirishima* and other ships on her starboard and by a Japanese destroyer to port. The cruiser would live to fight again but Admiral Callaghan was killed. *Portland* was hit, lost her steering gear and forced to travel in circles. Still, she was able to pump enough projectiles into *Yudachi* to explode and sink her. *Sterett* pitched in, after which she was hit and retired. Destroyers *Barton* and *Monssen* were sunk. *Akatsuki* was lost and *Yudachi* was abandoned south of Savo Island. By 0200 on November 13, Abe ordered *Hiei* and *Kirishima* north and away which meant Henderson Field was safe for another night. On the morning of November 14, remnants of the US task force sailed east, *Helena* and *Fletcher* unscathed along with *San Francisco*, being repaired even while underway. An enemy torpedo found light cruiser *Juneau,* killing almost 700, among them the five Sullivan Brothers. That morning, though, Avengers, Dauntlesses and Wildcats had a good run over the Slot, hitting *Kinugasa* and planting bombs on *Isuzu.* The battle continued.

Yamamoto reassigned Vice Admiral Hiroaki Abe to shore duty for his failures, including the final death knell to battleship *Hiei* that was delivered by Wildcats, Avengers and B-17s northwest of Savo the evening of November 14. The US battleships hit light cruiser *Sendai* and destroyer *Ayanami* that survived to fight again. Admiral Mikawa, now in charge, continued with what he thought was a successful attack on Henderson Field and retired without cover from Kondo's ships. US planes found him and managed to sink a cruiser and damage three others. Admiral Tanaka also took punishment from the Americans as he tried to land more transports at Tassafaronga where he lost most of the Special Naval Landing Force and other troops. US Admiral Lee with *Washington* and *South Dakota* returned to Iron Bottom Sound to intercept Tanaka and lost destroyers *Benham, Gwin, Preston* and *Walke* in the attempt. However, thanks to *Washington's* excellent radar, Lee left *Kirishima* burning to sink on November 15.

As both forces disengaged, both claimed victory, but it was the Americans who turned the tide from defensive to offensive. They landed troops while the Japanese transports were decimated. The Americans maintained air superiority and kept Henderson Field. The Americans lost more combat ships but the Japanese loss of two battleships and 11 transports was more serious. *Enterprise* continued to launch and retrieve her planes while carriers *Hiyo* and *Junyo* were held back. The waters north of Guadalcanal were in American hands and Vandegrift resumed a push to the west with enough troops and artillery to see the Japanese fight for every yard. By November 23, a stalemate settled in the land battle as Hyakutake held on with half of his men sick or wounded. Lt. General Hitoshi Imamura, new at Rabaul, determined a new offensive on Guadalcanal could not begin until mid-January 1943.

Battle of Tassafaronga

Because of American air superiority, the Japanese were unable to supply their troops on Guadalcanal by day so Tanaka the Terrible, as the Americans now called him, found a way. He would load his destroyers with cleaned oil drums filled with supplies, connect the drums with ropes and chains and throw them off his destroyers into the sea by night. They would float to shore or be retrieved by swimmers or men in small boats. In an operation such as this on November 30, after the Americans were alerted by encryption experts and coast watchers, Tanaka's force was surprised in Iron Bottom Sound by Task Force 67 from Espiritu Santo. It was led by Rear Admiral Carleton Wright who had recently taken over from Admiral Kincaid. TF 67 included destroyers sailing in this order: *Fletcher, Perkins, Maury* and *Drayton* followed by cruisers *Minneapolis, New Orleans, Pensacola, Honolulu* and *Northampton*. Destroyers *Lamson* and *Lardner,* headed east with a transport/supply group, were ordered by Halsey to join Wright at the rear. No pickets were sent ahead as had been planned but radar on *Fletcher* found the enemy. Tanaka, streaming east along the coast, had *Naganami, Makinami, Oyashio, Kuroshio, Kagero, Kawakaze* and *Suzukaze* with *Takanami* to port of the supply destroyers on lookout. Japanese and Americans were the proverbial ships passing in the night until at 2316 hours when *Fletcher* asked permission to fire. Wright hesitated to give an order because of distance, but Wright was wrong.

The unsuspecting Japanese were an easy target but the delay was fatal. At 2320, when order to fire was finally given, the Americans sent off a full barrage of torpedoes against targets that had advanced out of line. All torpedoes beached except two that sank *Takanami*. The Japanese, although surprised, carried off their attacks with speed and accuracy. *Minneapolis, New Orleans* and *Pensacola* were all hit and afire but made safe way to Tulagi Harbor. They would not return to action for a year. *Northampton* took no evasive action and was hit with two torpedoes that took out her propulsion and left her burning. She was abandoned and sank two hours later, her crew rescued by small craft from Tulagi. Tassafaronga was a horrific American failure with blame to go around. Four hundred sailors died with *Northampton*. Nevertheless, it was the last major sea battle in the Southern Solomons. Further visits by the Tokyo Express would serve only to evacuate Japanese troops.

Part Four

JANUARY 1943–
SEPTEMBER 1945

And now the old ships and their men are gone; the new ships and the new men, many of them bearing the old auspicious names, have taken up their watch on the stern and impartial sea, which offers no opportunities but to those who know how to grasp them with a ready hand and undaunted heart.

—Joseph Conrad, *The Mirror of the Sea*

Chapter XVI

GUADALCANAL TO TOKYO BAY

Pupuraka Hill—Withdrawal

Tassafaronga would be the last major sea battle in the southern Solomon Islands. General Vandegrift and the Marines said goodbye to Guadalcanal in December 1942 as General Patch and the Army's Americal Division took over. Unknown to the Americans, Imperial General Headquarters requested permission from Emperor Hirohito to evacuate the starving, sick and dying Japanese troops from the island. Hyakutake and his subordinates would have preferred to give their lives and the lives of their men in a final Banzai charge but the emperor was obeyed. As plans were being made in late January 1943 for Tanaka's transports to accomplish the evacuation, Patch ordered a reconnaissance party to march the Kokumbona Trail from the north shore of Guadalcanal to the southwest where landing craft would meet them with tanks and supplies. The battalion would set up an observation post in the northwest from which to observe the enemy. Destroyers *DeHaven*, *Fletcher*, *Nicholas* and *Radford* provided cover.

While rounding Cape Esperance to return to Tulagi, *DeHaven* was sunk with 167 of her crew. Soon alerts came in from coast watchers of 20 Tokyo Express destroyers heading for Iron Bottom Sound. The Americans were still unaware it was Tanaka arriving to begin the evacuation. Remaining Japanese troops on Guadalcanal assembled near Pupuraka Hill near Cape Esperance for three attempts at evacuation, January 1st, 4th and the last on the 7th. The operation was called KE. In it, the Japanese lost destroyer *Makigumo* early in the process and before the Americans realized this was a retreat, they lost four planes. In an air attack near Rennell Island, cruiser *Chicago* was sunk. On February 2, when American troops found an abandoned base at Tassafaronga, the evacuation became obvious. Of 35,000 Japanese who fought on Guadalcanal, 14,000 were killed, 9,000 died of disease, and 4,300 were wounded.

Issue No Longer in Doubt

Japanese expansion in the Pacific stopped at Guadalcanal. Allied supply lines to Australia and New Zealand were secure. For the next 24 months, the Allies would employ a military strategy of island hopping as they recovered lost territory and fought their way toward the Japanese mainland. Unlike General MacArthur's strategy of leapfrogging in which troops landed on lightly guarded beaches, Admiral Nimitz and the US Navy favored direct assaults on heavily defended islands. Thus, many know the names Tarawa, Peleliu, Saipan, Guam, Iwo Jima and Okinawa where fighting resulted in casualties on both sides and where the stars and stripes were flown in hard-won victories. US shipbuilding programs in the months of 1943 and 1944 moved forward at a rapid pace. The German Third Reich signed its surrender on May 7, 1945.

In July 1945, heavy cruiser USS *Indianapolis* left San Francisco on a secret, urgent mission. She carried two crates of components for nuclear weapons to the US naval base on Tinian in the Northern Mariana Islands. On July 30, she left Tinian for the Philippines on training duty, untracked and without destroyer escort. Midway to her destination and outside normal shipping lanes, *Indianapolis* was torpedoed by IJN submarine *I-58* and sank within minutes. Of her crew of over 1,200 officers and men, 300 went down with their ship and the rest were left at sea for four days with few lifeboats to suffer exposure, hunger, dehydration, hallucination and shark attacks. Only 316 were rescued to survive and learn the reason for their secret mission to Tinian, the August 6 bombing of Hiroshima and Nagasaki on August 9. The

Empire of Japan surrendered on August 15. On the morning of September 2, 1945, on the new battleship USS *Missouri* in Tokyo Bay, representatives of nine Allied nations watched as the following persons signed the Instrument of Surrender: Japanese Foreign Minister Mamoru Shigemitsu, General Yoshijiro Umezu, General Douglas MacArthur and Fleet Admiral Chester Nimitz.

War in the Pacific began when the first wave of 183 Japanese fighter and bomber aircraft arrived over Oahu on December 7, 1941. It ended when a single bomber dropped a solitary bomb on Nagasaki. In the 1,388 days separating those two events, the Empire of Japan and the United States of America relied on the warships and men of their navies to locate, engage and destroy the enemy. Even after their carrier attack on Pearl Harbor, the Imperial Japanese Navy held to the belief that war could not be won without the battleship, the Dreadnaught. Yet Admiral Yamamoto's battleship *Yamato* never saw action. It was the loss of carriers *Akagi, Kaga, Hiryu* and *Soryu* at the Battle of Midway in June 1942 that was the most significant turning point for the Japanese. It was the Battle of Tassafaronga on November 30, 1942, when Japanese reinforcements were kept from reaching Guadalcanal and retaking Henderson Field that signaled the issue was no longer in doubt.

BIBLIOGRAPHY

Ballard, Robert D. *Return to Midway*. The National Geographic Society, 1999.

Belote, James H. and William M. Belote. *Titans of the Sea*. Harper & Row Publishers, 1975.

Boatner, Mark M., III. *The Biographical Dictionary of World War II*. Presidio Press, 1996.

Bowman, Martin W. *Encyclopedia of U.S. Military Aircraft*. Bison Books, 1980.

Boyne, Walter J. *Clash of Titans*. Simon Schuster, 1995.

Chank, Christopher, Richard Holmes and William Koenig. *Two Centuries of Warfare*. Octopus Books Limited, 1978.

Cooper, Bryan and John Batchelor. *Fighter*. Charles Scribner's Sons, 1973.

Costello, John. *The Pacific War*. Rawson, Wade Publishers, 1981.

Dear, I.C.B., ed. *The Oxford Companion to World War II*. Oxford University Press, 1995.

Dull, Paul S. *A Battle History of the Imperial Japanese Navy (1941–1945)*. The United States Naval Institute, 1978.

Dunnigan, James F. and Albert A. Nofi. *Victory at Sea*. William Morrow, 1995.

Ewing, Steve and John B. Lundstrom. *Fateful Rendezvous: The Life of Butch O'Hare*. Naval Institute Press, 1997.

Fuchida, Mitsuo and Masatake Okumiya. *Midway, The Battle That Doomed Japan: The Japanese Navy's Story*. George Banta Publishing, 1955.

Gailey, Harry A. *The War in the Pacific.* Presidio Press, 1995.

Glines, Carroll V. *The Doolittle Raid.* Orion Books, 1988.

Griess, Thomas E., ed. *Atlas for the Second World War: Asia and the Pacific.* Avery Publishing Group, 1985.

Halsey, William F. *Admiral Halsey's Story.* McGraw-Hill, 1947.

Hamilton, John. *War at Sea.* Blandford Press, 1986.

Hara, Tameichi. *Japanese Destroyer Captain.* Ballantine Books, 1961.

Hart, Sir Basil Liddell. *World War II (Vol. 5).* Purnell Reference Books, 1977.

Hart, Sir Basil Liddell. *World War II (Vol. 6).* Purnell Reference Books, 1977.

Hewson, Robert. *The World War II Warship Guide.* Chartwell Books, 2000.

Hough, Richard. *The Longest Battle.* William Morrow, 1986.

Hoyt, Edwin P. *Blue Skies and Blood.* Paul S. Eriksson, 1975.

Hoyt, Edwin P. *Guadalcanal.* Stein and Day Publishers, 1981.

Hoyt, Edwin P. *Japan's War.* McGraw-Hill, 1986.

Hoyt, Edwin P. *The Lonely Ships: The Life and Death of the U.S. Asiatic Fleet.* David McKay, 1976.

Jane, Frederick Thomas. *All the World's Fighting Ships.* Arco Press, 1941.

Jane, Frederick Thomas. *Jane's Fighting Ships of World War II.* Random House, 2001.

Johnston, Stanley. *Queen of the Flat-Tops.* Nelson Doubleday, 1942.

Keegan, John. *Atlas of the Second World War.* Borders Press in association with Harper Collins, 1999.

Kohn, George C., ed. *Dictionary of Wars.* Facts on File Publications, 1986.

Latourette, Kenneth Scott. *A Short History of the Far East.* Macmillan, 1957.

Lawson, Theodore. *Thirty Seconds over Tokyo.* Random House, 1943.

Leonard, Jonathan Norton. *Early Japan.* Time, 1968.

Lodge, O.R. *The Recapture of Guam.* U.S. Marine Corps Historical Branch, 1954.

Lord, Walter. *Incredible Victory.* Harper & Row, 1967.

Manchester, William. *American Caesar.* Little, Brown, 1978.

Merrill, James M. *A Sailor's Admiral: A Biography of William F. Halsey.* Thomas Y. Crowell, 1976.

Milton, Joyce and Wendy B. Murphy. *Tradition and Revolt.* Macmillan, 1980.

Moody, Sidney C. Jr. *War Against Japan*. Presidio Press, 1994.

Morison, Samuel Eliot. *History of United States Naval Operations in World War II, The Rising Sun in the Pacific, Vol. III*. Castle Books, 2001.

Morison, Samuel Eliot. *History of United States Naval Operations in World War II, Coral Sea, Midway and Submarine Actions, Vol. IV*. Castle Books, 2001.

Morison, Samuel Eliot. *History of United States Naval Operations in World War II, The Struggle for Guadalcanal, Vol. V*. Castle Books, 2001.

Morison, Samuel Eliot. *"Old Bruin": Commodore Matthew Calbraith Perry*. Little, Brown, 1967.

Morison, Samuel Eliot. *The Two-Ocean War*. Little, Brown, 1963.

Moskin, J. Robert. *The U.S. Marine Corps Story*. McGraw-Hill, 1987.

Munson, Kenneth. *Blandford Book of War Planes*. Blandford Books, 1981.

Natkiel, Richard. *Atlas of the 20th Century*. Bison Books, 1982.

Parrish, Thomas, ed. *Encyclopedia of World War II*. Simon and Schuster, 1978.

Parsons, Iain, ed. *The Encyclopedia of Sea Warfare: From the First Ironclads to the Present Day (A Salamander Book)*. Crowell, 1975.

Pitt, Barrie, cons. ed. *The Military History of World War II*. Military Press, 1986.

Pogue, Forrest C. *George C. Marshall: Organizer of Victory 1943–1945*. Viking Press, 1973.

Polmar, Norman and Thomas B. Allen. *World War II: America at War 1941–1945*. Random House, 1991.

Potter, E.B. *Nimitz*. Naval Institute Press, 1976.

Prados, John. *Combined Fleet Decoded*. Random House, 1995.

Prange, Gordon W. *At Dawn We Slept*. McGraw-Hill, 1981.

Prange, Gordon W. *Dec. 7, 1941*. McGraw-Hill, 1988.

Prange, Gordon W. *Miracle at Midway*. McGraw-Hill, 1982.

Romulo, General Carlos P. *I Saw the Fall of the Philippines*. Doubleday, Doran, 1943.

Roscoe, Theodore. *United States Destroyer Operations in World War II*. Naval Institute Press, 1953.

Schultz, Duane. *Wake Island*. St. Martin's Press, 1978.

Seagrave, Sterling. *The Soong Dynasty*. Harper & Row, 1985.

Sharp & Dunnigan Publications. *The Congressional Medal of Honor*. Sharp & Dunnigan Publications, 1984.

Slackman, Michael. *Remembering Pearl Harbor*. Arizona Memorial Museum Association, 1984.

Smith, S.E., ed. *The United States Navy in World War II*. William Morrow, 1966.

Stoessinger, John G. *Why Nations Go to War*. St. Martin's Press, 1990.

Toland, John. *But Not in Shame*. Random House, 1961.

Toland, John. *The Rising Sun, Vol I*. Random House, 1970.

Tuchman, Barbara W. *The Guns of August*. Macmillan, 1962.

United States Naval Institute. *The Bluejacket's Manual*. United States Naval Institute, 1943.

Wainwright, General Jonathan M. *General Wainwright's Story*. Doubleday, 1946.

Westwood, J.N. *Fighting Ships of World War II*. Follett, 1975.

Wheal, Elizabeth-Anne, Stephen Pope and James Taylor. *Dictionary of the Second World War*. Peter Bedrick Books, 1989.

Whitley, M.J. *Cruisers of World War Two, an International Encyclopedia*. Brockhampton Press, 1999.

Whitley, M.J. *Destroyers of World War Two, an International Encyclopedia*. Naval Institute Press, 2000.

Winton, John. *War in the Pacific*. Mayflower Books, 1978.

Wood, Pamela G., ed. *Pearl Harbor Survivors*. Turner Publishing, 1992.

Worth, Richard. *Fleets of World War II*. Da Capo Press, 2001.

Yoshitaro, Takenobu, ed. *Kenkyusha's New Japanese-English Dictionary*. Harvard University Press, 1942.

Y'Blood, William T. *The Little Giants*. Naval Institute Press, 1987.

About the Author

Bares at Red Beach, original landing site of the 1st Marine Division on Guadalcanal, August 7, 1942.

Roger Bares was an amateur World War II historian with a special interest in the Pacific Theater.

Acknowledgements

My deep appreciation to and affection for Daniel Schmitt. Without his technological expertise and his kind generosity over several years and various geographic locations, this book would never have come to publication. Thank you to all the authors and writers listed in the bibliography and to a few who were not listed. I'm grateful to John Wemlinger who steered me to Doug Weaver at Mission Point Press and to all the staff there who took me under their collective wing: Zinzi, Jen, Darlene, Kirsten, Martha, Heather, Todd, and to Misha, who patiently and intelligently brought me through to the day I could hold Roger's book in my hand. And to family and friends, you each deserve a medal.